The British Bus and Truck Heritage

Cumberland Motor Services
1921 - 1996

by

Harry Postlethwaite

Venture *publications*

ISBN 1 898432 75 9

ACKNOWLEDGEMENTS

I am most grateful to Brian Pritchard for compiling the Fleet List, with his detailed records and my memories, in some cases quite vivid, particularly covering wartime, we hope we have got it right. The information available from the PSV Circle records has been invaluable. On the photographic side Bob Downham made available his enormous collection of high quality prints and Mr and Mrs Percy Duff of Kendal were also particularly helpful with photographs of that area. Dawn Webster at Tullie House Museum, Carlisle provided archive information and photographs for which we are grateful. Information and photographs for the Barrow area were provided by Geoff.Holme, Phil.Cousins and John Hambler and to them we express thanks. Mr A. B. Cross has made available photographs from his own collection and that of the late S. L. Poole and we gratefully acknowledge these together with those from Arnold Richardson of Photobus. With regard to photographs, we have endeavoured to acknowledge these individually but in some cases prints which have been purchased from rallies, do not have the photographers name or copyright holders name on them and if we have used any such photographs without permission we can only apologise. Mr T. W. W. Knowles provided information in relation to the Lancashire City Transport operation in Kendal and John Graham loaned very useful archive material. The assistance of John Senior and his staff at the publishers in bringing everything together has been invaluable. I am pleased to acknowledge the photographers as below:

CMS Collection	5, 6 (top & centre), 9, 10 (centre & bottom), 25 (bottom), 72, 73 (lower), 83, 84, 85, 86, 87 (top), 141 (lower).	Tullie House Museum	31, 32, 33, 34 (upper)
Margaret Duff Coll.	6 (bottom), 66, 67 (top & centre), 69 (lower)	J. Cooper Collection	36 (lower)
Whiteheaven Mus. Coll.	7 (top), 10 (top)	A. A. Townsin	37 (upper) 39 (upper)
P. Cowman Collection	7 (centre)	Late R. F. Mack	40 (top)
Venture Collection	7 (bottom, 8 (top & bottom), 11, 13 (centre), 15, 21, 35, 36 (upper), 39 (lower), 60 (upper), 65, 67 (bottom), 68 (upper)	Beamish Museum	40 (bottom)
		R. Downham	41 (bottom, 50, 62, 63, 70, 71 (lower), 119 (bottom), 122 (upper), 123 (lower), 124 (centre), 127 (top), 130 (3rd down), 140 (top), 142 (centre), 143 (top)
A. B. Cross/S. L. Poole	12, 14 (lower), 37 (lower), 38, 68 (lower), 69 (upper), 73 (centre)	R. Solyom	117 (upper)
Photobus	13 (top), 16, 17 (bottom), 74, 113, 114, 115 (lower), 116 (bottom)	K. Norman Coll.	57 (lower)
		Barrow C. T. Coll.	59, 60 (lower), 61
R. Marshall	13 (bottom)	Ribble Enthusiasts Club	34 (lower), 73 (top)
R. C. Davis	14 (upper, 40 (left centre), 41 (top), 115 (upper), 116 (top & centre)	Easter Coach Works	75
		J. A. Senior	77
R. H. G. Simpson	17 (centre)	Unknown	17 (top), 19, 40 (right centre), 41 (centre)
Ivor Nicholas for CMS	18, 22, 28, 30, 46, 47, 122 (lower)	J. Robinson	Front cover
Cumbrian Newspapers	20, 25 (bottom)	M. Bailey	126 (bottom), 136 (upper)
P. L. Barlow	26 (lower)		

All other photographs are by the Author.

Front Cover Illustration

The oldest surviving Cumberland vehicle is this 1936 Leyland TD4 which was rebodied by Eastern Coach Works in 1950. Now looked after by James Sunderland, it was posed for this atmospheric shot by John Robinson, recalling the austere early post-war years.

Produced for the Publishers
Venture Publications, Glossop, Derbyshire,
by Mopok Graphics, Glossop SK13 8EH
using computerised origination

CONTENTS

PREFACE

When British Bus Systems No.1 – Cumberland was published in May 1983 I suspected that at some date in the dim and distant future I may write a volume 2. That dim and distant future has now arrived, remarkably quickly it seems, and to celebrate the 75th anniversary of the name Cumberland Motor Services this volume has been prepared.

It could never have been anticipated in 1983 that in 1996 the company would be twice the size that it was then, or that the traditional red, so long associated with the company, would have given way to white with stripes. However, such is the change that has come upon the industry over the past thirteen years that this book covers a much larger company operating over a greatly increased area. The first sign of change came with the transfer of Ribble operations in Carlisle and Penrith to Cumberland and then, following privatisation of the National Bus Company and sale to Stagecoach, the transfer of the Barrow and South Lakes areas from Ribble to Cumberland.

My brief was to summarise the previous book in the first chapter and then deal with happenings since 1983 in the remaining chapters. This has given the opportunity to look at, albeit very briefly, the history of public transport in Carlisle, Barrow and Kendal areas. In covering these areas we have tried not to duplicate material already published in British Bus Systems No.2 – Ribble or in Ribble Volumes 1 and 2, except where this is necessary for continuity of the story.

A book such as this could not have been written without the co-operation and help of many people. The company chairman Barry Hinkley and managing director Les Warneford have provided encouragement and help in many ways. The finance director of Stagecoach Holdings plc, Derek Scott has also assisted together with his parents who have provided useful information from the time when they lived in Carlisle. I have appreciated the help of Steven Barber, operations manager at Barrow in providing access to company archives and to Douglas Haig, retired traffic manager who has assisted in various ways from his long service with the company extending to almost 40 years.

In the text we have tried to appeal to both the transport enthusiast and to those with an interest in the local history of the county of Cumbria. With this in mind we have tried to avoid being over detailed and technical and to explain terminology which may be obvious to transport specialists and enthusiasts.

Harry Postlethwaite,

Blackpool,

February 1996.

FOREWORD

I joined Stagecoach Cumberland in October 1994, knowing nothing of its history or geography. I found it slightly confusing that the staff and residents of West Cumbria insisted on referring to the company as CMS. I then found in my office a copy of British Bus Systems No. 1 – "Cumberland" by Harry Postlethwaite. I read this with great interest to find I was managing a company with an unusual and very individual background. Unfortunately, the story ended in 1983 when the book was published, and Stagecoach Cumberland was obviously a very different company to CMS.

I began to piece together the split of Ribble, the sale of CMS to Stagecoach, the sale of Ribble to Stagecoach, and the battles of long ago in Barrow, Kendal, West Cumbria and Carlisle, leading to the emergence of Stagecoach Cumberland.

I then met Harry Postlethwaite who gave me a full account of the recent history. His knowledge of events, services, vehicles and the people within the organisation was fascinating. Since then I have met Harry regularly, and have been privileged to read and discuss the draft of this new book bringing the story of Cumberland up to date. The reader will find not just details of dates and events but a lively and living story of people and places.

Seventy five years ago the far sighted Mr Henry Meageen, in conjunction with British Automobile Traction, changed the name of Whitehaven Motor Service Company Limited to Cumberland Motor Services Limited, with a vision of a large and enduring business providing bus services in the old county of Cumberland. I trust he would be proud that the business has grown to serve the whole of Cumbria. Harry Postlethwaite's first book has ensured that the history of growth and success will not be forgotten. This new book brings the history up to date and it is entirely appropriate that it should mark this 75th anniversary year.

L B Warneford,
Managing Director,
Stagecoach Cumberland,
Whitehaven.

February 1996.

STAGECOACH CUMBERLAND

MANAGEMENT STRUCTURE MARCH 1996

CHAIRMAN
Mr W B Hinkley
———————————————— OTHER COMPANIES

MANAGING DIRECTOR
Mr L B Warneford

CHIEF ENGINEER	TRAFFIC MANAGER	FINANCE DIRECTOR
Mr M Britten	Mr I Lyon	Mr M Clayton Cumberland and Ribble
DEPOT ENGINEER LILLYHALL Mr P Mc Intyre	OPERATIONS MANAGER WHITEHAVEN Mr J Bradley	
DEPOT ENGINEER CARLISLE Mr S Morris	OPERATIONS MANAGER WORKINGTON Mr A Anderson	
DEPOT ENGINEER BARROW Mr P O'Callaghan	OPERATIONS MANAGER CARLISLE Mr K Wilson	
DEPOT ENGINEER KENDAL Mr E Jones	OPERATIONS MANAGER BARROW Mr S Barber	
	OPERATIONS MANAGER KENDAL Mr T Pennington	

Chapter One
From Early Days to NBC

Origins and Development

Throughout its seventy five years of existence Cumberland Motor Services has had its headquarters in the West Cumbrian town of Whitehaven, a town with a long transport history going back to the times of sailing ships. In this period the town had a thriving shipbuilding industry and in the period between 1750 and 1772 is listed as being the second largest port in the country, behind London. In 1828 it was listed as fifth behind London, Newcastle, Liverpool and Sunderland. However, as larger ships came into being, its importance declined, a situation which was aggravated by its rather isolated location. Stagecoach services commenced in the eighteenth century and some information on these is given in Chapter 3.

Turning to bus services, Cumberland Motor Services Ltd was first registered on 1st June 1921, but for the origins of the Company we go back to 8th August 1912. This was the date of the registration of the Whitehaven Motor Service Company which was founded by a local man, Mr Henry Meageen who had started his working life in Lord Lonsdale's colliery office in Whitehaven where he became cashier. He was later appointed Relieving Officer and Registrar for Whitehaven, a position which he later relinquished in order to devote his full time to the bus company. Outside his business interests he was a member and trustee of the Lowther Street Methodist Church. Other shareholders in the company were his wife Sarah, Mr

George W. Cowin, a Whitehaven toy and glass dealer, Mr William Clark, a provision merchant of Whitehaven, and Mr T. S. Bell, an electrical engineer, also of Whitehaven. The registered office was at 33 King Street and the share capital was £1,500 in £1 shares of which £575 was issued.

Messrs Clark and Bell later sold their shares to Henry Meageen, leaving the company entirely in the hands of the Meageen family and their brother in law, George Cowin who continued as a director until his resignation from the Board in May 1949. George's son Arthur worked for the company until his retirement in 1972 when he was Depot Superintendent at Carlisle. The name Meageen was to become synonymous with buses in West Cumberland for many years and the influence which the family had was to be seen in its nonconformist policy, particularly with regard to vehicles. Henry's son Tom and Tom's son Harry played leading roles in the company for many years, Tom as Managing Director and Harry as Chief Engineer. At the time of his death at the age of 79 years on 3rd December 1941, Henry was Company Chairman and had visited the Whitehaven offices the previous day, apparently in good health.

The Whitehaven Motor Service Company commenced with excursion business and the first stage carriage service was from Whitehaven to Cleator Moor, commencing in October 1912. The timetable commencing 14th May 1914 for the Cleator Moor service, shows it operating on Thursdays and Saturdays only, these being Whitehaven Market Days. The Thursday service operated between 9-45am and 9-0pm but the Saturday service commenced at

Driver Bill Grey, with coach and four, waits outside the Tangier Street premises of the Whitehaven Cab and Posting Company Ltd. which was purchased by the Meageens. The registered office of the Whitehaven Motor Service Company Ltd. was transferred here from 33 King Street and the site was later developed as workshops becoming the Central Engineering Works for Cumberland Motor Services.

QUEEN MOTOR COACHES

The original 'Lady Betty' purchased in June 1919 is shown with N Hamilton, H. Davidson and T. Conway.

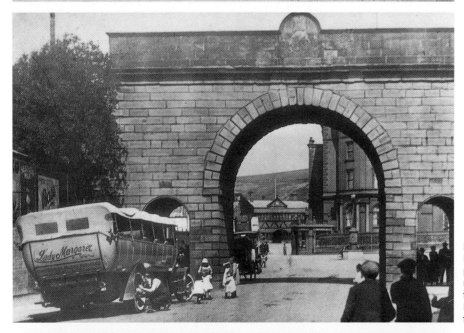

Bransty Arch, Whitehaven with 'Lady Margaret' receiving attention whilst children play around, something which they could not do safely to-day. Through the arch is the Grand Hotel and beyond that, Bransty Railway Station with covered walkway to the hotel.

Number 2, a Daimler 'Y' type with Dodson body, delivered to Whitehaven Motor Service Company in 1920, stands in Workington with its crew whilst operating on the Whitehaven to Carlisle service. This was one of the buses which passed to Armstrong and Siddle Motor Services Ltd of Penrith in 1928, later becoming Ribble No.705.

2-15pm then 4-0pm and hourly until 11-0pm reminding us that, in those days, Saturday evening was a busy shopping period with the Whitehaven Market open until late evening. The fares were 4 pence to Hensingham and 6 pence to Keekle and Cleator Moor. The first vehicles were an Arrol-Johnston charabanc, XS 102, purchased second-hand and a new Commercial Car charabanc, AO 1636, both seating 24 passengers. They were named Lady Favourite and Lady Florence respectively and were joined in September 1912 by another Commercial Car charabanc purchased secondhand from Davis of Bognor Regis and named Lady Nin.

Top: This early publicity postcard shows the extent of the Cumberland system at the time of publication, thought to be the early 'twenties.

Centre: This view of Workington Bus Station, standing somewhat in isolation without the Murrey Road shops, is thought to have been taken shortly after it was opened in 1926.

Below: Number 56, a Leyland SGH7 Special with Leyland body, photogaphed by the builder before delivery in 1924. Note the solid tyres which were later replaced by pneumatics. It was typical of vehicles delivered at that time and was soon made to look obsolete by vehicles purchased only a few years later.

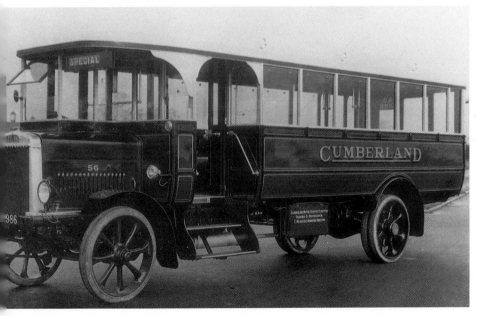

The First World War prevented expansion and the Cleator Moor service was suspended in September 1914 whilst at the end of this year the Registered Office of the company was transferred from 33 King Street to the Tangier Street premises of the Whitehaven Cab and Posting Company which the Meageens had purchased.

Following the end of the War and the lifting of restrictions, the company was able to expand, and by 1920 there were services from Whitehaven to Frizington via Cleator Moor, to Egremont and to Maryport via Workington. It was in 1920 that British Automobile Traction Co Ltd purchased a half interest in the company and arising from this the name was changed to Cumberland Motor Services Ltd with effect from 1st June 1921. This gave the company the backing it required and from this time expansion took place. The first 'Cumberland' timetable, issued in 1921, showed the following services as being operated:-

Whitehaven to Carlisle via Workington, Maryport, and Wigton.
Whitehaven to Keswick via Workington and Cockermouth.
Carlisle to Silloth via Wigton and Abbeytown.
Whitehaven to Frizington via Cleator Moor.
Whitehaven to Egremont via Bigrigg.
Maryport to Cockermouth.

By now the basic operating territory to the north of Whitehaven, which was to continue for many years, had been established and was added to in 1925 with a service from Cockermouth to Wigton, in 1928 with the Keswick to Penrith service and in 1929 with the service from Carlisle to Keswick. To the south of Whitehaven the Egremont service was extended to Thornhill in 1922 with extension to Gosforth in 1926 and further extension to Millom in 1928, operating initially via the main road between Gosforth and Holmrook but being diverted via Seascale in 1930. In 1925 a service was commenced from Whitehaven to St.Bees and by 1926 a route from Whitehaven to Egremont via Cleator Moor was operating and certain journeys on the St. Bees service were extended to Egremont. By 1930 the Frizington service had reached Lamplugh. town service operation was to form an important part of the company activities in West Cumberland and the first town service was operated from Workington to Harrington in 1922. The first Town Service in Whitehaven was from Bransty Row to Hensingham Square and this was followed in 1926 by a town service from Bransty Estate to Kells via the Town Centre. Use was made of the new road which had just been opened and the new service led to the

The first of a long line. Number 29, RM 2225, was numerically the first of the famous Leyland Lions to be delivered to Cumberland arriving in April 1926 – note the contrast with No.56 delivered only two years earlier. This batch, with bodies by Leyland, was rebodied by Massey Brothers in 1932, which was something of a surprise as Leyland's bodies were normally very durable, some lasting for fifteen years or more. The reason for the rebodying has never been discovered.

RM 6631, fleet No. 113, was one of four Leyland TS2 models with bodies by Massey Brothers purchased in 1930. They were later rebodied by Myers and Bowman of Distington. There is a photograph of 114 as rebodied in my earlier book *British Bus Systems No. 1.*

The Leyland TD1 double-decker with standard lowbridge 'Piano Front' body, also by Leyland, although in some instances built under licence by others, became a feature of many fleets in the early 'thirties. This official photograph shows Cumberland No. 18, RM 7544, delivered in 1931. Earlier examples had open staircase bodies.

Above: The 1933 Ambulance Team is pictured with Tom Meageen, Henry Meageen, Dr. Victor Harris and Dr. I Fletcher and W Rae Company Secretary, on the roof of the Head Office building in Whitehaven.

Left: Tom Meageen was the son of founder Henry Meageen and served with the company from its early days to his death in November 1949.

cessation of Mrs Wilson's service to Kells and the purchase of her business in 1927, this being the second company to be taken over. The first had been Star Bus Services Ltd of Workington, in 1926.

In 1921 four double-deckers were acquired from the London General Omnibus Company and two of the drivers who delivered them to Whitehaven remained with the company. One was William Field who became known as 'Cockney Bill' and the other was Daniel Steele who became Traffic Manager of the Company and whose son Alf Steele became Depot Superintendent at Keswick. A

Mr Williams, who for some years was manager of Marks and Spencer in Workington, recalled being employed as a boy in the office of CMS and being sacked by 'Cockney Bill' after being caught driving one of the buses around the garage.

The livery had been green and cream but in 1924 this was changed to red and cream, colours which were to continue in various shades and combinations up to the present-day Stagecoach era. Single-deck liveries tended to vary with body styles but the double-deck livery was more standard. In the prewar and immediate postwar period this was bright red with three cream bands and white roof. Beadings between the red and cream were black, the cream was lined out with red and the red was lined out with white. From the late 'forties, the lining out was omitted and as the Tilling influence became established the white roof was abandoned in favour of red and the number of cream bands reduced to two. Information on subsequent liveries is given later.

Manxland Bus Services Ltd was registered in the Isle of Man by British Automobile Traction Co Ltd in May 1927 and as Whitehaven is the nearest town in England to the Isle of Man, it was perhaps not surprising that the new company was placed under the control of Cumberland Motor Services Ltd. Cumberland provided a number of vehicles to commence the operation and some vehicles on order were diverted to the new company.

Control of Manxland Bus Services was taken over by the Isle of Man Railway Company in February 1929.

The 'twenties had been a period of expansion as the company grew from small beginnings to become the largest bus company based in the county of Cumberland. This expansion was followed in the 'thirties by a period of

Top: This photograph of Cleator Moor Square taken in the early 'thirties shows a Leyland Lion with Massey body heading towards Whitehaven whilst a Leyland TD1 with Leyland body on the other side of the road is heading to Lamplugh, the pronunciation of which has caused many problems to visitors to the area over the years. The second double-decker is probably going to Egremont via Cleator. This photograph always reminds the author of a Lowry painting.

Above: For many years the company had a cricket team and one such team is pictured comprising :-
Back Row L to R – T. Drake, R. Wilson, J. Thornthwaite, W. Kinrade,
Front Row L to R – G. Dawson, A. Sutcliffe, J. Kenny, W. Rae (Captain), W. Briggs, J. Douglas, ? Stone.

Left: Alf Steele seemed to like to have his photograph taken and this is one of a number taken when he was Depot Superintendent at Keswick. It shows him standing in front of Leyland TD1 No. 77 which is about to depart to Whitehaven.

One of the 1938 Leyland TS8s with Massey bodies numbered 138 to 142 is shown at Ullswater. These were particularly comfortable vehicles with higher than normal moquette covered seats. In later years they would probably have been classified as dual purpose.

consolidation when the company took over numerous small operators as listed in the Appendices. Perhaps the most dramatic change in this period was in vehicle design as vehicles produced in the mid-'twenties were obsolete by the early 'thirties. Vehicle policy in this period settled down to favour Leyland for double-deckers and both Leyland and AEC for single-deckers. On the body building side the Wigan based firm of Massey Brothers predominated; which was something of a surprise as this body builder tended to be associated with municipal and small operators rather than large companies. Other body builders regularly employed in prewar days were the Cockermouth firm of Tolsons and H. V. Burlingham of Blackpool for single-decks, whilst Leyland and East Lancashire Coachbuilders of Blackburn supplied double-deck bodies.

In addition to the publication of timetable booklets which were issued twice per year, the company issued an 'Official Handbook' which was updated every two years. This gave details of the company's services together with information on excursions and extended tours. In addition the handbooks gave details of places of intereest within the operating area and the wider area of the Lake District. The company operated a parcels service with agents in most of the towns and villages served, and a list of the agents was given in the Handbook and also in the timetable booklets. It was quite a usual sight to see a conductor leaving a bus in order to deliver a parcel but this is a service which could not be offered with one-person-operation.

By the outbreak of war in 1939, the company had seen off most of the opposition in the area and had very much a monopoly of services in West Cumberland. A notable exception to this was the Thursday and Saturday service operated by Billy Sim from his base at Boot, close to the terminus of the Ravenglass and Eskdale Railway, to Whitehaven. The relationship was a friendly one and Sim's bus would normally be parked at the Bus Station in Whitehaven during layover. Sim also operated a service from Eskdale to Seascale. The other case of operation by small operators was on the service from Keswick to Borrowdale where Cumberland operated jointly with a number of Keswick-based operators to a rather complicated schedule.

WARTIME

For Cumberland Motor Services, the wartime period was one of both expansion and restriction. There was restriction on the supply of fuel and on the supply of new vehicles whilst many of the staff had been called up into the armed forces. On the other hand, West Cumberland was regarded as a safe area with the result that many were evacuated into the area from other more vulnerable centres of population and there was also the establishment of munitions factories and other factories associated with the war effort. Many of these were established well away from local centres of population and transport was required to take workers to their places of employment.

The effect on fuel supplies was more or less immediate and the first wartime timetable came into effect on 7th October 1939. Seasonal services in the Lake District were eliminated, not to appear again until after the war, and other restrictions generally involved earlier finishing times, very restricted Sunday services and reduced frequencies. The timetable was published in two halves, the Northern Area covering services from Whitehaven northwards and the Southern Area covering services from Whitehaven

Above: Number 152, GW 550, was one of seven Leyland TD2s purchased from London Transport in 1940. It was new to A H Raper (Standard) of London SE16 and is shown about to depart on a Whitehaven Town Service to Woodhouse Estate, one of the routes on which these buses were regularly employed.

Left: Number 177, a Northern Counties bodied Leyland TD7 was one of two 'unfrozen' vehicles received in the early years of the war. The other, 176, is illustrated in *British Bus Systems No. 1*. It is shown approaching Workington bus station after postwar rebuilding.

southwards. Each timetable comprised a folded sheet, priced at one penny, rather than a booklet, and revised timetables were issued regularly as restrictions were either eased or increased. All street lighting was eliminated and vehicle lights both internally and externally had to be masked.

On the vehicle side there was little immediate change as vehicles which had been ordered prior to the outbreak of hostilities were delivered as planned. However, one sign

of the times was the diversion of four Leyland TD7 double-deckers with Park Royal bodies from a Southdown order to Cumberland. They had been built to Southdown specification and contrasted in details with the Cumberland, specified vehicles delivered at the same time. It was in late 1941 and early 1942 that the first signs of restriction on vehicle design became evident with the arrival of two Leyland TD7 double-deckers with semi-utility bodies, sometimes referred to as 'unfrozen' vehicles, one by Massey Brothers and the other by Northern Counties Motor and Engineering Co Ltd, also of Wigan. The other significant factor in the early years of wartime was the purchase of a number of second-hand vehicles from various sources, supplemented by a number of hired vehicles from other operators, details of which are given in the Fleet List.

The Brush bodied Guy Arab Mark 1s were rebuilt in the postwar period with curved frontal profile as illustrated in this view of 185 outside the former Grand Hotel in Whitehaven. A photograph of this vehicle when new appears in *British Bus Systems No.1*.

This photograph, although not of a Cumberland vehicle, illustrates features common on Cumberland utility vehicles for some years. It shows the wooden seats, a wartime feature, and also the side sunken gangway upstairs on lowbridge double-deckers. Also illustrated are the masked interior lighting fittings, another wartime feature.

Previously illustrated 152 was rebodied by H V Burlingham in 1948 with this highbridge body and returned to work on Whitehaven Town Services. It is shown at Whitehaven Bus Station on Town Service 05 to Bransty.

The first postwar double-deckers to be delivered were Leyland PD1s with Massey or Northern Coachbuilders bodies and one of the former, which was numerically the first postwar double-decker, No 218, is at Keswick bus station awaiting departure on the joint service with Ribble to Penrith. Behind is a typical Ribble prewar coach of the type used on that company's Express services from Keswick.

The Northern Coachbuilders bodies did not have the flair of the Massey bodies but were neat and well finished, spoiled only by the untidy arrangement of the windscreen, a feature of a number of early postwar bodies in which the body builder utilised the cab front supplied with the chassis. Number 230 is shown at Carlisle bus station awaiting departure to Silloth after the introduction of service numbers in 1950.

An event took place in 1942 which probably went unnoticed by the majority of the company's passengers but which had a significant effect on its future. In that year it was decided to disband the Tilling – British Automobile Traction Group to which Cumberland belonged, and to allocate the companies involved to either the Tilling or the British Electric Traction (BET) groups. Cumberland was allocated to the Tilling Group and became what was generally regarded as the most un-Tilling like member of the group. The main reason for this was that the Meageens still had a majority shareholding and were therefore able to dictate such matters as vehicle policy – it was a further twelve years before the company was made to conform to the Tilling Group vehicle policy of Bristol chassis and Eastern Coach Works bodies, but more about this later.

The effect of wartime restrictions on vehicle policy became evident in 1943 when the first buses to the Ministry of Supply wartime specification arrived in the fleet. Wartime commitments prevented Leyland Motors Ltd from building buses and the first utility double-deckers to enter the fleet were five Guy Arab Mark 1 examples with very austere bodies built by Brush

The 22 Leyland PD2/1 were followed by a total of 30 PD2/12 with synchromesh gearboxes and the later style of Leyland metal framed body. This scene in Keswick bus station shows No. 335 of the second and final batch about to depart for Penrith. Judging by the style of destination blind lettering, it was probably taken shortly after delivery. Behind is Ribble No 2101 a typical prewar single decker about to depart for Ambleside on service 555, possibly as duplicate to the Ribble PD2 double-decker behind on the through service to Lancaster.

Coachworks of Loughborough. They were followed by three Daimlers with preselector gearboxes and similar bodies. A further sixteen Guy Arabs of the Mark 2 variety followed, the first fourteen having bodies by Northern Counties Motor and Engineering Co Ltd of Wigan and the last two with bodies by Massey Brothers. All the Arab Mark 2 buses, except the first three, had the notorious wooden seats. On the single-deck side the standard wartime single-decker was the Bedford OWB, most of the bodies for which were built by Duple to the Ministry of Supply specification and Cumberland received fifteen of these, all of which had wooden seats. More detailed general information on bus manufacture in this period is given in Alan Townsin's book *The Best of British Buses – The Utilities* published by Transport Publishing Co Ltd.

The livery was changed from red and cream to grey with limited white relief and the Cumberland fleetname was replaced by a CMS monogram.

Many older vehicles were rebodied in this period, some being from the original Cumberland fleet and some being vehicles acquired. The double-deck bodies were supplied by Northern Coachbuilders Ltd, Newcastle upon Tyne, and the single-decks by H. V. Burlingham Ltd of Blackpool. Details of new and rebodied vehicles are given in the Fleet List.

There was certainly variety in the fleet at this time and one never knew what colour of bus would turn up with so many hired vehicles in operation, from London Transport

ST types complete with anti-shatter material on the windows, to more familiar Leyland TD1s from East Kent.

Services were often full and it was not unusual to have to wait for the next bus although the company did provide duplicates where possible. The condition of the fleet deteriorated considerably, due to restrictions on the supply of materials, and staff shortages brought about by conscription to the forces. However, despite these problems, service continued to operate and the fact that they did is credit to all concerned.

THE POST WAR BOOM AND DECLINE.

Once the war had ended, and restrictions were lifted, the company was able to concentrate on fleet renewal, the restoration of suspended services and the provision of new services to serve housing estates which grew up in the west Cumbrian towns. With the exception of six Bedford OB coaches with Duple bodies, all new vehicles in the immediate postwar period were Leylands with bodies by Northern Coachbuilders, Massey Brothers and Leyland Motors for double-decks and H. V. Burlingham, Massey Brothers and Associated Coachbuilders of Sunderland for single-decks and coaches. In addition to the provision of new vehicles, many chassis were rebodied by either Eastern Coach Works or H. V. Burlingham and others were extensively rebuilt either by the company itself, by Myers and Bowman of Distington or by Lancashire Aircraft

An example of the excellent bodies built by the company to replace coach bodies on Leyland PS1 chassis is illustrated by No.113, formerly No.34, stopped at the Moot Hall, Keswick, on the service to Seatoller.

Corporation (later Samlesbury Engineering). In many cases where bodies were scrapped, the seats were in reasonable condition and were used to replace wooden seats in the Guy utility double-deckers. All the utility bodies on the Guys were rebuilt to a greater or lesser extent, the Brush bodies receiving curved front profiles and the Northern Counties and Massey bodies recieving rubber mounted glazing. All except one (No. 217) received postwar style destination displays. The Daimlers, being very much non-standard to the fleet, were disposed of and were not rebuilt. It was always easy to identify bodies which had been rebuilt by Lancashire Aircraft/Samlesbury Engineering as they were rebuilt exactly as they had been previously with regard to destination displays, and the rebuilding was so thorough, with seats and all lining panels completely recovered, and polished timbers to the window surrounds replaced, that they were like new bodies.

The extent of the fleet renewal can be seen from the fleet list, and between 1947 and 1953 almost 150 new vehicles arrived in the fleet. A significant development as far as single-deck buses and coaches were concerned was the arrival of the underfloor-engined chassis, giving opportunity for greater seating capacity, and Cumberland received five Leyland Royal Tiger chassis with Eastern Coach Works bodies, followed by a further seven with Leyland bodies and a further three with Leyland coach bodies, these being the last new Leyland vehicles to arrive in the fleet for many years.

To revert to postwar services, demand for travel increased and extensive housing developments, particularly in Whitehaven and Workington, led to the establishment of new services. At this time it was the policy to use the oldest vehicles on Town Services and, as many of these were in very poor condition, there was some criticism

particularly from the Borough Council in Whitehaven where there was talk of attempting to establish a municipal service. However, as rebodied vehicles became available, standards improved and in the early 'fifties, the rebodied vehicle were replaced by much newer vehicles and the criticism subsided. Seasonal services in the Lake District were restored in 1947.

Another important event, of which the travelling public of West Cumberland was probably also unaware, took effect from 8th November 1948 when the Tilling Group sold out to the British Transport Commission for £24,800,000, which meant that Cumberland became state-owned from that date. This had little or no effect on the operation of the company, indeed it could be said that the companies which suffered were those outside the Tilling Group, as they were no longer allowed to purchase Bristol chassis and Eastern Coach Works bodies as these Tilling Group companies were now state-owned and not allowed to trade on the open market.

In November 1949 Tom Meageen died and in June 1950 Harry Meageen resigned. Thus the Meageen era came to an end. H. H. Merchant became General Manager from January 1950 and served in this position until his retirement in January 1963, being succeeded in February 1963 by W. T. Skinner. In mid 1965 Mr Skinner was succeeded by Mr I. Campbell who took the company into the National Bus Company era.

Up to 1953 the policy on new vehicles had followed prewar practice with Leyland predominating as this supplier fulfilled long established advance orders placed under the Meageen regime. The frustration of the Tilling management at this situation is evident from the minutes of the Tilling board meetings and eventually it was decreed that, to fulfil outstanding orders from Leyland, the General Manager should place orders for twenty Leyland Royal Tiger chassis

Once obligations to Leyland had been satisfied with regard to the advance orders placed by the Meageens, Tilling influence prevailed and the first Bristol double-deckers were five LD6G of the revolutionary low floor design which enabled a normal upper saloon seating arrangement to be provided within the height of a lowbridge vehicle. One of the first batch was No. 402 formerly numbered 355 and shown at Keswick having arrived from Thornthwaite on 22nd January 1964.

A number of Lodekkas with four speed gearboxes and without platform doors was introduced for Town Services and to distinguish them from the others they were given 'T' prefixes to their fleet numbers as illustrated by T388 a Bristol engined example on a Whitehaven Town Service.

When the Town Service Lodekkas were given 'T' prefixes to their fleet numbers, the others were given 'C' prefixes for Country Operation. C419, an example of the later FS type of Lodekka is shown at Carlisle bus station on service 30 to Egremont.

which would be allocated in accordance with the Tilling Chairman's instructions. In the end United Automobile Services Ltd placed a direct order for ten Royal Tigers, and Cumberland took ten, seven with Leyland service bus bodies and three with Leyland coach bodies. An arrangement was made whereby Central SMT would take ten PD2 double-deck chassis – others went to Crosville. In this way responsibilities to Leyland were fulfilled and Cumberland was brought into line with Tilling Group vehicle policy.

The first Bristols to arrive entered service in 1954 and comprised three LS6G chassis with the classic Eastern Coach Works coach body of that time. They were followed later in the year by five Bristol LD6G 'Lodekka' type double-deckers to the revolutionary design recently introduced by Bristol, with a low floor enabling a standard upper saloon seating arrangement to be incorporated in a vehicle conforming to 'lowbridge' height of 13ft 5ins. This was particularly attractive to Cumberland where the lowbridge double-decker with inconvenient sunken side gangway had predominated for so long. The fact that they all had Gardner engines must have pleased the Cumberland engineers who held this power unit in high esteem. Initially, all Bristols delivered to Cumberland had Gardner engines but in 1959 the first Bristol engined examples arrived and these also gave a good account of themselves, being described many years later by engineering staff as 'the next best engine to a Gardner'.

The company took delivery of both new and second-hand examples of the Bristol SC4LK, a lightweight design of single-decker intended for rural services. They were known locally as the 'Sputniks' as the initial examples arrived in the fleet at the time when the first Sputnik had been launched into orbit and it is alleged that the first driver to take one out brought it back and said "It's a pity they did not send that up in the Sputnik." One of the engineers, speaking of these buses many years later conceded, "They were dreadful buses, the only good thing about them was that they had Gardner engines." Having said all that, it has to be said that they were economic on fuel and some operators in flat territory obtained fuel consumption figures of around 25 miles to the gallon.

The author recalls walking along Tangier Street, Whitehaven, one day in 1958 and seeing an unfamiliar single-decker approaching. As it came closer it was obvious that it was Leyland PS1 No. 180 which had had its Associated Coachbuilders coach body replaced with a new bus body. The design of the new body was unfamiliar, although it did bear some resemblance in overall shape to the Weymann bodies of the early 'fifties. It transpired that this body had been built by Cumberland in the body shop at Whitehaven under the expert direction of John Twentyman, the body shop foreman. A further nine similar bodies were built and in talking to John about these bodies, many years later, it was revealed that they were built

The lightweight SC4LK Bristol single-deckers were generally used on lightly loaded rural services and 206, ONV 429, is shown en route to Millom from Seascale where it would have made connection with the vehicle from Whitehaven. It was purchesed second-hand from United Counties Omnibus Company in 1963.

without any drawings and the first one was built in the body shop before the old body was removed. The only part of the old body to be retained was the windscreen.

In the early years the fleet numbering system had been based on a 'gap filling' policy with new vehicles taking numbers vacated by withdrawn vehicles. From 1950 onwards a chronological system was employed and previously-vacated numbers were not re-used on new vehicles. A system of prefix letters was introduced in December 1959 for the Bristol Lodekkas, 'T' for Town Service being used for those with four-speed gearboxes and without platform doors and 'C' for Country Service being used for those with five-speed gearboxes and platform doors. In 1961 the complete fleet was renumbered with series of numbers allocated according to vehicle type. At the same time cast metal fleet number plates were introduced, originally with a yellow background but this was later changed to black which gave a much better contrast with the bright metal characters.

When Bristol stopped manufacturing its own engine, it wanted to offer an alternative unit to the Gardner and in 1964 Cumberland received three Bristol FLF double-deckers with Leyland engines. At this time Cumberland still had a number of Leyland vehicles in the fleet and this may have influenced the allocation of these vehicles to the company. They were set to work on Whitehaven town services and comparative tests were carried out against similar vehicles with Gardner engines. The Gardner came

out very much on top, no more FLF chassis were built with Leyland engines and one of the Cumberland examples was retrofitted with a Gardner engine in 1976.

The Leyland engine was offered however by Bristol in its RE single-deck chassis and, as mentioned elsewhere, most of the Cumberland examples of this model had Leyland engines. These single-deckers, built to the maximum length of 36ft and with a seating capacity of 53, took over many of the duties previously operated by double-deckers and brought to an end the dominance of the double-decker in the fleet.

This was a period which saw both the rise and fall in public transport and Cumberland was no exception to this. Business peaked in 1955 when the total number of passengers carried in the year was almost 40 million. Following this, as car ownership increased, the number of passengers declined and by 1973 was down to 20 million although the mileage operated had fallen by a little more than one fifth.

With effect from 1st January 1963, the British Transport Commission was abolished and a new organisation – the Transport Holding Company – was formed to take over the road transport interests of the BTC including the Tilling bus group. On 22nd November 1967 it was announced that the other major bus group, the BET Group, had sold out to the Transport Holding Company and the scene was now set for the Labour Government of the time to progress towards the formation of the National Bus Company.

The first Leyland National to enter service was ERM 35K, fleet No. 350, and it operated on service 41 from Workington to Whitehaven via Lowca with invited guests before taking up its regular duties on Whitehaven town service 05 on 16th March 1972. It is shown here before departure from Workington bus station annexe with driver Barry Taylor, the mayors and mayoresses of Workington and Whitehaven and other guests. One heading in a local press report was 'Super Bus Enters Service'. It seems unlikely that CMS would have described it in this way.

THE NATIONAL BUS COMPANY ERA.

The Transport Act of 1968 included the establishment of the National Bus Company and this organisation came into being on 1st January 1969 to take over the bus operating subsidiaries of the Transport Holding Company. Cumberland found itself in the North West Area of NBC along with Crosville Motor Services Ltd, North Western Road Car Company Ltd, Ribble Motor Services Ltd and the Ribble subsidiary of W. C. Standerwick Ltd. One immediate local effect in Cumberland was that the Carlisle based operations of United Automobile Services Ltd passed to Ribble and the number of major operators in Carlisle was reduced from four to three. There was no other obvious immediate effect, particularly for former Tilling Group Companies, and vehicle policy continued very much as before. At the time the General Manager was Mr I Campbell and during the early years of NBC General Managers tended to change regularly as NBC pursued a policy of moving its management around. Another factor in this respect was that Cumberland, being one of the smaller subsidiary companies, was used as a training ground for general managers. This is thought to have been one reason why Cumberland was maintained as a separate company, rather than being merged with Ribble. The other reason which has been suggested for this is that the company was profitable and no one would therefore make the decision to disband it. General managers who served during the NBC era were :-

– 1969	Mr I Campbell.
1970 – 1971	Mr S H Morris.
1972 – 1974	Mr W H Jelpke.
1975 – 1977	Mr H B Sessford.
1978 – 1984	Mr P A Townley.
1985 – 1987	Mr J M Wadsworth.

Of the above only Mr Wadsworth had been a general manager of an NBC subsidiary company before arriving at Cumberland.

This view of Leyland National No. 350 shows it at the West Cumberland Hospital, Whitehaven, the southern terminus of town service 05, shortly after entering service.

On the vehicle side the National Bus Company had two major effects. In conjunction with British Leyland, a standard single-deck service bus was developed and a new factory to build this revolutionary vehicle was constructed at Lillyhall in West Cumberland in the heart of CMS operating territory. It is worth mentioning that one man who was influential in the choice of Lillyhall was Sir Frank Schon, who with his partner Mr Fred Marzillier, had founded Marchon Products (later part of Albright and Wilson) in Whitehaven in the early 'forties.

The vehicle was of integral construction and left operators with little or no choice as to specification detail. A sophisticated heating and ventilation system was provided but the interior finish was rather spartan with seating covered in a plastic material and has been described by Alan Townsin in the *British Bus Story – The Early 'Seventies* as rather like a hospital waiting room. A new engine was developed by British Leyland for this bus and it soon gained a reputation for being noisy, dirty and inefficient, both from the fuel consumption and life between major overhauls aspects. It has been reported that one company replaced a Bristol RE with a Leyland National, on one particular duty, and found that the daily fuel consumption rose from 15 to 22 gallons. Cumberland took the first production Leyland National to enter service with an operator, ERM 35K, and set it to work on town service 05 in Whitehaven. It seems that the manufacturer was keen to test one of the vehicles on an arduous town or city service and 05 was chosen because of its hilly character. One of the problems with this vehicle, in the early days of operation, was that when it traversed Bransty Brow in wet weather it rained in over the driver's area and he got wet. It seems that British Leyland took some convincing that this problem existed. The 'clatter' of the Leyland National 1 engine became a feature of bus operation in many parts of the country. On the other hand, the Leyland National body was a very strong box and the fact that some operators had examples extensively refurbished when they were approching twenty years old is testimony to this, although it should be mentioned that this refurbishment generally included replacement of the 500 series engine.

Cumberland did not however carry out any such refurbishment but disposed of its Leyland Nationals 'en bloc' as covered later.

A less sophisticated version, known as the 'B' type, was developed and the fifteen examples of this type which Cumberland purchased became known as the 'Country Cousins'.

A later version known as the National 2 was offered with the more conventional Leyland 680 bus engine and use of the original 500 series engine was discontinued. Operators were also given the choice of moquette covered seating, which was a great improvement on the original material, and apart from its first batch of National 2s, this was an option which Cumberland took up.

Operators asked Leyland to offer the Gardner engine as an alternative but it was claimed that it would not fit. Two operators, Eastern Counties and Crosville, then retrofitted Gardner engines into Nationals and following that Leyland offered it as an alternative, Cumberland received the first National built with a Gardner engine, Fleet No. 395.

The other effect which NBC had on the vehicles concerned the corporate livery. The Prime Minister of the time, Harold Wilson, brought in Mr Freddie (later Sir Frederick) Wood as Chairman of NBC and he was keen to establish a corporate identity covering the various fleets across the country. He introduced the white coach for the express operations of National Express and also red, green and blue standard liveries for service buses. The blue was later dropped and Cumberland, whose basic livery had been red, adopted the NBC red, described as Poppy Red, which was a very insipid shade which lacked 'body'. It looked particularly drab when applied to older vehicles which had previously carried attractive liveries. The relief was a single white band between decks on double-deckers and a single white band below the windows on single-deckers. The Leyland Nationals, however, had no relief and later an edict was issued by NBC that white bands were to be omitted on all single-deckers on repaint, to save money. Speaking about this in an interview with the authors of the the *National Bus Company history*, the late

Michael Wadsworth, the last General Manager of Cumberland in the NBC era stated, 'We were told at one stage that white waistbands around single-deck vehicles had to be removed at repaint because this saved a few pounds, but somehow they never seemed to need repainting in some companies.' Despite having these drab liveries imposed upon it by NBC, Cumberland and its neighbour Ribble did strive to maintain a good standard of appearance in the fleet.

The year 1974 brought a major reorganisation of local government with the abolition of County Boroughs and the rearrangement of Distict and County Councils. The County of Cumbria was created by the amalgamation of the counties of Cumberland, Westmorland and the Furness area of Lancashire together with other minor boundary changes.

A joint report was prepared by Peter Townley, General Manager of Cumberland Motor Services and Ian Chapman, General Manager of Ribble Motor Services, covering the provision of bus services in the new County and details regarding the vehicles and staff employed at that time are given in the Appendices.

A significant event of this period was the 1980 Transport Act which brought about the deregulation of long distance coach services. Generally the Act had little effect on stage carriage services, as local bus services were called in those days, but there were a few notable exceptions to this and one concerned CMS in Whitehaven. Here, Yeowarts Coaches applied for a licence to operate two circular town services covering the large Mirehouse Estate and this application was objected to by Cumberland Motor Services and Cumbria County Council. The application was refused by the Northern Area Traffic Commissioners and went to appeal where the appointed inspector recommended confirmation of the refusal.

In a foretaste of things to come, however, the Secretary of State for Transport decided to allow the appeal and the licence was granted. The service commenced on 19th October 1981 with fares below those charged by CMS, which reacted by introducing its 'Haven Link' services and cutting its fares. These services combined existing town services providing, in some cases, circular facilities. For instance Haven Link Service 7-9 operated outward by service 7 to Mirehouse Estate and returned by service 9. The name 'Haven Link' was applied to some vehicles and Whitehaven must have had the cheapest town services in the country at this time. The loss of revenue was partly offset by the withdrawal of a number of loss making rural services. The Yeowart service operated until January 1983 and the ultimate outcome is covered in the next Chapter.

The greater problem facing Cumberland, and all other NBC subsidiaries, however, was yet to come. The 1984 *Buses* White Paper and the *Transport Act of 1985* created a situation in which the National Bus Company had no future, for the Act was designed to speed up the growth of competition in the bus industry.

Those opposed to Nationalisation would perhaps shed no tears over the break up of an organisation which at its peak operated over 21,000 vehicles and employed over 84,000 staff throughout England and Wales (by the breakup of NBC these figures had reduced to 14,083 and 48,857). If, however, they believed that the Government's forced sale of NBC would create a host of small operators, thereby providing profitable opportunities for small entrepreneurs, they were – in the main – to be sadly mistaken.

In little more than a decade the two new giants of the bus industry would have grown to a point where they were operating almost as many vehicles as the National Bus Company had in 1984 (though with considerably fewer staff), and they were still growing.

The last Leyland National 1 to enter service was number 369, shown here at Salterbeck Cemetery, Workington on service 34 from Whitehaven to Keswick.

Chapter Two
Towards Privatisation

The Author's earlier history of CMS – *British Bus Systems No. 1 - Cumberland* – went to press in early 1983 and this chapter picks up the story at that point. The book was launched on 18th May 1983 at a buffet luncheon organised by the company at Roseneath Country Hotel, Low Moresby, Whitehaven, attended by representatives of local government, local industry and commerce and the transport industry. To mark the occasion, the company restored 1961 Bristol FS double-decker 109 DRM and repainted it in the pre- and early postwar livery of bright red with three cream bands and white roof with full lining out to the red and the cream. The vehicle had been delivered in 1961 as C416, becoming No. 550 in the 1961 renumbering scheme. More details regarding the history of this vehicle and its subsequent sale for preservation are given in the Appendices.

The major issue facing the company at that time, however, was the operation of local services in Whitehaven by Yeowarts Coaches. Objections to the granting of a licence had been raised by Cumbria County Council on the grounds that the Yeowart services were having an adverse effect on the revenue of Cumberland Motor Services Ltd which had reacted by withdrawing certain rural services. The County took the matter to the Court of Appeal and as a result of this, the Yeowart licence was withdrawn and the services ceased on Friday 21st January 1983 when a free service was operated. However, Yeowarts had previously expressed interest in operating further services in the Whitehaven area and application had been made to the Northern Traffic Commissioners, in whose area Cumbria was situated at that time, for three licences. The hearing commenced in Whitehaven in early March 1983 and was

This was the period of the demise of the Bristol RE, a vehicle which had served Cumberland for many years in various forms and on most types of service. Here No. 301 of the final batch leaves Whitehaven bus station on town service 09 on Sunday 24th May 1981. Two similar vehicles, formerly numbers 293 and 295 have recently been purchased for preservation and are in the process of being restored to the pre-NBC Cumberland livery in which they were delivered.

then postponed until 28th and 29th April 1983 by which time reorganisation of the Traffic Areas had taken place and Cumbria had been transferred from the Northern to the North Western Area.

This application was opposed by Cumberland Motor Services Ltd, Cumbria County Council, Copeland Borough Council, Allerdale District Council and local Members of Parliament. In announcing his decision not to allow the application, the Chairman of the Commissioners, Mr Roy Hutchings, stated that he had been swayed by the possible loss of rural services if competition was allowed to take away revenue from Cumberland Motor Services Ltd. As a result of this decision Cumberland Motor Services Ltd regained the monopoly of services which it had enjoyed for so long.

LOCAL DEVELOPMENTS

The 1983 timetable was introduced on 5th June and followed the same format as the 1982 issue with a drawing of Cockermouth Main Street on the front and a vehicle inset in a circle. In this case the vehicle was Bristol VR 419 in the National Holidays advertiser livery. The timetable incorporated the changes introduced in August 1982 as a consequence of the closing of Wigton garage and also other minor variations.

Another development at this time concerned the Company's Bristol REs, a model which was generally regarded in the industry as the most successful of the rear engined single-deckers introduced in the 'sixties. Cumberland had purchased a total of 53 of these vehicles between 1966 and 1972 and had been pleased with their performance, although the fact that, apart from the first two examples, they had Leyland rather than Gardner engines, did not please the engineers who had been told by the management that the reason for the Leyland engines was that they were cheaper on initial cost. As previously mentioned the Gardner engine had always been held in high esteem by Cumberland engineers. On the other hand, the first two had manual gearboxes which made them unpopular with drivers. However, be that as it may, it was decided to embark on a programme of major rebuilding of the early models with flat front and shallow windscreen.

Number 271 was selected as the first example and it was rebuilt in the body shop at Whitehaven under the direction of John Twentyman, the body shop foreman who had been responsible many years previously, for the design and construction of the excellent new bodies built for the Leyland PS 1 chassis which had previously carried coach bodies. Number 271 was rebuilt with bow front, as fitted to later REs, and also with flat floor and with the seating recovered in standard NBC moquette. The result was an excellent job but the programme to rebuild further examples was abandoned due to a decline in service requirements.

Cumberland employees in the news at this time included Roger Burge of Workington depot, winner of the 'United Kingdom Bus Driver of the Year' competition, the final of which was held in Blackpool in September.

Whitehaven driver Luke Ryan was included in the 1984 Birthday Honours list and received the BEM, the award being made just after his retirement following 38 years service with the Cumberland company. From 1956 until 1983, Mr Ryan was Branch Secretary of the Whitehaven CMS Passenger Services Branch of the Transport and General Workers Union.

In May 1984 Barry Hinkley was appointed Chief Engineer in succession to Jim Weeks who had been appointed Chief Engineer of the Northern General Transport Company Ltd, Gateshead. Like his predecessor, Mr Hinkley took great interest in the appearance of Company vehicles and re-introduced the white bands on the single-deck NBC livery with a consequent improvement in appearance.

THE BORDER CLIPPER

For some time the company had been considering the introduction of a limited stop service between West Cumbria and Carlisle with possible extension of some workings to the north east. This emerged under the title of 'Border Clipper' with vehicles being presented to the press at Whitehaven on 21st August 1984, four days before commencement of the service on 25th August 1984. In its original form this comprised a limited stop service with most northbound journeys commencing at Egremont and operating as service 22 to Whitehaven before continuing as either service 300 or service 600 to Carlisle. One journey started from Kirkland as service 17 and one of the southbound journeys continued beyond Whitehaven to Cross Gates as service 17, the others continuing to Egremont as service 22. North of Whitehaven service 300 operated to Carlisle via the 'high way' to Workington and then via Maryport, Aspatria and Wigton. Service 600 operated via the 'high way' to Workington then via Cockermouth and Wigton. In addition there was a return working from Whitehaven to Sunderland operating to Carlisle via service 300 route, then via Hexham and Newcastle upon Tyne. In order to protect the services of United Automobile Services Ltd, passengers were not carried point to point between Carlisle and Newcastle or between Hexham and Sunderland.

To operate the service, the five Willowbrook bodied Leyland Leopards, numbered 628 – 632 which had been new in 1981, were repainted in a special livery of white with black window surrounds and broad bands of blue and red swept up towards the rear. The name 'Border Clipper' was applied in script to both sides, front and rear, whilst the normal NBC style CUMBERLAND name was applied towards the rear of both sides.

This was the only concession to NBC which the livery gave and this is understood to have brought forth some comment from the NBC hierarchy! 'Border Clipper' nameboards were also prepared for fitting to other coaches for occasional use as necessary. The five coaches, which had received river names when new, were renamed as follows :-

River Calder, River Cocker, River Eden, River Waver, River Derwent (628 – 632). Coach No. 632 was the only one to retain its original name.

Willowbrook-bodied Leyland Leopard number 632 in Border Clipper livery is shown near Arlecdon heading towards Kirkland to operate the Border Clipper service to Carlisle on 14th March 1985.

Below left: Leyland National 2 number 376 stands in Keswick bus station on 29th May 1985 in 'Advertiser' livery loading on route 35 to Frizington. The Lakeland hills can be seen above the top of the original bus station – now demolished to make way for a supermarket. Note the 'Cumberland Advertiser' fleetname.

The service became popular, particularly on the section between Cockermouth and Carlisle where there was no rail alternative, so much so that duplicates had to be provided on some workings. In view of this it was decided to fit coach seating to the two Leyland Olympian double-deckers which had been delivered in 1983 and paint them in 'Border Clipper' livery. The first to be dealt with was No. 801, being repainted in September 1985 and this was followed shortly afterwards by No. 802. On repainting, the vehicles were renumbered 1001 and 1002.

MORE CHANGES

As a consequence of 'Border Clipper', service 30 between Whitehaven and Carlisle was reduced in frequency from 30 minutes to 60 minutes but a new service 31 was introduced at intermediate timings to operate between Whitehaven and Maryport with extension beyond Maryport to Broughton Moor. This gave the villages of Broughton Moor and Dearham their first direct regular bus service with Whitehaven. However, at the same time, service 56 Workington – Broughton Moor – Maryport was withdrawn. Another important change in the 1984 timetable concerned services 34 and 35 between Whitehaven and Keswick. These were diverted to operate between Whitehaven and Workington via Lowca instead of Distington and most journeys were extended south of Whitehaven to terminate at Frizington. Between Whitehaven Bus Station and Frizington the service operated via West Cumberland Hospital to give places north of Whitehaven a regular daytime service to the Hospital. The extension of services 34 and 35 south of Whitehaven when combined with

Left: Roger Burge winner in 1983 left and Roy Blaikie winner in 1984 of the United Kingdom Bus Driver of the Year Competition, stand with Driving Instructor Peter Cremins, displaying their trophies in front of one of the Leyland Leopards with Duple Dominant 2 body.

'Border Clipper' workings on service 22 and journeys from Whitehaven on service 17 provided, for most of the day, a regular 20 minute headway between Whitehaven, Cleator Moor and Wath Brow. As a result of the operation of services 34 and 35 via Lowca, service 41 Whitehaven – Lowca – Workington was withdrawn.

During 1984, one of the 1977 Duple Dominant 1 bodied Leyland Leopards (No. 616) was taken into the body shop at Whitehaven for body repairs following a minor accident. On removal of panels it was noted that there was extensive corrosion of the body framework and major rebuilding had to take place. Other vehicles in the same batch were examined and all in turn received extensive rebuilding with the exception of No. 618 on which work commenced but it was then decided to sell the vehicle. Subsequent to this the body was scrapped and the chassis was rebodied by Plaxton, entering the fleet of J. & F.

Aspden (Blackburn) Ltd which re-registered it GEY 273 shortly after purchase. Number 613 of this batch had previously been sold to Midland Red, along with No. 610. Numbers 614, 615 and 617 were rebuilt without the brightwork surrounds to the windows and were finished in white livery with black window surrounds and NBC red and blue stripes. Large CUMBERLAND fleetnames were applied.

For some time, consideration had been given to possible replacement vehicles for the ageing ex-Trent Leyland Leopards to operate through the Seascale railway arch and on the service to Netherwasdale. Dennis Lancets and the Leyland DAB, later renamed Leyland Tiger Cub, were considered but in the end it was decided to rebuild the ex-Trent Leopards. This work was undertaken by Ribble Motor Services Ltd at Preston and the vehicles were dealt with in number order 606 – 609. On completion Nos. 606

A representative of the period of white band restoration for single-deckers under the influence of Barry Hinkley when he was Chief Engineer. Leyland National 2 No. 394 is shown in the body shop at Whitehaven having just emerged from the paint shop, visible in the background, The white band was a feature which these vehicles had not previously carried. The date is 22nd June 1985 on the occasion of an Omnibus Society visit to the company. The Haven Link symbol is clearly visible on the destination and service number blinds.

– 608 received standard NBC red and white local coach livery but No. 609, which was not rebuilt until mid 1985, received 'Border Clipper' livery for operation on a new service from Keswick to Carlisle, mentioned later.

In November 1984, the company received five Duple Laser bodied Leyland Tigers more details of which are given in Chapter 7 but two of these, Nos. 103 and 104 received 'Border Clipper' livery and were set to work on this service. However, their usage on this service was to be short lived as, following an increase in National Express work in Spring 1985, they were repainted into National Express or National Holidays livery as detailed in Chapter 7.

The company entered the 1984 'United Kingdom Bus Driver of the Year' competition and at the final at Blackpool in September came out winners for the second year in succession. This time the winner was Roy Blaikie, also of Workington Depot.In February 1985 a dinner was held to mark the retirement of Gerry Carruthers, after 48 years service with the company. Gerry had joined CMS as a fitter at Keswick depot, transferring to Central Works in Whitehaven in 1964. He was promoted to Assistant Chief Engineer in 1980 and held this position until his retirement.

In 1985, the revenue support grant from Cumbria County Council was reduced by £500,000 and this forced the company to make some major changes. These changes included a revised management structure with the General Manager, Peter Townley, taking a more active role in the Traffic Department which was renamed Customer Service Department. The Traffic Manager, David Dickinson, left after 14 years with the Company, the Assistant Traffic Manager, Douglas Haig became Operations Manager and Stuart Bear, formerly Chief Traffic Officer, became Chief Operations Officer. Maryport Depot was closed on 25th May 1985 and a new timetable was introduced on 26th

May which incorporated some major changes; the timetable booklet was circulated free in the company's area, being financed by advertising.

Service 12 between Whitehaven and Millom was truncated south of Seascale with a new service 16 operating between Bootle and Millom with school service extensions to/from Ravenglass. Service 11 from Gosforth to Netherwasdale was withdrawn and the need for short vehicles was therefore eliminated. Service 71 from Keswick to Wigton was withdrawn but some replacement for this was provided by two new 'Border Clipper' services from Keswick to Carlisle numbered 710 and 720.

Service 710 operated via Cockermouth and then via the same route as service 600 to Carlisle where it connected with service 300 to Sunderland. Service 720 operated via Castle Inn. Ex-Trent Leyland Leopard No. 609 on rebuilding and repainting in 'Border Clipper' livery was the regular vehicle for this service although initially one of the other vehicles from this batch was used pending completion of No. 609. Services 710 and 720 operated Mondays to Fridays but a Saturdays only service from Keswick to Newcastle upon Tyne was introduced shortly afterwards. In 1986 Duple Dominant 2 bodied Leyland Leopard No. 619 received extensive body rebuilding and was repainted in 'Border Clipper' livery and later became the regular vehicle on this service.

This timetable introduced an interesting change on the Whitehaven Town Service 01, Bus Station to Kells, in that it was linked to certain workings on Town Service 05 under the 'Haven Link' banner to provide a 1-5 and a 5-1 operation thus restoring a link which had last operated in 1931. Town Service 03 from Whitehaven Bus Station to Sandwith was withdrawn thus ending a long established although infrequent service.

Sandwith was and still is very much a 'small country village' which had market day connections on Thursdays and Saturdays to the Town as well as schools services but it was within the Borough of Whitehaven and the services were therefore town services. At this time service No. 03 was re-allocated to the long, circuitous town service, previously 08, Bus Station, Loop Road, Fairfield Estate, Hospital, Mirehouse, Greenbank, Woodhouse, Kells. Service 23 from Whitehaven to Moor Row was withdrawn with certain workings on service 12 being diverted via Moor Row,

In Workington, Town Service 46, Bus Station to Brierydale, was linked with Local Service 47, Bus Station to Seaton, to provide a cross town facility. Service 44 from Workington to Moresby Parks was withdrawn.

There was an important change on Service 74 between Keswick and Penrith as Cumberland withdrew from the service which had been jointly operated with Ribble, leaving Ribble to work a much reduced service.

The Bristol RE made a return to the fleet in 1986 when nine were purchased from Bristol Omnibus Company Ltd for the operation of a site service for British Nuclear Fuels Ltd at Sellafield. They were painted in NBC leaf green with white band to meet the request of BNFL that they be in a livery other than red. No fleetnames were applied and they were numbered 900 to 908 with a painted front destination display 'Site Bus Service', The centre track of the three track service number display was retained, the outer tracks being painted out. They were withdrawn in mid-1987 and sold to Belfast Citibus where they resumed normal service operation. They were replaced on the Sellafield Site service with four Sherpa minibuses hired from Carlyle Works and these in turn were replaced with minibuses from the CMS fleet.

With the forthcoming demise of the National Bus Company, subsidiary companies were freed from the obligation to use the National Bus Company corporate livery and began to adopt their own schemes. Cumberland adopted a very attractive livery of Ayres red and sandstone with brown skirt and this was first applied to dual-purpose ECW-bodied Leyland Leopard No. 635. The first double-decker to receive the new livery was Bristol VR No. 435. There were three basic versions of the livery. Double-deckers received sandstone roof, upper saloon window surrounds and central band, dual-purpose single-deckers were red below the waistrail and sandstone above whilst single-deckers were red with sandstone roof. In addition two of the coach-seated Bristol VRs, Nos. 436 and 437

General Manager Peter Townley on the extreme left, with management, staff and partners, gathered to say farewell to Chief Engineer Jim Weeks and Mrs Weeks, on his right, at the time of his departure to Northern General Transport Company Limited, Gateshead.

received red lower saloon and sandstone upper saloon with slight variation in the dividing line between the red and sandstone. Coach seated No. 435 retained the standard double-deck version. All vehicles initially received a brown skirt but this was later abandoned. The fleetname CMS Cumberland was used and this was applied in Sandstone between Sandstone stripes, except in the case of single-deckers where it was in red between red stripes on the sandstone cove panels. The CMS Cumberland name was also adopted for publicity. The livery was very attractive and received much admiration.

The Company was very keen to promote bus services in the Lake District and to this end a special leaflet was produced for the Borrowdale service describing it as the most beautiful bus ride in England. The summer timetable was retained for the winter period in 1986/87.

POLITICAL IMPLICATIONS

The early indications of government plans for the privatisation of the National Bus Company subsidiaries such as Cumberland began to filter through in 1983 through General Managers conferences and regional meetings. At many of these meetings general managers were exposed to a series of what could best be described as 'business briefings' as a preparation for the new brave world ahead. It was quickly becoming clear that the ethic of providing excellence of service to generate profit would soon be replaced by profit targets dictating the quality of service. The shadow of privatisation began to overshadow all sorts of other issues such as fleet renewals and replacing national level agreements with local agreements. Confusion and uncertainty began to slowly undermine morale at all levels within the company and senior management was viewed with a suspicion never previously evident.

Company management teams began to sit round the table to discuss issues such as who should be involved in management buyouts and the size of stake that each manager would need to raise. This was an unenviable task. Those included began to worry about raising the required stake and those excluded began to think they had been excluded from a wonderful opportunity. Everyone began to dwell on other questions such as continuity of employment and pension rights, this regardless of their age or proximity to retirements. Meetings started to take place with these mysterious creatures from the City called merchant bankers.

By May 1984 subsidiaries were visited by a consultant appointed by NBC to review progress and advise on issues arising. The advice was somewhat too independent in nature for NBC's tastes; hence that assignment came to a rapid conclusion.

The form of privatisation envisaged within NBC circles went through sudden changes of form, no doubt influenced by DoT officials' latest thinking on the subject. Originally NBC had hoped privatisation could have taken a form similar to that used for National Freight Corporation; in other words a transfer as a whole with NBC senior officials remaining in the driving seat. This was generally well received as it preserved the hierarchy with which senior managers were familiar and

had been evolved through past promotions. It would have avoided all the upheaval which customarily dissipates productive effort when a major restructuring is effected. But that scheme was too easy and was soon dismissed. It failed to leave a method of entry for the new entrepreneur from outside the bus industry.

Another scheme involved groupings of companies according to geographical considerations, but presumably it would have been seen as creating local monopolies. The answer then presented was diverse groupings of companies presenting no adjoining boundaries.

As far as Cumberland was concerned an interesting NBC proposal emerged which provided for it to become part of Ribble. This was a repeat of similar suggestions which had been made in earlier times and by dint of vigorous representation this proposal was eventually reversed. It was then decided that the large subsidiary companies would be split into smaller units in order to make them more attractive to prospective purchasers and as part of this policy it was declared towards the end of 1985 that Cumberland would take over the Ribble depots in Carlisle and Penrith 'in the near future'. The actual transfer took place on 22/23rd February 1986 and involved 74 vehicles.

Initially, the name 'CARLISLEBUS' was adopted for the local services in Carlisle and this name was applied to vehicles. Penrith-based vehicles and coaches based at Carlisle received 'CUMBERLAND' fleetnames. Further information on the operations in Carlisle and Penrith prior to the Cumberland takeover is given in Chapter 3.

In this giddy atmosphere heads began to whirl and it was almost necessary to put a reminder in the diary to remember to attend to the daily business of running the bus service.

As 1984 passed and 1985, the year of the Transport Act, emerged the 'club' atmosphere of working as a senior manager within the NBC began to evaporate. Early indications began to show in the individuals who were prepared to consider 'dog eat dog' tactics. Meantime the new entrepreneurs began to show their colours. It quickly became clear to senior management teams of the best run companies in the NBC group that there would be a lot of new contenders, well provided with finance, ready to acquire the 'plum' companies such as Cumberland. Its worth was considerably increased by the addition of the former Ribble depot at Carlisle with its highly profitable city services network.

At the end of 1985, Peter Townley, the longest serving General Manager since H. H. Merchant, left the company to take up a similar position with the Manchester company A. Mayne and Son Ltd. He was succeeded in January 1986 by Michael Wadsworth. One of Mr Wadsworth's major tasks was to continue the process of preparing the company for privatisation and he mounted a management bid for the enlarged Cumberland undertaking. The initial response from company employees to a management/employee buyout proposal had shown a majority of three to one in favour of this but the bid was unsuccessful the race being won by the newly emerging Statgecoach group with effect from 23rd July 1987.

ENJOY THE MOST BEAUTIFUL BUS RIDE IN ENGLAND

THE BORROWDALE · BUS ·

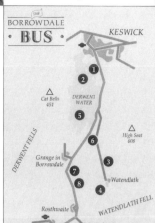

The bus journey from Keswick to Seatoller along the shores of Derwentwater, "Queen of the Lakes", and through the Jaws of Borrowdale, is the most spectacular in England: Eight miles of grandeur to be enjoyed at leisure. Leave your car behind and relish the freedom of "hopping on and off" the frequent buses.

The 'Hail and Ride' facility of the Borrowdale bus enables passengers to visit the many beauty spots en route, some of which are listed below.

1 Friar's Crag and Calf Close Bay. A short lakeside walk from the Keswick boat landings to Friar's Crag leads to one of Lakeland's most famous views. A stone memorial records how impressed John Ruskin was with this unique combination of lake, mountains and trees. The bay beyond is Calf Close, originally Scarfclose, from the old norse "skarf" meaning a cormorant.

2 The Islands. Largely neglected today, the four islands of Derwentwater have enjoyed a glorious past. Derwent Isle provided some bizarre attractions for 18th century tourists — mock ruins, make believe battles and vast regattas. By contrast, the island in the middle of the lake was the hermitage of St Herbert, and later became a place of pilgrimage.

3 Ashness Bridge & Surprise View. A rambler's dream but a motorist's nightmare, the steep twisting road up to Watendlath Tarn is rarely wide enough to allow more than single file traffic. The panorama from Ashness Bridge and the even more dizzying vista of Surprise View has made the road famous the world over. Be sure to take your camera!

4 Watendlath Tarn. Walkers who persevere beyond Surprise View to the tiny hamlet of Watendlath are well rewarded. Here by the mountain tarn is Fold Head Farm, fictional home of Judith Paris in Sir Hugh Walpole's "Herries Chronicles". Among the cluster of whitewashed farms and cottages sleek sheepdogs welcome visitors. Farmhouse teas are served.

5 Floating Islands. The mysterious floating islands of Derwentwater appear and disappear from time to time at the southern end of the lake. They are often not seen for several years. Dorothy Wordsworth saw them and was inspired to write one of her few poems. Legend surrounds their significance, but scientists now believe them to be rafts of rotting vegetation made buoyant by marsh gas.

6 Lodore Falls.
Dividing and gliding and sliding,
And falling and brawling and sprawling,
And driving and riving and striving,
And sprinkling and twinkling and wrinkling,
And sounding and bounding and rounding,
And bubbling and troubling and doubling,
And grumbling and rambling and tumbling,
And clattering and battering and shattering;
From the Cataract of Lodore by Robert Southey.

7 The Jaws of Borrowdale. Just south of the village of Grange with its graceful twin arched bridge, the fells close in on the valley to form the romantically named Jaws of Borrowdale. Early travellers were so impressed that they imagined a kind of alpine pass where speaking was disallowed lest the sound bring down an avalanche!

8 The Bowder Stone. The massive boulder over 30 feet high seems to perch precariously on its narrow base. But it has probably been standing like this for the last 12,000 years, since Lakeland's glaciers melted and left the rock stranded. A substantial ladder staircase climbs to the "summit" for those who can manage 29 steps!

The leaflet produced to promote the Borrowdale Bus.

Driver Luke Ryan was presented with the British Empire Medal in June 1984 and is pictured here at Mirehouse Estate, Whitehaven in May 1984, with Mr P. Wyke Smith, Mr R. Brook, Mr D. G. F. Rawlinson, all of NBC, Mr P. A. Townley, CMS General Manager and Lord Shepherd PC, Chairman of NBC. 550 is in the background.

Chapter Three
Carlisle and Penrith

In the Beginning

The city of Carlisle has a long and interesting history, its Ccstle was founded in the year 1092 and its Cathedral dates from 1133. Its growth accelerated in the middle of the 18th century following the establishment of cotton and other industries. Located at a junction of the north-south and east-west routes its growth as a transport centre was assured and embraced within its general history is a fascinating transport history.

Stagecoach services are thought to have commenced in the 1760s and by the year 1810 considerable expansion had taken place, Carlisle, Kendal and west Cumberland all having regular services by this time. It is recorded that by now Carlisle had seven daily stage coach departures with a further seven leaving twice per week. At the same time Whitehaven had 30 departures per week including a daily service to Carlisle leaving at 5am and returning from Carlisle at 5pm, serving Workington, Maryport and Wigton en route. By 1829 there had been further expansion with services as follows :-

Kendal-Carlisle-Glasgow	Daily
Carlisle-Edinburgh	3 times/week
Carlisle-London	3 times/week
Carlisle-Manchester	Daily
Carlisle-Liverpool	Daily
Carlisle-Newcastle	Daily
Carlisle-Whitehaven	Daily

Reproduced opposite is a copy of an announcement by a Mr Kirkbride of the Globe Inn, Whitehaven regarding a service by 'Tub' from Whitehaven to Carlisle and dated 1822. Competition between operators became intense, many resorting to dangerously fast speeds and racing, with the result that safety tended to suffer. As a result of this some operators issued notices that they would not indulge in the 'disgraceful and dangerous practice of racing against other operators.' Increased speeds brought other problems in that they were not uniform across the routes resulting in the deterioration of connection facilities. This period of racing was followed by one of greater co-operation, with operators advertising connections with other operators' services.

Travel by road was at this time expensive and only the rich could afford it. A fare of 18 shillings has been quoted from Whitehaven to Kendal, plus tips for the driver and guard. Competition for the stagecoach came first on

TUB TO CARLISLE.

J. KIRKBRIDE,

GLOBE INN, WHITEHAVEN,

RESPECTFULLY informs his Friends and the Public in general, that he has commenced running a TUB between WHITEHAVEN and CARLISLE by way of *Allonby, Wigton, &c.* at very reasonable Fares.

The TUB leaves WHITEHAVEN every MONDAY, WEDNESDAY, and SATURDAY, and returns every TUESDAY, THURSDAY, and SUNDAY.

PARCELS, &c. carried through, or left at any part of the Road, and delivered with the greatest care and punctuality.

The TUB leaves WHITEHAVEN at 7 o'Clock in the Morning, and arrives the same Evening at Mrs. IRVING's, Blue Bell Inn, Scotch-street, CARLISLE, which Place it leaves at 8 o'Clock in the Morning, and arrives here the same Evening.

Whitehaven. July 10, 1822.

coastal routes and whilst this did not directly affect Carlisle it did provide competition between Whitehaven and Liverpool. On inland routes it was the railways that provided competition and these certainly had their effect on Carlisle.

The first railway to arrive in Carlisle was the Newcastle and Carlisle Railway in July 1836 and from that time Carlisle grew as an important railway centre and continues as such to-day.

THE CARLISLE ELECTRIC TRAMWAYS COMPANY LTD

The first suggestion of a tramway for the City of Carlisle came in 1880 when a horse tramway was proposed but this was not proceeded with.

It was in 1898 that the Carlisle Tramways Order was made, its promoters being Messrs. Needham, Horton, Gittings and Kershaw, all from Birmingham. They obtained powers to operate a tramway and were backed in this by Manchester Traction Company Ltd. The Order authorised construction of 5.5 miles of 3ft 6ins gauge tramway with a track mileage of 7.75 miles.

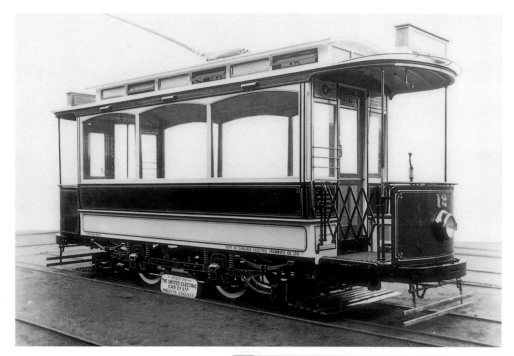

Left: Single deck tramcar No.12 photographed when new by the builder, The United Electric Car Company Ltd. of Preston, for service under the Denton Street railway bridge on the route to Denton Holme.

Below: An early view of English Street, looking north with an unidentified tramcar operating along the single track section.

The consent of Carlisle City Council was received but was conditional on all electric power being purchased from the municipal power station with a guaranteed minimum consumption of 1,000,000 units per year. The charge was to be 2 pence per unit for the first 50,000 units, 1.75 pence for the next 100,000 units with the remainder at 1.5 pence. The Corporation had power to purchase the system after 21 years and thereafter at intervals of seven years.

The Order authorised the construction of 28 sections of tramway. One section was rejected and five sections were not constructed whilst one section was partially constructed. A company was formed and named The City of Carlisle Electric Tramways Company Limited. It was first registered on 16th June 1899 and acquired the rights of the 1898 Order.

The first directors were :-

English Street, Carlisle

> R. Barningham, also a director of Manchester Traction Co Ltd and G. F. Milnes.
> T. D. Lingard, also a director of Dick, Kerr and Co Ltd
> G. Readman, also a director of the Blackpool and Fleetwood Tramroad Company.
> L. R. Creighton, a local director.
> George Cook was Company Secretary and the registered office was at 23 London Road, Carlisle. The depot was also built in London Road.

Invitation for share capital was issued on 3rd July 1899 and the majority was taken by the Manchester and Liverpool District Banking Company and the Clydesdale Bank, with few local applications.

The joint consulting engineers for the construction were Alfred Dickinson and Company of Birmingham and Pritchard, Green and Company also of Birmingham. Mesrs Dick, Kerr and Company Limited were awarded the contract for the construction of the tramway including overhead and rolling stock. Construction commenced on 4th September 1899 in Lowther Street and was completed ready for inspection in June 1900.

The construction involved three river bridges, five railway bridges, two under railway bridges, that on Denton Street being only 12ft 11ins high and making necessary the use of single-deck trams on this route. The power supply was 500 volts DC and the completed system was inspected by Mr A. P. Trotter of the Board of Trade on 28th June 1900, being operated the following day for driver training. The system was opened to the public on 30th June 1900.

Rolling stock comprised twelve tramcars, three single-deck and nine open-top double-deck. The first timetable contained six services as shown opposite :-

Citadel Station to Stanwix.
Citadel Station to Denton Holme.
Citadel Station to London Road.
Citadel Station to Boundary Road.
Citadel Station to Warwick Road.
Citadel Station to Newtown.

The basic frequency was ten minutes and in practice the system operated as three cross city routes as follows :-

Boundary Road to Newtown.
Stanwix to Warwick Road.
London Road to Denton Holme.

The Denton Holme service required single-deck trams because of the low bridge in Denton Street and this was a factor which was to influence Carlisle city services for the next 50 years with Ribble's standard pre-war single-deckers being a feature of these, followed by underfloor engined Sentinels until the road was lowered under the bridge in 1954.

The system was not a financial success and the last dividend was paid in 1906. By 1910 the financial situation had become serious due to lack of passengers and also to the high cost of power purchased from the Corporation. As a result, maintenance suffered, leading to deterioration of the system and rolling stock and the directors recommended that the system be sold. The company was finally purchased in November 1911 by Balfour Beatty and Company Limited which already had experience of tramway operation in other places.

In 1912 agreement was reached with the Corporation for a reduction in the price of power and the new company then proceeded to update the track and rolling stock, eight double-deck and four single-deck cars being purchased from United Electric Car Company Limited. The overhead was also improved and the upgraded system was opened on 9th December 1912, having cost £18,172.

The First World War brought further problems as a shortage of labour and materials affected maintenance and by 1917 the City Watch Committee expressed concern over the condition of the tramway. Call up for service had also led to a shortage of tram drivers but, despite this, the Watch Committee refused to sanction the use of women drivers. However, over a year later, the Committee relented and this enabled the company to improve the service.

Following the end of the war there was considerable building development on the outskirts of the city, but despite requests from the Corporation, the company refused to extend the system. By now the motor bus was becoming popular and this mode of transport was introduced to service these new areas. The Tramways Act of 1870 required tramway companies to maintain the roadway between the tracks and also for a distance of 18in beyond the outer rails, so the company was in the position of having to maintain at least part of the roadway for use by its competitors. Despite this competition, the company managed to survive and with the prospect of embracing other forms of transport, changed its name in March 1926 to Carlisle and District Transport Company Limited. By this time it had taken over Percivals Motor Bus Services with services to Annan, Dumfries, Langholm and Brampton.

In 1930 it was announced that Ribble Motor Services Ltd had arranged to buy the company and replace the trams with buses but this did not meet with the approval of the City Council which was keen to establish a municipal transport system. Accordingly, in March 1931, the City Council decided to purchase Carlisle and District Transport Company Ltd and a Transport Committee was formed and elected a member of the Municipal Tramways and Transport Association. However, the Northern Traffic Commissioners refused to grant the Corporation's application to operate buses. In view of this the Corporation agreed to the Commissioners' suggestion that talks be held with transport operators to discuss the possiblity of providing a co-ordinated transport system for the city. The outcome of this is covered later but it was the beginning of the end for the tramway system and although it had been intended that the tramway would continue until April 1932, the final date was brought forward to Saturday 21st November 1931. Thus ended the Carlisle tramway system.

A horse bus en route from Boundary Road to the Infirmary with advert for Robinson's store. This store later became Binns, a firm which was to feature for many years in bus advertising in the north and particularly north east England where every bus seemed to carry a 'Shop at Binns' message.

A line up of early buses in Bowness on Solway, the first two at least belonging to local operator Hodgsons of that village.

THE MOTOR BUS.

Horse buses were introduced in Carlisle around 1866 by a Mr Joseph Carlisle but the service did not last very long and the next service was introduced in 1886 by the Carlisle Carriage Company Ltd with two routes, Harraby to Stanwix and Newtown to Boundary Road, and later in 1896, a service from Botcherby Lane to Cemetery Lane. Some competition was provided by a Mr Crosbie, a taxi proprietor of West Walls but this was short-lived. The horse bus services ceased in January 1900.

It was on 30th May 1921 that the first regular motor omnibus service into Carlisle was established. This was the service by Cumberland Motor Services Ltd from its headquarters at Whitehaven, linking en route the towns of Workington, Maryport, Aspatria and Wigton and initially involving a change of vehicle at Maryport. The basic frequency was two-hourly and the time taken for the 42

mile journey was 3hrs 25mins, although the 8am departure ex-Whitehaven was scheduled to complete the journey in 3hrs. The service terminated at The Crescent in Carlisle and it is appropriate that it should have been the first country service into the city for, over the years, it has remained the most frequent of these services and provided a 'Northern Backbone' to the Cumberland Motor Services Ltd system. Premises were rented in Carlisle in order to avoid 'dead mileage'. In 1925 CMS opened its first branch depot in the small town of Wigton, ten miles to the south west of Carlisle and housed its northern allocation there, the use of the rented premises in Carlisle being discontinued. This is evident in the 1926 and subsequent timetables which show early morning positioning journeys from Wigton to Carlisle to operate the Whitehaven service and also the reverse happening in the evening.

The other service which CMS commenced from the city in 1921 was to Silloth and an unusual feature of this service was that the timetable showed two departures from Silloth to Carlisle at 8pm and a footnote confirmed that two vehicles would be provided.

Circular tours were offered by CMS whereby passengers could travel from Whitehaven to Carlisle and return via Silloth. The fare was 12 shillings and 7 pence or in modern terms about 63 pence. It is worth noting that with inflation the equivalent cost to-day would be over £13! In 1922 special excursions were offered by CMS from West Cumberland in conjunction with Robinsons (later Binns) store.

The 1926 CMS timetable contained a note which proclaimed 'Through services between Whitehaven and Carlisle by the latest pneumatic tyred saloon buses.' The frequency of the service was still two hourly but the

Carlisle and District Motor Services Ltd received these two Daimler CF6 with bodies by Northern Counties Motor and Engineering Co Ltd in 1930. They are shown in Wigan when photogrphed by the builder before delivery.

This Lion was No. 3 in the fleet of Alfred Fidler of Carlisle and operated on the Carlisle to Wetheral service. It carries the fleet emblem 'Wetheral'.

journey time had been reduced to 2hrs 45mins. A new addition to this timetable was a service from Carlisle to Cockermouth via Wigton, Mealsgate and Bothel.

In the 1927 timetable the note regarding pneumatic tyres was supplemented by another which read *Travel in comfort by the famous 'Lion' bus*. This was a reference to the Leyland Lion single-deck buses which the company had introduced in 1926 and of which further examples were purchased in 1927 and 1928. The note speaks volumes for the reliable simplicity of these vehicles which provided the foundation on which many bus companies were built. The author recalls travelling on some of these 'Lions' in the postwar period when they were twenty years old.

In 1929 the frequency of the Whitehaven service was increased to hourly and the journey time reduced to 2hrs 20mins but this must have been too ambitious as it was increased to 2hrs 25mins in the 1930 timetable. A service from Carlisle to Keswick was introduced on 22nd March 1929 to operate during the Summer only.

During this period when CMS had been concentrating on its services from the south west, things had not been standing still in the city. The scene in city and local services was dominated by a large number of small independent operators, many of whom had only one or two vehicles, some being owner driven. A schedule of these operators and the routes covered is provided in Table 3.1. Many of them also operated weekend and holiday charabanc services. The first of these operators was Mr Bert Everard who commenced a service between Lowther Street and St.Ann's Hill on 26th February 1922 and was followed two months later on 25th April by Mr J. J. Foster who operated between the Town Hall and Kingstown. One of the largest of these operators was Richard Percival Ltd, incorporated on 21st April 1922 and later becoming a subsidiary of the Tramway Company.

Eighteen miles south of Carlisle in the small town of Penrith, two hoteliers, George Armstrong of the George

Hotel and Tom Siddle of the Crown Hotel, had been involved in the provision of horse drawn carriage services for their guests and in 1920 they formed Armstrong and Siddle Motor and Transport Co Ltd. From this they built up bus services over a wide area, details of which are given in *Ribble Volume 2* published by Venture Publications Ltd in 1994. In March 1925 an approach was made to Cumberland Motor Services Ltd regarding a possible takeover but following an investigation CMS decided not to proceed, mainly because of the poor condition of the Armstrong and Siddle fleet. In June 1927 further negotiations took place and it is suspected that these were initiated by British Automobile Traction Ltd and as a result, the takeover was agreed, the date being 31st March 1928. However, on the night of 19th March 1928 there was a fire at the Brunswick Road depot and several vehicles were destroyed. This resulted in the takeover being postponed until 30th April 1928 and CMS supplied six secondhand Daimlers to replace those destroyed. A new company named Armstrong and Siddle Motor Services Ltd was formed and commenced trading on 18th May 1928. The association with CMS was short-lived and Armstrong and Siddle Motor Services Ltd passed to Ribble control with effect from 1st April 1929. The assets included the Brunswick Road premises which Ribble used as its Penrith depot and which subsequently passed to CMS in 1986.

The Caledonian Omnibus Company Ltd, with headquarters in Dumfries, was formed in April 1927 as a subsidiary of British Automobile Traction Company Ltd, later Tilling and BAT, to take over five small bus companies including that of G. P.Bell of Ecclefechan who had a service from Lockerbie to Carlisle. This gave the company an entry into Carlisle from which an attempt was made to extend southwards by taking over, in February 1928, the business of T. G. Wood of Cumwhinton with services to Cotehill, Wetheral Pastures and High Hesket. An attempt

Above: Penrith was a staging post on the early express services, being used for refreshment breaks. Here a Ribble single decker halts en route to Glasgow and another Ribble single decker awaits departure on the local service to Carlisle.

Right: Ribble Leyland TD1 awaits departure from the City Centre to Raffles on the first City Service to be operated by Ribble, having been taken over from S P & T Adair. Alongside, an unidentified single-decker awaits departure to Bowness on Solway.

was made to extend operations to Penrith but this was never achieved and in January 1929 the services to Wetheral and High Hesket were transferred to the other BAT company in the area, Armstrong and Siddle of Penrith, which was at that time controlled by CMS. Following this, Caledonian, which had become the second major operator to enter Carlisle, then concentrated on the development of routes from the north and in the 1930 Agreement became the dominant operator from the north. Within its network of routes to the north was a service operated by Lochinvar Motor Services Ltd of Carlisle with operations to Longtown and a Sunday service to Gretna via Longtown which continued until December 1939 when the company was taken over by Caledonian.

Ribble Motor Services Ltd, which was to become the dominant operator in the Carlisle area for many years, arrived in the summer of 1929 with the establishment of Lancashire – Scottish Express Services, jointly operated with Scottish Motor Traction Co. Ltd. However, a more significant event was that, as previously mentioned, Ribble had taken over from Cumberland, Armstrong and Siddle Motor Services Ltd of Penrith, and this had given it a very definite presence in the north Cumberland area with

services into Carlisle from Penrith and Wetheral. Obviously the company had its sights on Carlisle city services and in November 1929 gained its first foothold in this direction when it took over the Town Hall to Raffles service from S.P.& T.Adair, whose partners were Mr S P "Sid" Adair and his younger brother Mr T "Tommy" Adair. The service was known as 'The White Star.' Ribble had now arrived in Carlisle and the fact that it intended to stay there is obvious from subsequent events.

The Scottish Motor Traction Company Ltd commenced operation into Carlisle from Edinburgh on 13th April 1929 but did not make any attempt to use this presence as a basis for expansion in the area. The other major operator which was to have a presence in the area for many years was United Automobile Services Ltd of Darlington. This operator arrived in January 1930 with the takeover of the Emmerson service from Newcastle to Carlisle. The situation now was that there were four major bus operators all with varying degrees of interest in expansion in the area and a

Ribble required lightweight vehicles for operation on the service from Carlisle to Bowness on Solway because of a weight restriction on a bridge. Six Dennis Ace with English Electric bodies were purchased in 1934 for this purpose and the last of them, No.1416 is shown at Carlisle Bus Station with another in the background. Because of the shape of the bonnet, these buses became known as the Flying Pigs.

multiplicity of small operators. In addition there was a small tramway system in poor condition and serving a very limited part of the city.

Reference has already been made to the refusal of the Traffic Commissioners to grant an Operator Licence to Carlisle City Council. In the meantime, the Tilling and BAT Companies had set up the Carlisle Joint Transaction in an attempt to bring some order into the situation and agree plans for the operation of services. Arising from this Ribble was to purchase the tramway system and Carlisle and District Motor Services together with most of the smaller operators and services were to be allocated on a geographical basis. Ribble would operate services to the south together with most of the city services,

Cumberland would operate to the west, Caledonian to the north and United to the east including two city services in that direction.

The main exception to this concerned the service to Bowness on Solway which, although in Cumberland territory, was to be operated by Ribble as Cumberland was not interested in operating small 20-seat buses, use of which was dictated by a weight restriction on the road.

From this time the Carlisle area services settled down in a pattern which was to remain with very limited change over the next 40 years or so. Initially Ribble adopted the Carlisle City Council route letters and in addition allocated its own service numbers, which, at that time, were issued for administrative purposes and were not displayed on vehicles. Details of these are given in the Appendices. In

Because of the low bridge in Denton Street and the interworking by buses between various routes, single-deckers featured prominently on Carlisle city services for many years. Ribble, being a large company, had its own design of body, built by various fmanufacturers. RN 8732, shown here at the Town Hall on service C2 in 1944 was a 1939 Leyland TS8 with body by H V Burlingham of Blackpool.

June 1935, prior to the general allocation of displayed service numbers, Ribble allocated numbers with a 'C' prefix to city services as detailed in the Appendices and this system continued until 1968 when it was replaced with a system having numbers in the 6XX series.

Following the agreement on services it would have seemed logical for the four companies to co-operate on the provision of one central bus station for the city but this was not to be. Ribble took over the Corporation Road depot of Carlisle and District Motor Services and in June 1935 opened a new bus station in Lowther Street which it shared with Cumberland. A depot building within the bus station was used by Cumberland for its Carlisle allocation which was always small, most of the vehicles required for use in the northern area of the county being based at Wigton. Originally United used its Peter Street depot as a terminus before opening a new bus station in Scotch Street in May 1938, but services for Houghton, Kirklinton, Crosby and Irthington left from the Town Hall. Caledonian built a combined bus station and depot on the site of the former Hodgson's garage in Lonsdale Street adjacent to the rear entrance of the Ribble bus station which made interchange very convenient. The city then had three bus stations, none of which was used by city services.

The Denton Street bridge with its height restriction continued to have its effect on vehicle allocation and as a result of this, the standard prewar Ribble single-decker was a familiar sight on city services for many years. Due to interworking of routes C2, C5, C8 and C11, these services were also affected by this restriction as the operating schedule below indicates. A vehicle would thus work as follows :-

C2	Harraby to Kingstown
C5	Kingstown to Holme Head
C8/11	Holme Head to Harraby
C5	Harraby to Kingstown
C2	Kingstown to Harraby

It was not until 1947, following service reorganisation, that double-deckers took over on the Harraby service. In 1954 the road under the Denton Street bridge was lowered and the restriction removed.

The post-war period was one of fleet renewal for most operators and this included Cumberland as reported elsewhere, also Ribble and United. The exception to this general rule was Caledonian which continued to use vintage double-deck and single-deck vehicles on services

ACK 769 fleet No.2404 was a Guy Arab Mark 2 delivered in 1944 with lowbrdge utility body by Northern Counties. It was quite new when this view was taken whilst on service C17. CMS had fourteen similar vehicles, one of which is illustrated in *British Bus Systems No.1*. Note the white edging to the mudguards to assist visibility in the blackout.

into Carlisle. By 1949 when most operators had received substantial numbers of new vehicles, Caledonian had received four new double-deckers and ten new single-deckers with the result that services from the north into Carlisle in the immediate post-war period resembled a real life vintage bus rally being operated mainly by rebuilt Leyland TD1 double-deckers, some of which remained in service for about 27 years. Caledonian, which had been the only Tilling Group company in Scotland, was taken over by Western SMT in 1950 and its General Manager, H. H. Merchant, became General Manager of Cumberland in January 1950, following the death of Tom Meageen in November 1949. He was the first person outside the Meageen family to occupy this position. In 1953 Western amalgamated the Carlisle to Dumfries service with those from Dumfries to Ayr and Dumfries to Glasgow to form what was the longest stage carriage service in the United Kingdom, being 110 miles in length. However, this created practical difficulties and from 1959 the services were again split at Dumfries although initially vehicles continued to show the ultimate destination of the connecting service.

In the post-war boom period for bus operation, the Cumberland service from Whitehaven, numbered 30 in the 1950 service numbering scheme, continued to thrive and from 1953, following a time when vehicles were often duplicated, the frequency was increased from hourly to half hourly and the journey time was reduced from 2hrs 20mins to 2hrs 5mins but no attempt was made to provide a limited stop service other than a connection facility to the Western SMT express services from Carlisle to London. The first Bristol Lodekkas, introduced in 1954, brought new standards of comfort to the service with platform doors and particularly comfortable moquette covered seats with higher than normal backs. Unfortunately, subsequent

Typical of Ribble's standard pre-war single decksers is No.1850 a Leyland Cheetah with body by Eastern Coach Works and dating from 1938. When photographed in Carlisle Bus Station in 1948 it still had its petrol engine. In the background is the solitary Dennis Ace with Dennis body, delivered in 1936.

Leyland double-deckers, were used regularly on shorter distance and rural services.

Leyland-bodied PD2s and Royal Tigers also featured regularly on Ribble country workings into Carlisle giving the rather unusual situation of the Tilling and BET operators in the area using the same type of vehicle. In the post-war period city services were initially operated by examples of the Ribble standard prewar single-decker together with prewar Leyland TD4 double-deckers, which had received new highbridge bodies by H. V. Burlingham, and a number of wartime Guy Arabs. Ribble took advantage of the higher seating capacity afforded by underfloor engined single-deckers and introduced a fleet of twenty Sentinels to serve on those city services which were restricted to single-deckers. This was Ribble's entire Sentinel fleet and comprised six four-cylinder 40-seat models, generally found on the service to Bowness on Solway, and fourteen of the later six-cylinder 44-seat model. In 1955 a batch of 25 Leyland PD2s with MCW 'Orion' bodies was introduced on city services replacing the wartime Guys.

From July 1957 the maximum length of double-deck buses on two axles was increased to 30ft and Ribble was quick to take advantage of this, ordering a fleet of Leyland PD3s with attractive full fronted bodies by H. V. Burlingham. The prototype was tried out on Carlisle city services in September 1957 and following the success of this, further examples were introduced and these vehicles together with later similar vehicles with MCW bodies dominated the Ribble city services in Carlisle until the advent of one-person-operation.

In June 1968 revisions were carried out to city services to suit the newly introduced one way traffic system and at the same time the numbering system was changed to eliminate the 'C' prefix and replace it with a system in the 6XX series, details of which are given in the Appendices.

deliveries reverted to normal bus seating. Service 30 was also extended south from Whitehaven, initially once per hour to Egremont and Thornhill from 1954, then from 1955 alternate journeys were extended to Frizington. These extensions operated until 1971 when Whitehaven again became the southern terminus. Crews always changed at Whitehaven and vehicles heading for Thornhill displayed Egremont on the destination display until Whitehaven was reached when the display was changed to Thornhill. Until the advent of the Bristols in 1954, Leyland PD2s and Leyland Royal Tiger single-deckers had been the mainstay of the vehicles operating Cumberland services into Carlisle although Leyland PD1 double-deckers and Leyland PS1 single-deckers, together with rebodied and rebuilt pre-war

The rebuilt front coupled with the neat windscreen arrangement and the Cov Rad radiator conversion do much to disguise the true age of Caledonian 246 but the side elevation tends to give the game away. The bus was new in 1928 to Keighley Corporation, later passing to Keighley - West Yorkshire and to Caledonian in 1939. It was one of many vehicle of similar vintage operated by Caledonian in the postwar period and after takeover by Western SMT survived in that fleet until 1955. The radiator carries the Tiger name at the bottom.

Following the formation of the National Bus Company, with effect from 1st January 1969, it was decreed that Ribble should take over the United operations in Carlisle and this became effective from the same date. United Carlisle fleet was, at this time, 100% Bristol and, with the exception of the three 'K' type double-deckers, was transferred to Ribble, bringing into that fleet vehicle types which were not normally associated with an ex BET company. Details of the services taken over from United are given in the Appendices.

The final major event to take place in Carlisle prior to the transfer of Ribble operations to Cumberland occurred in June

Right: Ribble 1732, RN 8093, a 1937 Leyland TD4 with 1947 Burlingham body heads from the city centre to St.Anns Hill. These vehicles were regular performers on Carlisle city services in the postwar period.

Centre left: CRN 214 was one of six Sentinel STC 4 underfloor engined vehicles of integral construction with Beadle 40 seat bodies and they were the first underfloor engined buses in the Ribble fleet. All were allocated to Carlisle and operated regularly on services to Bowness on Solway.

Centre right: The six Sentinel STC4s were followed by fourteen STC6s built to the newly legalised length of 30ft and seating 44 in their Sentinel bodies. All were allocated to Carlisle and operated on those city service workings which were restricted to single-deckers. DRN 343, fleet No. 286, is shown parked at the Bus Station.

Foot: This 1950s scene in English Street shows United Guy Arab GHN 385 on the city service between the Town Hall and Botcherby, whilst in the background is one of the Ribble pre-war Leyland TD4s with new body by H V Burlingham which featured in city services for many years.

1972 with the completion of the conversion to one-person-operation. To provide for this change a fleet of 23 new Bristol VRT double-deckers with ECW 70-seat bodies was introduced and supplemented by Leyland Atlanteans with low height MCW bodies brought in from other Ribble areas. Between this time and the takeover by Cumberland, rural services continued to decline but City Services remained substantially the same. The Atlanteans and the original Bristol VRTs were replaced by later standard NBC Bristol VRTs and Leyland Atlanteans.

Further reading on the history of Passenger Road Transport in Carlisle can be found in :-

Tramways of the City of Carlisle by G. S. Hearse. Published by G. S. Hearse.
Ribble in Carlisle by DAG Published by Ribble Enthusiasts Club.
British Bus Systems No. 2 – Ribble by Eric Ogden. Published by Transport Publishing Company.
Ribble Volumes 1 & 2 by Bruce Maund. Published by Venture Publications.

Above: United had only one Willowbrook-bodied Guy double-decker, RHN 69, and this was a regular vehicle on its Carlisle city services for some years. It is shown on service 24, being followed by one of the Ribble standard single-deckers.

Right: The rebodied Leyland TD4s and the remainder of the wartime Guys were replaced on Carlisle City services in 1955 with a batch of Leyland PD2s carrying austere MCW bodies. Number 1472 picks up on route C9 to Harraby with one of the Sentinel STC6s behind.

Below: Ribble 1805, a Leyland Atlantean with lowbridge MCW body dating from 1962, leaves Penrith Bus Station for the depot on 22nd September 1979, having worked the 1607 departure ex Carlisle on service 615. Similar vehicles were a feature of Carlisle city services alongside new Bristol VRs following the introduction of one-person-operation. This vehicle is now preserved.

Chapter Four
Deregulation

The 1985 Transport Act included provision for the Deregulation of local bus services, thus ending the system which had existed since 1930 whereby the existing operator of a service was protected from competition from a new operator. Deregulation Day was to be Sunday 26th October 1986 and it was expected that many new operators would register services for commencement at this time. In addition 'blanket subsidies' for the provision of services were withdrawn and County Councils and Passenger Transport Authorities were required to advertise services which were considered to be socially desirable, subsidies being applied to these services rather than to an operator. As far as Cumberland Motor Services was concerned, Whitehaven was again to be the main centre of competition with competing services registered by J. D. Yeowart, S. H. Brownrigg of Egremont who operated under the title of 'Country Bus Service' and Andy Vine of Cleator Moor. The services registered were :-

J. D. YEOWART :–	W Whitehaven Bus Station-Woodhouse.
S. H. BROWNRIGG:–	1 Whitehaven Bus Station-Bigrigg-Egremont-Thornhill
	2 Whitehaven Bus Station-Cleator-Egremont-Thornhill
ANDY VINE:–	Whitehaven Bus Station-Cleator Moor-Ennerdale Bridge

In addition, Brownrigg obtained, on tender from Cumbria County Council the service from Egremont to St. Bees and the Egremont Town Service.

Brownrigg, Andy Vine and Yeowart took joint advertising space in the Whitehaven News in the form of a half page advertising feature to promote their services and on the same date, Thursday 23rd October 1986, CMS had a similar half page advertising feature in the same newspaper. CMS also took similar space in the Times and

This scene in Whitehaven on 27th October 1986 shows minibus 21 turning from Tangier Street into George Street on Town Service 01 to Kells. In the background is minibus number 26 parked outside the 1932 workshops.

Left: Minibus No.30 travels along Oxford Street, Workington towards the Bus Station on Town Service 51 on Monday 27th October 1986, the first day of minibus operation.

Below left: The first vehicle to be painted in the new CMS Cumberland livery was ECW-bodied Leyland Leopard No. 635 and it is shown entering Oxford Street, Workington on Monday 27th October 1986.

Star and in the Cumberland News. In these adverts Michael Wadsworth proclaimed "With more than half a century of experience and a reputation for reliability, we've introduced new ideas, new services and taken on more staff at Whitehaven and Workington – we're ready for Deregulation."

This was certainly the impression created at Whitehaven on Monday morning 27th October 1986, the first operational day under Deregulation.

The CMS minibuses in their red and sandstone livery and with drivers smartly turned out in red vee neck sweaters, grey trousers, fawn shirts and ties created a business-like impression. Michael Wadsworth and other members of the management were around to sample and supervise operations.

The Yeowart service was operated by an ex-Western National Bristol RE, VOD 102K, in Yeowart's livery of yellow with fawn waistband and skirt. The destination indicator was set at W TOWN SERVICE and there was a board in the windscreen reading WOODHOUSE.

Brownrigg used Leyland Leopards and a Bedford with Duple Dominant bodies, including PWK 6W, PWK 7W, and PWK 9W in a variety of liveries and without use of destination blinds. Route information was carried on boards in the windscreen although one of the vehicles which had a destination blind, had this set at 'SPECIAL PARTY' which seemed odd on the first day of a new public service.

There seemed to be some confusion among drivers as to where they should pick up at Whitehaven Bus Station and loadings for the new operators were low although perhaps this was to be expected on the first day. They certainly improved in the following months.

The Vine service was operated by an old type Ford Transit minibus in a brown livery with no indication of the fact that it was in public service. It did not therefore pose much competition to CMS and it was not surprising that it was withdrawn after only a few months, ceasing on 24th January 1987. The other services were very much a threat particularly as they were expanded in the coming months as we shall see later.

The only other initial threat to CMS was in Carlisle where Palmer of Carlisle Ltd had registered services as follows :-

C1	Morton Park to Morton Park via Wigton Road, West Tower Street, English Street, Longsowerby.
C2	Operating in the opposite direction to C1.
C8	Belle Vue, City Centre, Belle Vue via Newtown Road, West Tower Street, Warwick Road, English St., Lowther St., Newtown Road.

Cumberland introduced new timetables on Deregulation Day and for the first time broke away from the tradition of

Whilst there was considerable activity centred around the new minibus services on 'D' Day, Border Clipper continued to thrive and Leyland Olympian 1001 was carrying a good load on this day as it left Workington Bus Station for Whitehaven and Egremont. In the background is a new minibus entering the bus station and also coach seated Leyland National 2 No. 384 in dual-purpose livery loading on Town Service 48 to Harrington.

a combined booklet for all services, introducing area booklets as follows :–Whitehaven: Millom: Workington, Cockermouth, and Maryport: Keswick: Penrith: Carlisle City Services: Carlisle Country Services. The main changes were centred on Whitehaven and Workington Town Services where minibuses were introduced for the first time. Initially these were :–

01	Whitehaven Bus Station to Kells with day time journeys returning via Basket Road and Rosemary Lane, something which had not been possible with full size buses due to road restrictions.
02	Whitehaven Bus Station to Woodhouse. With effect from 1st May 1988 this service was extended to Greenbank Estate.
50	Workington Bus Station to Moorclose Hotel via Ashfield Road.
51	Workington Bus Station to Moorclose Hotel via Harrington Road.

There were complaints from residents over the use of Basket Road and as a result of this the service was altered with effect from 2nd February 1987 to return via the outward route and it operated in this way until 30th April 1988 when it was again rerouted via Rosemary Lane but without using Basket Road. Further minibus services were introduced on 2nd February 1987 and these were :–

| 05 | Whitehaven Lowther Street to Bransty Crescent. This service was extended to Parton with effect from 27th April 1987. |
| 08 | Whitehaven Lowther Street to Hillcrest Estate via Sunnyhill and Loop Road South. This route was short lived and with effect from 16th November 1987 the route was changed to operate via Inkerman Terrace. |

On 30th November 1987 a minibus service was introduced on Town Service 09 in Whitehaven to operate from Lowther Street to Mirehouse Latrigg Road in between the fifteen-minutes frequency of the normal full size bus service.

In Workington, minibus services 50 and 51 ceased on 2nd January 1988, being replaced with full size buses on modified routes.

In Carlisle there had been very few changes to services on Deregulation Day and the minibus era began on 9th February 1987 when two services were introduced. These were :-

| M3 | Kingstown or Lowry Hill-City Centre-Morton Park via Nelson St. |
| M4 | Kingstown or Lowry Hill-City Centre-Morton Park via Longsowerby |

These services replaced services 663 and 664 operating until 24th October 1987 when they were replaced with the

Left: Yeowart's Bristol RE, VOD 102K on Town Service W to Woodhouse travels along George Street, Whitehaven on the morning of Monday 27th October 1986, not carrying many passengers on this journey, but the start of something which was to develop in the following months.

Below left: The other main deregulation threat to CMS came from Brownrigg's Coaches of Egremont, operating as 'Country Bus Service' and its PWK 6W is shown on Duke Street, Whitehaven on service 2 to Egremont via Cleator Moor, in direct competition with CMS service 22. Note the destination display 'Special Party', a surprising display for a vehicle operating a new local service.

chassis with coachbuilt bodies by Reeve Burgess seating 23 and numbered 21-32. When the Carlisle operation was commenced fourteen Mercedes L608D with conversions by Reeve Burgess and seating 20 were purchased. These were numbered 33-46. Since that time, all minibuses purchased new have been Mercedes.

To return to the question of competition, this continued to threaten, particularly in Whitehaven and to a lesser extent in Workington. On 7th April 1987 Yeowart modified its original service extending it to Greenbank and renumbering it Y1. On 13th April two new services were introduced:–

following :-

| 64 | City Centre to Morton Park via Nelson Street with evening journeys extended to Kingstown. |
| 65 | City Centre to Blackwell with some extensions to Durdar. |

The Maryport Town service 57 was converted to minibus operation from 3rd January 1988 and a new minibus service 52 from Workington to Distington was introduced on 28th March 1988.

Since this time minibuses have played an important part in the operations of the company but after the initial setting up of the services the division between minibus services and full size or midibus services has tended to become less rigid although there are certain services which are entirely minibus operated, particularly where road conditions dictate this.

The initial minibus fleet comprised twelve Dodge S50

| Y2 | Whitehaven Bus Station to West Cumberland Hospital via Mirehouse. |
| Y3 | Whitehaven Lowther Street to Lowca via Bransty and Parton. |

A further service had been introduced on 5th April 1987 but this was an evening only journey and did not pose competition to CMS; indeed it was introduced following the withdrawal of the evening working on Town Service 03. The service was :–

| Y4 | Kells to West Cumberland Hospital via Woodhouse, Greenbank, Mirehouse. |

At the same time Brownrigg introduced a service from Whitehaven Bus Station to Frizington via Cleator Moor in direct competition with CMS service 17.

On 4th March 1987 Whitehaven Depot was visited by this party of children with parents and helpers from St. Gregory's and St. Patrick's Nursery School. They are pictured with Inspector Bob Daglish, the late Brian Dickinson and Pat Turnbull. In the background is a CMS minibus behind a Brownrigg's coach, whilst to the right is a Leyland National 2 on Haven Link service 9-7.

At Deregulation Cumberland commenced a Fridays only 'Shoppers Service' between Penrith and Carlisle via Caldbeck, numbered 640. Leyland National 1 number 362 is shown in the village of Hesket Newmarket operating this service. Unfortunately the service did not turn out to be a financial success and had to be withdrawn.

One way in which CMS attempted to counter this competition was to introduce its 'Bargain Bus Services'. Three Duple Dominant bodied Leyland Leopard coaches, Nos. 626, 1118 and 1119 were painted in an all-white livery without fleetnames and set to operate between Whitehaven and Frizington and between Whitehaven and Thornhill via Bigrigg. Destination blinds were set at black blank and boards were carried in the windscreen detailing the destination and route, similar to the boards used by Brownrigg. In addition a further board was lettered 'Bargain Bus Service'. Reduced fares were charged on these services.

Further competition arose in the Workington-Cockermouth area on 9th March 1987 when Kirkpatrick's Coaches, Brigham, near Cockermouth introduced two services. These were :-

003	Cockermouth Rose Lane to West Cumberland Hospital, Whitehaven via Main Steet, Brigham, Broughton Cross, Greysouthen, Bridgefoot, Great Clifton, Distington, Moresby.
004	Cockermouth Rose Lane to Workington via Broughton Cross, Greysouthen, Bridgefoot, Clifton, Stainburn.

To that date competition had not affected services in Maryport but this was to change on 19th May 1987 when Richard Smith of Dearham, a former Cumberland Motor Services Ltd employee, commenced two services :–

1.	Maryport Town Service operating Senhouse Street, Curzon Street, Ewanrigg Road, Ellenfoot Drive, Fleming Square, Senhouse Street.
2.	Dearham to Maryport.

To revert to Deregulation Day, Cumberland Motor Services Ltd had made the decision not to register any Sunday services other than the single working on 'Border Clipper' service 300. Consequently, Cumbria County Council advertised for tender, services which were considered to be socially desirable and quotations were received for these from numerous operators.

The services advertised were however determined by social need rather than by staff and vehicle utilisation. As a result of this Cumberland decided to base its offer on what had been its normal Sunday service and this was accepted by Cumbria County Council. It was accepted on the basis of 'best value for money' rather than lowest cost and the result was that that most Cumberland Sunday services continued very much as before.

Another move by the company was the introduction of a range of multi journey tickets. These comprised 'Commutacards' which were available for unlimited travel between chosen points for one, four, eight or twelve weeks, and 'Supersavers' which were available for one or four weeks and gave unlimited travel in either Whitehaven, Workington or Carlisle.

Competition continued and the ultimate outcome of this is covered in Chapter 5.

Safe Driving Awards were presented by Pat Turnbull (third from left) on 10th January 1987 to:- Derek Glaister, Ted Biggins, Gordon Grey, Albert Ryan, John Kennedy, Cyril Gordon, and Ken Jenkinson.

Chapter Five
The Stagecoach Era

Cumberland Motor Services Ltd was sold to Stagecoach Holdings Ltd of Perth with effect from 23rd July 1987, this company having outbid the local management/employee offer. The Pleasurama Group, which at that time owned Shearings, was also interested but dropped out of the bidding between indicative and final bids.

Early changes were made to the management structure, S. T. Sanderson, Operations Manager North left to join Lincolnshire Road Car Company Ltd and Michael Wadsworth, Managing Director, resigned. Paul Coupar, Business Development Manager became Operations Superintendent at Workington and Barry Hinkley, Chief Engineer became General Manager, becoming a director of the company on 6th October 1987 and Managing Director in January 1988. He joined the main board of Stagecoach Holdings plc on 19th October 1992 in preparation for the company's stock market flotation in April 1993. In May 1993 he was appointed Company Chairman, being succeeded as Managing Director by Paul Southgate. In October 1994 when Paul Southgate moved on to Selkent, Les Warneford was appointed to succeed him.

The new owner expressed at an early stage its intention to re-introduce conductors using ex London Transport Routemaster double-deckers. By 14th August 1987 three Routemasters had arrived from Kelvin Scottish and one from London Transport. These were followed by a further three from Kelvin Scottish and another one from London Transport, making a total of eight. The ex-Kelvin Scottish vehicles were in that operator's blue livery and the other two were still in London Transport red. The arrival of these vehicles brought back memories of the occasion 47 years previously when seven ex-London Transport Leyland TD2s arrived. The Routemasters were quickly prepared for service on Carlisle city services and received their own version of the CMS Cumberland red and sandstone livery,

An early effect of the Stagecoach takeover was the introduction of ex-London Transport Routemaster double-deckers on Carlisle city service number 61. Bus No.900 passes through Court Square en route from Harraby to Morton Park on 5th November 1987 with a Bristol VR in the new CMS Carlislebus livery in the background.

Displaying the CMS Carlislebus livery, Leyland Atlantean No. 1479 passes through Carlisle city centre on city service 69 to Upperby on 7th March 1990. By this time, the former Ribble lower case destination blinds had been replaced by new upper case ones.

Bristol VR No. 434 was working Border Clipper Service 300 from Whitehaven to Carlisle when photogrphed in Lowther Street Carlisle, approaching the Bus Station on 7th March 1990.

This former Ribble ECW-bodied Leyland Olympian with coach seating was still carrying Ribble fleetnames when photogrphed in Ambleside whilst operating on service 555 from Lancaster to Keswick on 4th October 1989.

The first new buses to be received under Stagecoach ownership were four Mercedes 709 minibuses with Alexander bodies numbered 47 to 50. They were delivered in all white livery and Stagecoach stripes were added at Whitehaven. No. 47 is outside Whitehaven Bus Station operating town service 02 to Woodhouse Estate with evidence in the background of work in progress on the former Grand Hotel site development.

the repainting being undertaken by Leyland Bus Ltd at the Leyland National plant at Lillyhall. Other work was carried out by CMS at Whitehaven and the author recalls being in the workshops at Whitehaven at this time and noting the excellent condition of the bodywork beneath the panels. There was no sign of corrosion on the metalwork or of rot in the timber inserts. Destination and route number blinds were made by London Transport, the full blind display being used including the small number blind above the lower saloon bulkhead window. The Routemasters were the first AEC double-deckers to join the fleet since 1936, apart from some hired during the war. Fleet numbers 900-907 were allocated to these vehicles, this series having previously been used by the Bristol RE single-deckers used on the Sellafield site services.

It was planned to introduce the Routemasters on Carlisle city service 61 on 26th October 1987, the first anniversary of Deregulation Day. A dispute over pay and conditions with former Ribble drivers at Carlisle had threatened to disrupt this but the dispute was settled and the vehicles introduced as planned. On the same date services in Carlisle and Penrith were reorganised and a complete new system of service numbering was introduced to supersede that inherited from Ribble. Details of this renumbering system are given in the Appendices.

The Routemasters were not the only changes in Carlisle at this time for at the end of September the seventeen ex-Ribble highbridge Bristol VRs were transferred to another Stagecoach company, Hampshire Bus at Southampton, and Cumberland received in return ten Daimler Fleetline DMS double-deckers which had started life with London Transport and also four Ailsa double-deckers which were unusual among modern double-deckers in having a front mounted engine. All came from Hampshire Bus and retained their Hampshire Bus fleet numbers. The Ailsas, which had been new to South Yorkshire PTE, were not popular and remained in the fleet for only three months before passing on.

A surprise move in 1987 was the sale of ten Leyland National 2 single-deckers to Shearings Ltd for operation on local bus services in which it had become involved since Deregulation. Eight of these had come from Ribble but the other two, Nos. 395 and 399, were from the original Cumberland fleet. They were painted in Shearings livery and fitted with electronic destination equipment by Leyland Bus Ltd at Lillyhall before going to Shearings.These were replaced in the Cumberland fleet with four Leyland National 2 and three Leyland National B type from Kelvin Scottish, all of which required extensive refurbishment at Whitehaven before entering service.

Competition continued, particularly in the Whitehaven area, where Brownrigg ventured into town service operation with services to Richmond Estate and to Sunnyhill. Encouraged by success in the Whitehaven area, this operator commenced a service from Workington to Seaton on 16th December 1987 and followed this with services from Workington to Distington, Thornhill to Workington via Whitehaven and Whitehaven to Workington via Parton and Distington. Kirkpatrick's Coaches also turned to Workington and operated a service to Moorclose Estate.

This gathering of momentum by smaller operators was of some concern to Stagecoach and two operators, J. D. Yeowart of Whitehaven and Kirkpatrick's Coaches of Brigham were taken over with effect from 12th May 1988.

Following on from this Brownrigg ceased local service operation with effect from 21st September 1988 and the monopoly which Cumberland had enjoyed in the area for many years was once again restored.

In early 1988 Cumbria County Council announced a further reduction in public transport subsidies including withdrawal of support for Sunday services. An article in the Whitehaven News on 9th June 1988 claimed that this would lead to the virtual elimination of Sunday services in West Cumbria but this was corrected in the same newspaper the following week when the company declared that despite the withdrawal of subsidies it would maintain the services.

Two former Barrow Borough Transport Leyland Nationals, UEO 478T and NEO 829R, repainted in Stagecoach livery and with Cumberland fleetnames at the Town Hall stop in the town centre. They became CMS 761 and 755 respectively.

A number of services were however withdrawn on or about 6th August 1988 and these included :-

15	Millom-Festival Road
38	Maryport-Silloth
45	Workington-Dean-Ullock
92	Carlisle-Caldbeck-Penrith
101	Carlisle-Calthwaite-Penrith

It was announced in mid 1988 that in future all vehicles would be painted in the Stagecoach livery of white with red, orange and blue stripes and the first Cumberland vehicle to receive this livery was Leyland National 369. Somehow there seemed to be reluctance locally to see the end of the CMS Cumberland livery and it was some time before a substantial proportion of the fleet was in the Stagecoach livery, many of the repaints in the meantime being in special liveries or the subject of extensive 'touching up'.

The first new vehicles to arrive under Stagecoach ownership were four Mercedes Benz 709D minibuses with Alexander bodies which arrived in July 1988 in an all-white livery, Stagecoach stripes being added later at Whitehaven. These were followed in September 1988 by what was to become the Stagecoach standard double-decker, Alexander bodied Leyland Olympians. Nine were received, numbered 1003 to 1011, and all were allocated to Carlisle city services, replacing the Daimler Fleetlines.

In April 1989 there was a further reduction by Cumbria County Council from £290,000 to £152,000 in the public transport subsidy and this had its effect on the level of services provided by the company.

In May 1989 another local coach operator was purchased, this time it was Stephensons of Maryport. This firm was not involved in local service operation.

On Friday 21st April 1989, Stagecoach purchased Cumberland's southern neighbour, Ribble Motor Services Ltd, and as a consequence of this, it was later announced that, with effect from 18th June 1989, Cumberland would take over the Ribble operations in the South Lakes and Furness areas. This involved the Ribble depots at Kendal, Ulverston and Barrow together with outstations at Sedbergh, Grange over Sands, Ambleside and Appleby.

Barrow Borough Transport Ltd had ceased operation on 26th May 1989 following intense competition from Ribble and the monopoly of town services which Ribble had gained as a result passed to Cumberland. This meant that Cumberland became the major operator throughout the county of Cumbria with regular operations extending from Carlisle in the north to Lancaster in the south. Although many of the services in the South Lakes and Furness areas were infrequent rural services, there were profitable town services in Barrow and Kendal together with the long standing 555 service through the Central Lakes linking Keswick with Lancaster via Ambleside, Windermere and Kendal. The legal lettering on the vehicles had of course to be changed immediately on takeover, but it was some considerable time before fleetnames were changed, unlike the situation in Carlisle and Penrith where fleetnames had been changed overnight. This led to

the rather unusual situation of vehicles operating with Ribble fleetnames and Cumberland Motor Services Ltd legal lettering. At the time of takeover some rationalisation of Ribble vehicles in the area was carried out to give a degree of standardisation. The Park Royal bodied Leyland Atlanteans were replaced with Eastern Coach Works bodied examples, similar to those already received in the Cumberland fleet with the take over of Ribble operations in Carlisle and Penrith. The two ex-Potteries low height Bristol VRs Nos. 2033 and 2034 based at Kendal and required for the service 552 which passed under Arnside railway bridge were transferred to Chorley and replaced at Kendal with similar Cumberland Bristol VRs Nos. 422 and 423. One result of this move was to introduce the attractive Cumberland Ayres red and sandstone livery to the Kendal area, this being carried by 422.

The main source of competition in this area was Lancaster City Transport Ltd which, in response to the registration by Ribble of local services in Lancaster and Morecambe, had commenced, on 30th November 1987, a service from Lancaster to Kendal together with town services in Kendal. Initially Barrow Borough Transport Ltd was also involved in the venture, which was marketed as 'Blue Bus', but Barrow's involvement was short-lived, ceasing after 6th February 1988. An outstation was opened at Mintsfeet Industrial Estate on 31st May 1988 and the operation was under the control of a leading driver. On this date the Kendal service was extended to Ambleside and services operated in Cumbria were :–

Two of the ex-Bluebird Leyland Olympians, Nos. 1092 and 1094, proceed along Duke Street, Barrow on 15th July 1992. The coloured destination blind is evident on 1092.

4	Levens Village-Kendal Queen Catherine School
5	Lancaster-Kendal via Milnthorpe.
6	Morecambe/Lancaster-Ambleside via Kendal, Bowness.
7	Morecambe/Lancaster-Ambleside via Kendal.
X6	Ambleside-Blackpool via Bowness, Kendal, Lancaster.
X7	Ambleside-Blackpool via Oxenholme, Lancaster.
8	Kendal Town Service. Town Hall-Hall Garth.
9	Kendal Town Service. Town Hall-Sandylands.
81	Lancaster-Settle via Kirkby Lonsdale.
125	Lancaster-Kirkby Lonsdale via The Kelletts.
126	Morecambe-Kirkby Lonsdale via Euston Road.
127	Morecambe-Kirkby Lonsdale via Promenade.
573	Lancaster-Kirkby Lonsdale via Halton, Wennington. Su. & B.Hols.

This competition continued until 29th July 1989 when the Kendal town services were withdrawn, and the depot closed. The Ambleside service ceased on 2nd September 1989.

On the vehicle side three new Leyland Lynx, the locally built replacement for the Leyland National, were purchased in 1989 together with an ex-demonstrator of the same model and these were allocated to Barrow, being the first new full size single-deckers to enter service in the town for some years. A further example of the same model was purchased from Ribble in 1991. Expansion of the coaching fleet at this time is covered in Chapter 7, whilst expansion of the minibus fleet between 1988 and 1993 involved secondhand, albeit modern, examples purchased from other Stagecoach companies namely Magicbus and Hampshire Bus and comprising the standard Alexander body on Mercedes or Renault chassis. The exceptions to this were two Metroriders, a Robin Hood bodied Iveco and a Ford Transit purchased from S. H. Brownrigg in 1988 following that operator's cessation of local bus services.

A notable event in 1989 was the entry into service of two three-axle Leyland Olympian double-deckers with bodies by Alexander, fitted with 97 coach seats. They were used initially, but not entirely, on the 'Border Clipper' service between Whitehaven and Carlisle and were later transferred to Barrow depot. They became known as the 'Meggadeckers.'

Palmer of Carlisle Ltd was taken over in December 1989 and this gave CMS its first regular local service operation into Scotland with the occasional service from Carlisle to Gretna via Longtown.

A further eight Alexander-bodied Leyland Olympians arrived in 1990 and apart from one which was allocated to Kendal, the remainder were allocated to Whitehaven and Workington depots.

In early 1990, four open-top ECW-bodied Bristol VRs arrived from Southdown in that operator's attractive green and cream livery together with an open top MCW bodied Leyland Atlantean from Ribble, this vehicle having commenced its service with Devon General in 1961. These were all repainted at Whitehaven in the 'Southdown' green and cream livery, with signwriting and name 'Lakeland Experience' for the Lake District service between Bowness on Windermere and Ambleside which had previously been operated by conventional buses. The Atlantean was regarded as a standby vehicle and it was replaced the following year by another MCW-bodied Atlantean, ERV 251D, which had commenced its life with Portsmouth City Transport.

On 20th July 1992, Olympian 1019, the only one of the batch allocated to Kendal, arrives at Windermere Station on service 555 from Grasmere to Lancaster. Note the advert on the side for the 555 'Lakes Link' service.

The service commenced on 19th May 1990 operating every twenty minutes, and from 26th May 1990, it faced competition from 'Guide Friday,' an operator specialising in open-top bus tours in places of historic interest. However, whilst Cumberland offered a true local service with local service fares, Guide Friday only offered a 'Day Ticket' priced at £3.50 which was all right for anyone wanting to spend a whole day on and off the service but expensive for anyone wanting to make only a single journey. Initially the Guide Friday service, which carried guides giving commentaries, operated every 20 minutes but this was reduced to every 30 minutes in August, when under normal circumstances an increase in demand could have been expected, and was withdrawn completely in September. By contrast the Cumberland service thrived and in 1994 was extended beyond Ambleside to Grasmere. This required an additional vehicle and it so happened that Bristol VR 2002 had been involved in an accident with a low canopy causing extensive damage to the upper deck. It was therefore an ideal candidate for conversion to open top and this was carried out by Cumberland at Lillyhall.

The use of the green and cream livery was extended in 1991 when it was applied to Leyland National B type No. 810 for use on the 'Borrowdale Bus' service between Keswick and Seatoller and also to minibuses Nos. 520, 558 and 560 for the new 'Coniston Rambler' service between Bowness, Ambleside and Coniston. In 1992 the name 'Langdale Rambler' was adopted for the service between Ambleside and Dungeon Ghyll.

A sad event in February 1991 was the death of Algie Corlett. He spent his entire working life with CMS, including a short period with CMS developments in the Isle of Man, retiring as Works Superintendent, and could recall many interesting tales of early years.

In August 1991 a major change took place with regard to the Whitehaven to Carlisle service in that the 'Border Clipper' workings were withdrawn, with the exception of the single return journey to Gateshead, and the original service 30 was speeded up and renumbered 300, with most workings between Whitehaven and Workington being via the 'High Way' rather than via Harrington. Service 30 was then used for workings between Whitehaven and Maryport. A number of Duple Laser bodied Leyland Tiger coaches was obtained from Ribble in exchange for Alexander bodied Leyland Tigers and these were used on service 300. A feature of them was the use of a large 'Cumberland' fleetname which looked particularly effective on these coaches.

The next batch of eight Alexander bodied Leyland Olympian double-deckers arrived in 1991 and differed from previous deliveries in having high backed seats, twin destination blinds at the front allowing the display of intermediate points and electronic service number displays at the side and rear. They were allocated to Kendal depot for the 555 trunk service betwen Keswick and Lancaster.

At the Coach and Bus Show in October 1991, Alexander exhibited an example of its 'Dash' single-deck body on the increasingly popular Dennis Dart chassis. It was finished in Stagecoach livery and had 'Cumberland' fleetnames

Bristol VR 2037 arrives at Bowness on Windermere from Ambleside in July 1992.

applied but it never entered service with Cumberland. However, three Alexander bodied Dennis Darts did arrive at Cumberland in December 1991 and entered service in Whitehaven with fleet numbers 701 to 703. In 1992 all three were transferred to another Stagecoach company, Hampshire Bus, and it was decided that Cumberland would receive 100 Volvo B6 single-deckers, the initial batch being used to carry out a major fleet replacement and service reorganisation in Carlisle. The B6 was to be Volvo's answer to the Dennis Dart and its first entry into what became known as the 'Midibus' sector.

Five Alexander bodied Leyland Olympians were purchased from another Stagecoach subsidiary, Bluebird Buses Ltd, Aberdeen. Three arrived in December 1991 and the other two in February 1992 and all were allocated to Barrow depot. The first three were unusual in that they had been re-registered with earlier registration numbers GSO 3-5V, having originally been registered C473-4 and D375 XRS when new in 1986 and 1987. The remaining two had their original registrations D380-1 XRS. The first three were subsequently re registered by Cumberland C382/3 SAO and D384 XAO to reflect their true age.

In February 1992 the Western Scottish operations from Carlisle to Annan and from Carlisle to Longtown were taken over. Under Western Scottish the Annan service had operated through to Dumfries but it was now necessary to change vehicles at Annan, the Annan to Dumfries section

being retained by Western Scottish. A reduction in the return fare from Carlisle to Annan from £3.60 to £2.50 generated new passengers.

The first Volvo B6s were built at the plant of an associate company of Volvo, Steyr, in Austria and the first Cumberland example, No. 704, arrived in June 1992 for presentation to guests at the official opening of the new depot at Lillyhall on 26th June 1992. En route from Alexander's works at Falkirk to Whitehaven, it broke down at Carlisle and had to be towed to Whitehaven. This was only the beginning of a long saga of mechanical problems related to the chassis, one result of which was that Volvo temporarily withdrew the model from the market and Cumberland ordered 100 of the well tried and tested Volvo B10M chassis in place of the B6. By this time the remaining three of the initial batch of four B6 arrived and proved to be as unreliable as the first example. All four vehicles were subsequently replaced by Volvo in 1994.

A further batch of eight Olympian double-deckers with Alexander bodies and dual-purpose seating arrived in 1992 and were employed mainly on the Whitehaven to Carlisle and Carlisle to Annan services.

A new system of Town Minibus Services was introduced in Cockermouth with effect from 14th December 1992, a free service having been operated on the previous Saturday, 12th December. This comprised five routes as follows, operated by one minibus :-

```
101  Main Street-Slatefell-Rose Lane-Main Street
102  Main Street-Slatefell-Highfield Road-Main Street
103  Main Street-Slatefell-Gable Avenue-Main Street
104  Main Street-The Moor-Main Street
105  Main Street-Beech Lane-Main Street
```

The first Volvo B10M single-deckers arrived in December 1992 and were used to launch a new service pattern in Carlisle under the name 'Goldline'. Total mileage remained broadly unchanged and routes were simplified to improve regular headways. Discounted cross city fares were introduced and a 4% increase in passengers was recorded. To assist passengers and traffic flows, on street conductors were introduced in the city centre. The new buses replaced the Routemasters and the Leyland Atlantean double-deckers and also some Leyland National single-deckers. The next batch was allocated to Barrow and the third batch to West Cumbria. A total of 92, numbered 699 to 746 and 748 to 791, was taken into service initially, three later being sold to East Kent, and this enabled the company to dispose of all its Leyland Nationals with the exception of 810 in Lakeland Experience livery which was retained for the Borrowdale service. Most of the Leyland Nationals were sold to Ribble Motor Services Ltd. The reason for not using fleet number 747 on the new buses was the non availability of the corresponding registration number. The last twenty were fitted with dual-purpose seating. Electronically operated destination displays were fitted and similar equipment was retrofitted to the latest Olympians, 1020 to 1035. Following this all Olympians numbered from 1003 to 1019 were also retrofitted with this equipment. The balance of the original order for 100 Volvo B10M was made up with the delivery of eight Volvo B6 in 1994, four of which subsequently passed to Ribble in a deal involving eight ex-Ribble Mercedes 709 minibuses coming to Cumberland.

The arrival of 132 new vehicles between 1992 and 1994, out of a fleet total of around 300, gave the company the most modern large bus fleet in the country and this high percentage of new vehicles combined with modern premises and revised methods of working led to a reduction in maintenance costs from 23p per mile in 1988/89 to 17p per mile in 1994/95. The average fleet age in mid 1995 was well below the national average at :–

Double-deck	9.1 years
Single-deck	3.9 years
Minibuses	6.1 years
Coaches	7.7 years
Fleet Total	6.1 years

This investment also led to improved reliability giving an exceptional record in 1994/95 of 0.1% of mileage lost for all reasons. In the same year there was only one first time MOT failure and six defect notices out of a 300 vehicle fleet.

With effect from 23rd May 1992 service 555 was extended north from Keswick to Carlisle involving three operations per day during the Summer timetable period. Kendal drivers continued to operate only to Keswick, with Carlisle drivers taking over from there. This extension giving a route mileage of the order of 80 miles made the service a candidate for the title of longest local bus service in the country.

In 1993 Stagecoach introduced the term 'Network 2000' and applied this to certain premium services, initially with Ribble but the term was then extended to Cumberland's 555 'Lakes Link' service and appropriate lettering to promote this was applied to the sides of the vehicles operating the service.

A further 'Lakes Link' service, also classified as a 'Network 2000' service, was introduced on 16th May 1993 numbered X5 with the basic service operating between Whitehaven and Penrith with some journeys extended to/from Carlisle. During the Summer period there was also an extension from Penrith to Langwathby for connection to the Carlisle to Settle railway and at the other end of the service an extension to the Sellafield Visitor Centre. Neither of these extensions was repeated in 1994 and the extension to/from Carlisle which had operated through the Winter 1993/94 timetable was withdrawn, connection being made at Penrith with service 104. The service connects at Keswick with the other 'Lakes Link' service 555 and is normally operated by Volvo B10M single-deckers with dual-purpose seating and with lettering on the sides to advertise the service. Connection is also made at Penrith railway station with trains on the West Coast Main Line.

At the beginning of 1994 a Central Telephone Enquiry Service was opened, based in Whitehaven bus station, and manned by specially trained staff to cover the complete operating area of the company. The unit was housed in the former travel office, which was moved to a smaller adjacent office, and operated seven days per week using what had previously been the head office telephone number, Whitehaven (0946) 63222. The number was applied to all bus stop signs and was of course quoted on all publicity.

The local service 15 from Millom to Haverigg was revised with effect from 26th June 1995 to provide three services, M1 operating Millom-Queens Park-Haverigg, M2 operating Millom-Festival Road-Queens Park-Haverigg, and M3 operating Millom-Haverigg Direct.

The summer of 1995 saw a change in the vehicles operating the Coniston Rambler service in that the Mercedes minibuses previously used were replaced by two Volvo B6 midibuses transferred from Lillyhall depot. The main reason for the change was to alleviate the problem caused by a considerable proportion of the passengers being accompanied by large rucksacks in the very limited space in the minibuses. Due to shortage of time, it was not possible to paint these vehicles in the green and cream livery but this work was undertaken during the winter in readiness for the 1996 season.

Also in 1995 the Traffic Regulation Order for Honister Pass was relaxed to allow the use of 25-seat vehicles. Cumberland responded to this by extending the Keswick to Buttermere service into a circular route, operating

outward via Whinlatter Pass and Buttermere and returning via Honister Pass and the west side of Derwentwater-service 77 or operating in the opposite direction-service 77A. The service was operated by one of the Mercedes 709 minibuses and again, due to shortage of time, a standard vehicle in Stagecoach livery was used. During the winter period a vehicle was repainted green and cream in readiness for the 1996 season. This is the latest addition to a series of initiatives to increase tourist traffic in the Lake District. On transfer from Ribble in 1989 the Kendal depot had a poor financial performance but as a result of these initiatives an increase of 16% in passenger numbers was recorded between 1992 and 1994.

In addition to the improvements to Lake District services, there was co-ordination of timetables to provide interchange facilities at Keswick, with services to Whitehaven, Carlisle, Penrith, Central Lakes, Lancaster, Borrowdale and Buttermere.

In 1995 a number of Stagecoach subsidiary companies introduced interurban express services marketed as 'Stagecoach Express'. In September of that year Cumberland in conjunction with Stagecoach Western Scottish introduced an hourly express service X75 between Carlisle and Dumfries and repainted DAF coach 509 into Stagecoach livery with route vinyls applied for the service. Similar treatment was given to Volvo coach 159 which was repainted from Coachline to Stagecoach livery with vinyls applied for the X3 service from Whitehaven to Gateshead.

As we conclude this chapter, which is the latest in the company's 75 years history, the question is "Where do we go from here ?" The company has shown a willingness to respond to passenger demand and has introduced commercial services at a time when subsidies and tendered work have been falling. In the winter of 1995/96 the 555 service between Lancaster and Keswick maintained its hourly frequency north of Ambleside for the first time in recent years. In its traditional operating area of West Cumbria there have been some interesting changes with some services showing a considerable increase in frequency whilst other once popular services are either much reduced or have been withdrawn. The service from Whitehaven to Lowca which, in the heyday of the bus, operated about twelve times per day, now has a daytime frequency of 30 minutes and Parton which had no service at all for many years now has a twenty minute service. On the other side of Whitehaven, the service to Frizington which in 1955 had two journeys per hour for most of the day now has a frequency of twelve minutes but services beyond Frizington are greatly reduced.

Similarly, the service to Egremont has increased but once popular services, particularly on fine summer days, to St. Bees and Seascale are reduced to infrequent Monday to Friday operation. There has been a reduction in Whitehaven town services particularly to Rosebank and Richmond, but these areas are catered for with the increased frequencies to Frizington and Egremont.

The situation can be summarised by saying that where there are passengers to be carried, the company will provide services but unless services are used they will, in the absence of subsidy, be withdrawn.

Details of the present company structure and its relationship to Stagecoach Holdings are given in the diagram but a brief word of explanation with regard to Company Numbers and Registrations may help to clarify the diagram.

Company Number:– 123665
Registered Office:– Tangier Street, Whitehaven

Name changes since original registration:-
8th August 1912:– Whitehaven Motor Service Company Ltd
1st June 1921:– Cumberland Motor Services Ltd
22nd May 1991:– Stagecoach (North West) Ltd

The name Cumberland Motor Services Ltd is retained for a dormant Company Number:– 211159. This was formerly named:–

Stagecoach (North West) Ltd
Bee Line Buzz Company Ltd
Bulwark Transport Company Ltd

Against a background of building work on the former Grand Hotel site at Whitehaven, Dennis Dart No. 701 leaves the bus station for the Hospital on Haven-Link Service 9-3 on 18th May 1992. In the background former Ribble Leyland Tiger No. 1154 heads for the bus station to operate on service 300 to Carlisle. Note the lower case lettering of the new destination blinds recently fitted to West Cumbria based vehicles. This was something of a surprise as lower case blinds inherited from Ribble in Carlisle and Penrith had been replaced with upper case blinds. A peculiarity of these new blinds was the variation in letter size from one display to another which seemed to be random and not related to length of the display.

Chapter Six
Barrow and South Lakes

BARROW IN FURNESS

Barrow in Furness is an isolated town; in fact it has been described as being situated at the end of the longest cul de sac in the country. Nevertheless it is a substantial community and is the largest town in Cumbria as distinct from Carlisle which is the county's only city.

Until local government reorganisation in 1974, it was in Lancashire and on becoming part of Cumbria at that time, brought with it the county's only municipal transport system.

The town had been built on the shipbuilding industry and throughout its history the shipyard has been the predominant employer and continues as such to-day. It was also the headquarters of the Furness Railway Company, the first lines of which were opened in 1846 to link Dalton with Barrow and Kirkby with Piel, on Roa Island, from where there was a steamer service to Fleetwood. A line to Broughton in Furness was opened in 1848 and this connected in 1850 with the Whitehaven and Furness Junction Railway to provide a service along the Cumberland Coast terminating originally at Preston Street Station in Whitehaven.

Progress was also made southwards, Lindal being reached in 1851 and Ulverston in 1854. The link from Ulverston to the Lancaster and Carlisle Railway at Carnforth was provided by the Ulverston and Lancaster Railway, being completed in 1857 and becoming part of the Furness Railway in 1862. Barrow was now linked to Whitehaven in the north and to Lancaster in the south. The original Barrow station was at the

Strand but this was replaced by the new Central Station in 1882. This station was extensively damaged in 1941 by enemy action and the present station was completed in

The first trams in Barrow were steam driven and this view shows one of these complete with top-covered trailer car and crew at an unidentified location.

Passengers and crew of No. 16, pictured here with No. 15 behind appear to be fascinated by the photographer. The location is thought to be Biggar Bank.

1959. The driving personality behind the Furness Railway Company was James Ramsden who became Locomotive Superintendent in 1846 at the age of 23 and four years later became Secretary and General Manager. In 1865 he became Managing Director and his name remains linked to this day with transport in Barrow as many bus services terminate at Ramsden Square.

Turning to transport within the town and its immediate environs, the Barrow in Furness Corporation Act of 1881 authorised the establishment of a tramway system and a special committee formed in 1883 sent a deputation to inspect tramway systems at Middlesbrough, Stockton, Sunderland, South Shields, Tynemouth, Portrush, Preston, Bolton, Southport and Birkenhead. Their recommendation was the establishment of a steam tramway system of 4ft-gauge and on 27th February 1884 the Tramways Order Confirmation promoted by Barrow in Furness Tramways Company Limited authorised construction of the tramway with routes as follows :–

> Abbey to Town Hall
> Ironworks/Steelworks to Ramsden Square
> Roose to Town Hall
> Ramsden Dock Station to Town Hall

It was on 11th July 1885 that the system was opened to the public with Mr William Parsons driving the first tram. Rolling stock comprised eight locomotives by Kitson of Leeds and eight trailers by Falcon Works, Loughborough. The depot was in Salthouse Road. On 28th July 1886, on completion of the original high level bridge, the tramway to Ramsden Dock was opened. In 1897 the total route length was 5.5 miles with a track length of six miles but all was not well financially. In 1898 the Company went into liquidation and was purchased on 23rd December 1899 by British Electric Traction Ltd with the intention of converting the entire system to electric traction.

The changeover from steam to electric traction was commenced in 1903 and by 6th February 1904 electric trams were operating on the following routes :-

> Town Hall to Abbey with short workings to White House and Hawcoat Lane
> Town Hall to Roose with short workings to Washington Hotel
>
> On 29th June 1904 electric cars were operating on :–
>
> Town Hall to Ramsden Dock with short workings to Tea House
>
> By about 24th October 1904 another route was operating, this being :–
>
> Town Hall to Ferry Road

Livery was maroon and cream but this was later changed to red and cream. The fleet at this time comprised 12 Brush tramcars, numbered 1-12 and these were followed in 1905 by two BEC cars (13 & 14) and two Brush cars (15 & 16). Work commenced in 1905 on the construction of the Jubilee Bridge linking Walney Island to the mainland and this was opened on 30th July 1908. On 8th January 1909 a tramway service was commenced to Walney Promenade, this being an extension of the previous service to Ferry Road. This service was extended on 4th August 1911 to Biggar Bank with short workings to Walney Promenade and Amphritite Street. The fleet was enlarged in 1910 and 1911 with the arrival of 4 Brush cars in each of these years to bring the fleet total to 24.

Outbreak of the First World War in 1914 placed restriction on further expansion and also saw the introduction of women as conductresses. In 1915 two second-hand Brush cars were purchased from Potteries Electric Traction Co Ltd and two trailer cars were purchased in 1917 for cars 22 and 23.

On 23rd September 1919 the Corporation resolved to take up its option to purchase the tramway system from British Electric Traction Ltd and this took place with effect from 1st January 1920, the cost being £96,250. Four of the original electric cars, numbers 1 to 4, together with number 25, were withdrawn in 1920 and six second-hand cars were purchased from Sheffield and four from Southport. These were followed in 1921 by ten new Brush cars, these being the last to be purchased.

In 1930, consideration was given to the replacement of the tramway and an inspection was made of the trolley bus system at Wolverhampton. However, it was eventually decided that the replacement should be by motor buses and the last tram service operated from the Abbey terminus on 5th April 1932, three trams being used, one of which was driven by Mr William Parsons who had driven the first tram in 1885. Mr Thomas Smalley was General Manager at the time.

As a postscript to the trams, just as this book was going to press, two tram bodies were discovered forming part of holiday chalets at Saltcoats Caravan Park near Ravenglass. They were Nos. 38 and 45 and both have been saved for restoration and preservation by Mr Alec Stott of Widnes. There had been two others on the site but, unfortunately, the owner burned these without realising their interest to enthusiasts. One thing which has come from this discovery is confirmation that, at some time, they were painted green and cream and this is thought to have been on takeover by Barrow Corporation whose colours were green and cream.

MOTOR BUSES

To look at the origin of motor buses in Barrow we have to go back to 1914 when British Electric Traction applied for a licence to operate a service from Barrow Town Hall to Dalton and Ulverston, and this commenced in 1915 using six Daimler CD vehicles purchased for the service. These were followed in 1916 by three Belsize vehicles which were disposed of in 1919. It was in 1919 that British Electric Traction offered to sell the bus undertaking to the Corporation for £15,000 but this was declined and on 1st January 1920 the undertaking was transferred to British Automobile Traction Co Ltd. In 1920 three Daimler Y type were purchased and had registrations transferred from the Belsize vehicles. Two further Daimler Y type arrived in 1920 and a further two in 1921. British Automobile Traction Ltd abandoned its service on 29th January 1922.

The Leyland Titan double decker figured prominently in the Barrow Corporation fleet throughout most of its history and this view taken near the Town Hall shows one of the first to be delivered in 1929 with open staircase bodies, also built by Leyland.

The commencement of municipal bus operation in Barrow goes back to 1920 when first proposals for a bus service were made but it was not until 17th August 1923 that the first service was operated from Roose tram terminus to Rampside. A small Ford bus was used for this. Two small Chevrolet buses followed.

The Barrow in Furness Corporation Act 1925 contained general powers to operate bus services and an expansion of services followed. The first was an extension in May 1925 of the Roose to Rampside service to Whitehall on the Coast Road, this being further extended along the Coast Road to Ulverston in July 1925. New Guy single-deck buses were used for this. In August 1925 two further services were commenced :-

Town Hall to Ormsgill and Town Hall to Hawcoat.

In October 1925 a garage was purchased in Salthouse Road, adjacent the tram depot and this was used as the bus depot. On abandonment of the tramway, the tram depot was converted to a bus depot and this site continued in use until 10th January 1936 when the new bus depot in Hindpool Road, built at a cost of £20,360, was formally opened.

In the meantime, further expansion of services had taken place with the opening in 1929 of routes Roose to Tea House, North Scale to Hawcoat and later Old Newbarns to Town Hall and North Scale.

In 1930 the blue and cream livery, so long associated with buses in Barrow, was introduced.

With the abandonment of the tramway in 1932, buses operated on the undementioned routes.

The colours refer to coloured destination screens introduced in 1934 which were a feature of Barrow buses until the 1960s although some of these screens continued in use on double-deck vehicles until the 1970s. They featured either white lettering on a coloured background or coloured lettering on a white background. This practice was again restored in February 1990 but was phased out by 1993 in favour of high visibility yellow on black blinds.

A new route, Oxford Street to Risedale was introduced in 1936 and was operated by single-deckers.

Early buses were lightweight single-deckers but in 1929 the almost inevitable Leyland Titan TD1 made its appearance when four with Leyland lowbridge bodies arrived and these were followed in 1931 by four Leyland TS3 single-deckers with Leyland bodies. Between 1932 and 1935 orders were split between Leyland and Crossley, bodies up to 1934 being either by Leyland or Northern Counties Motor and Engineering Co Ltd.

In 1935 there was a change of bodybuilder to English Electric Co Ltd, and thereafter up to and including 1941 all bodies were supplied by this firm. It is thought, however, that the 1941 deliveries, although to English Electric design, were subcontracted to East Lancashire Coachbuilders Ltd. The final pre-utility vehicles arrived in 1942 and comprised three Leyland Titan TD7 double-deckers, one with body by East Lancashire Coachbuilders and the others with bodies by Brush Coachworks. This same year also saw the arrival of the first utility vehicles in the form of six Guy Arab 1 5LW with bodies by Park Royal. These were followed in 1943 by 2 Daimler CWG5 and three further Guy Arab 1 5LW, all with bodies by Massey Brothers. A Massey-bodied Guy Arab 2 6LW which arrived in 1943 completed the wartime deliveries.

ABBEY TO BIGGAR BANK	via TOWN HALL	:-	Green
ROOSE TO TEA HOUSE	via TOWN HALL	:-	Blue
HAWCOAT TO THE SHORE	via TOWN HALL	:-	Red
ORMSGILL TO HARREL LANE	via TOWN HALL	:-	Yellow
CEMETERY TO NORTH SCALE		:-	Black/White

In the early postwar period Barrow became well known for having one of the most modern and standardised bus fleets in the country. The first new vehicles arrived in 1948 and comprised twenty Crossley DD42 double-deckers with Crossley bodies. These vehicles had relatively short lives with Barrow and it was for subsequent deliveries that the operator became well known. Between 1949 and 195 50 Leyland Titan PD2 double-deckers with Park Royal bodies was purchased, a sizeable intake over two years for a small operator, and all built to the new maximum width of 8ft. In their attractive blue and cream livery they were splendid vehicles. The ten vehicles delivered in 1950, Nos. 141 to 150 were rebodied by Roe in 1959/60.

Following the delivery of three single-deckers in the mid-'fifties, a further ten Park Royal bodied Leyland Titan PD2s arrived in 1958, these being the last Park Royal bodies to be purchased by Barrow. It was around this time that Park Royal changed from its attractive and well proportioned body to a boxlike design with frameless front and rear domes, regarded by many as the ugliest bus of the period. Following this a number of operators which had been regular Park Royal customers looked elsewhere for their bodies and Barrow turned to Massey Brothers for bodies on ten Leyland Titan PD2s delivered in 1961. These had front entrance bodies, a feature new to Barrow on double-deckers.

With the introduction in the early 'fifties of underfloor engined single-deckers and the subsequent increase in maximum permitted length to 36ft in July 1961, many operators turned from double to single-deckers and Barrow was among these. All deliveries after 1961 and in the 'seventies were single-deckers and included Leyland Leopards, Daimler Fleetlines, Leyland Nationals and Dennis Dominators. It was not until 1982 that further double-deckers were acquired and these comprised three Leyland Fleetlines with MCW bodies purchased second hand from London Transport with two further similar vehicles arriving in 1984. The first new double-deckers since 1961 were three Leyland Atlanteans with Northern Counties bodies which arrived in 1983 and were followed by a further similar vehicle in 1984.

This view of part of the Barrow Corporation Transport workshops at Hindpool Road shows postwar Crossley bodied Crossleys and Park Royal bodied Leylands. This section of the site was in the old Jute Works and pre-dates the 1936 development by many years as illustrated by the cast iron pillars.

Barrow ventured into coaching on 7th January 1973 when the coaching business of E. N. Hadwin, Ulverston was purchased with ten coaches. The business was operated as Hadwin's Luxury Coaches but was sold on 31st March 1977 to John Shaw & Son (Silverdale) Ltd which now operates as Shaw Hadwin thus perpetuating the Hadwin name.

To revert to the subject of services, on 11th April 1950, alterations were made to the Ormsgill to Harrel Lane and the Oxford Street to Risedale services to provide a circular service Oxford Street – Harrel Lane and Town Hall via Friars Lane and Ormsgill was linked to Risedale. Double-

deck vehicles were introduced on the Ormsgill to Risedale service and on 1st February 1953 this service was extended to a new housing estate at Newbarns. One-man-operation was introduced on 6th October 1958 on the Coast Road service to Ulverston.

Ribble used ten new Mercedes minibuses with Reeve Burgess conversion bodies and housed these at a depot in Emlyn Street. Ribble offered return fares at one and a half times the single fares which were generally the same as the single fares charged by Barrow Borough Transport. Prior to Deregulation, Barrow had operated jointly with Ribble to Ireleth, on the main service to Ulverston and also on the Coast Road service to Ulverston but the latter service was obtained on tender by Ribble which also became the sole operator on the service to Ulverston via Dalton. This provided further competition for Barrow Borough Transport which now operated no

---

BARROW BOROUGH TRANSPORT SERVICES ON DEREGULATION DAY

ROUTE	NOTES
Biggar Bank, Walney Island, Town Centre, Greystone Estate, Dalton	M-S No evns.
Holbeck Farm, Holbeck Park Ave., Town Centre, North Scale	M-S evenings
Lakes Parade, Hawcoat, Town Centre, Newbarns	M-S No evens.
Ravenglass Road, Town Centre, North Scale	M-S No evens.
Lesh Lane, Newbarns, Town Centre, West Shore	M-S Evenings.
Holbeck Farm, Holbeck Park Ave. Town Centre, Tea House	M-S No evens
Flass Lane/Harrel Lane, Town Centre, West Shore	Daily
Middlefield, Ormsgill, Town Centre, Lesh Lane, Newbarns	Daily
Biggar Bank, Town Centre, Lakes Parade, Hawcoat.	Daily
Middlefield, Ormsgill, Town Centre, Flass Lane / Harrel Lane	Daily

In addition several works and schools services were registered by Barrow Borough Transport Services..

Ribble Motor Services had decided to move into the local service scene in Barrow following deregulation and registered the following services:–

RIBBLE MOTOR SERVICES – ROUTES REGISTERED IN BARROW ON DEREGULATION

SERV.	ROUTE	NOTES
B1	Ocean Road Walney, Town Centre, Ormsgill	M-S.
B2	Middle Hill Newbarns, Town Centre, Furness Hospital	M-S.
B3	West Shore Walney, Town Centre	One early am working only
B4	Holbeck, Town Centre, North Scale	Su. afternoons only
B4	Town Centre, North Scale	M-F. early am only

Left: Barrow's claim to fame in the transport world concerned its large fleet of Park Royal-bodied Leyland PD2 double-deckers operated in the immediate postwar years. Number 169, one of the final batch of such vehicles delivered in 1958 is shown here in the town centre on 6th July 1972 in the later livery where a greater area of cream was employed. It has subsequently been preserved along with sister vehicle number 170.

Below left: When Park Royal produced a much less attractive design of double-decker in the late 'fifties and early 'sixties, many operators looked elsewhere for bodywork and Barrow turned to Massey Brothers of Wigan for ten bodies for Leyland PD2 chassis delivered in 1961. They were very attractive vehicles and were the first front entrance double-deckers for Barrow. Number 108 is shown in the town centre on 6th July 1972.

Despite these efforts the writing was very much 'on the wall' for Barrow Borough Transport. A proposal for a management/employee co-operative buyout was made in October 1988 and was approved in principle by the Borough Council and the trade unions but was not proceeded with and an Administrative Receiver was appointed in January 1989. The Company ceased to trade at 1530hrs. on 26th May 1989 with buses being withdrawn at just 2hrs notice. Ribble had won the battle but there was another interesting development to come.

Stagecoach had purchased Ribble in April 1989 and decided that Ribble operations in Cumbria should be transferred to sister company, Cumberland Motor Services Ltd, thus bringing all its operations in the County of Cumbria under the control of one company. This change took place with effect from 18th June 1989 and Ribble found itself in the situation of having spent almost three years establishing its presence in Barrow, only to be driven out of the town by its parent company one month after its victory over the opposition.

Although Ribble had purchased the depot and 24 vehicles there seemed to be a policy of not operating in Barrow any vehicles in the Barrow Borough Transport livery of blue and cream. Two Leyland Nationals, Barrow Nos. 16 & 17 were sent to Whitehaven for repaint into Stagecoach livery whilst Nos. 11,15,20-23 were repainted by Ribble. Number 13 and the Atlanteans were used by Ribble from Preston still in Barrow livery but with Ribble fleetnames applied. Cumberland sent Leyland Nationals Nos. 351,353,357,369 and 811 to Barrow to help out. All except 357 had their Cumberland fleetnames removed although 811 had not at that time received fleetnames following a recent repaint.

When it was decided that Cumberland would take over from Ribble, some further change of vehicles took place in that the Park Royal-bodied Atlanteans were transferred to other Ribble depots and replaced with Eastern Coach Works-bodied examples similar to those inherited by Cumberland with the Carlisle and Penrith depots of Ribble.

Legal lettering on vehicles had to be changed immediately ,but most vehicles retained their Ribble fleetnames for some time with the result that they carried

further than Dalton. This had its effect on fleet size which was reduced from 41 to 31.

Barrow recognised that it was now up against it and attempted to retaliate against Ribble by joining forces with Lancaster City Transport, which had also experienced the intrusion of Ribble into its traditional territory, and introduced services in Kendal. The services commenced on 30th November 1987 and whilst the Lancaster operations continued for some time as reported later, Barrow pulled out after 6th February 1988. The other action which was taken by Barrow was the introduction of minibuses, the first comprising five Dodge S56 with East Lancashire bodies, two of which were dual-purpose, arriving in 1986. A further Dodge S56 but with Reeve Burgess body arrived in 1987 and this also had coach seating. In 1988 fourteen Talbot Pullman six-wheeled minibuses arrived, these being on lease and offering the advantage of a low floor with easier access than the conventional minibuses. This easier access was welcomed by passengers and Ribble then reacted by bringing into Barrow ten similar vehicles which had been taken over with the United Transport Zippy operations in Preston and Bee Line Buzz operations in Manchester.

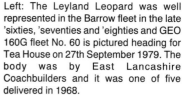

Left: The Leyland Leopard was well represented in the Barrow fleet in the late 'sixties, 'seventies and 'eighties and GEO 160G fleet No. 60 is pictured heading for Tea House on 27th September 1979. The body was by East Lancashire Coachbuilders and it was one of five delivered in 1968.

Centre left: The 1971 deliveries comprised five single-deckers on Daimler Fleetline chassis, a unit normally associated with double-deckers. East Lancashire Coachbuilders produced these rather odd looking bodies for them. Number 1 is heading for the Abbey on 6th July 1972.

Lower left: The Leyland National first appeared in the Barrow fleet in 1974. Number 14 was one of five delivered in 1977 and it is shown leaving Ulverston Victoria Road on the 1015 to Barrow via the Coast Road on 25th March 1978. Alongside and behind are Ribble vehicles.

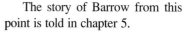

Ribble fleetnames and Cumberland legal lettering until such time as fleetnames were replaced.

Repainted Barrow Nationals received Cumberland fleetnames with the exception of 760 (ex Barrow 15) which received Ribble fleetnames, having been repainted prior to the change from Ribble to Cumberland being announced with the consequence that for a period it also carried Ribble fleetnames and Cumberland legal lettering. With the return of the former Barrow Nationals to service the Cumberland vehicles were returned to Whitehaven where they were prepared for the journey north to Perth to join the fleet of Perth Panthers.

The story of Barrow from this point is told in chapter 5.

THE FURNESS AREA AND GRANGE OVER SANDS.

Whilst the story of transport in Barrow had been unfolding there was also considerable activity in the rural areas comprising the Furness Peninsula and the small seaside resort of Grange over Sands. The largest company was the Furness Omnibus Company Ltd first registered on 9th January 1926 by sixteen owner drivers, and with a depot in Dalton in Furness. Services operated included Barrow to Ulverston, Ulverston to

BARROW CORPORATION TRANSPORT / BARROW BOROUGH TRANSPORTFLEET SUMMARY – MOTOR BUSES.

FLEET NO.	REG. NO.	CHASSIS	BODY	BODY TYPE	DATE
	EO 3070	Ford	Allen	B14F	1923
1-2	EO 3152/74	Chevrolet	MacPherson	B14/12F	1923
1	EO 3463	Guy B	Guy	B26F	1925
2-5	EO 3482-5	Guy B	Guy	B26F	1925
6-9	EO 3755-8	Guy B	Vickers	B26F	1926
10-11	EO 3775-6	Guy JA	Guy	B14F	1926
12	EO 4197	Guy BB	Guy	B26F	1927
14	EO 4198	Guy BB	Guy	B26F	1927
1-2	EO 4441-2	Guy B	Guy	B26F	1928
15-18	EO 4678-81	Leyland TD1	Leyland	L24/24R	1929
7	EO 4998	Leyland TS3	Leyland	B32R	1931
9-10	EO 5030-1	Leyland TS3	Leyland	B32R	1931
19	EO 5162	Leyland TS3	Leyland	B32R	1931
31-39	EO 5234-42	Crossley Con.	N.C.M.E.	H24/24	1932
40-48	EO 5243-51	Crossley Con.	N.C.M.E.	H24/24	1932
5	EO 5264	Crossley Al.	Crossley	B32R	1932
1-4	EO 5400-3	Leyland TS4	Leyland	B32R	1933
6	EO 5404	Leyland TS4	Leyland	B32R	1933
49-50	EO 5514-5	Crossley Con.	N.C.M.E.	H24/24R	1933
20-21	EO 5758-9	Leyland TD3c	N.C.M.E.	H24/24R	1934
22	EO 6065	Leyland TD4c	E.E.C.	H24/24R	1935
23	EO 6066	Crossley Con.	E.E.C.	H26/22R	1935
24-27	EO 6373-6	Leyland TD4c	E.E.C.	H26/26R	1936
11-14	EO 6634-7	Leyland TD4c	E.E.C.	H26/26R	1937
8	EO 6842	Leyland TD4c	E.E.C.	H26/26R	1937
28	EO 6843	Leyland TD4c	E.E.C.	L26/26R	1937
29-30	EO 6886-7	Leyland TD5c	E.E.C.	L26/26R	1937
51-54	EO 7066-9	Leyland TD5c	E.E.C.	L26/26R	1938
55-56	EO 7141-2	Leyland TD5c	E.E.C.	L26/26R	1938
57-59	EO 7143-5	Leyland TD5c	E.E.C.	H30/26R	1938
60	EO 7146	Leyland TD5c	E.E.C.	L26/26R	1938
67-72	EO 7368-73	Leyland TD5c	E.E.C.	H29/23R	1939
62-66	EO 7520-4	Leyland TD5c	E.E.C.	H29/23R	1939
61	EO 7525	Leyland TD5c	E.E.C.	H29/23R	1939
73-78	EO 7732-7	Leyland TD5c	E.E.C.	H29/23R	1940
15-18	EO 7802-5	Leyland TD7	E.Lancs.	H29/23R	1941
79	EO 7859	Leyland TD7	E.Lancs.	H29/23R	1942
80-81	EO 7882-3	Leyland TD7	Brush	H30/26R	1942
82-85	EO 7893-6	Guy Arab 1	Park Royal	H30/26R	1942
86-87	EO 7901-2	Guy Arab 1	Park Royal	H30/26R	1942
91-92	EO 7904-5	Guy Arab 1	Massey	H30/26R	1943
88-90	EO 7906-8	Guy Arab 1	Massey	H30/26R	1943
93	EO 7932	Guy Arab 2	Massey	H30/26R	1944
40-49	EO 8650-9	Crossley DD42	Crossley	H32/26R	1948
101-110	EO 8788-97	Crossley DD42	Crossley	H32/26R	1948
111-122	EO 8890-01	Leyland PD2/3	Park Royal	H30/26R	1949
123-140	EO 9050-67	Leyland PD2/3	Park Royal	H30/26R	1949
141-150	EO 9171-80	Leyland PD2/3	Park Royal	H30/26R	1950
151-158	EO 9502-09	Leyland PD2/3	Park Royal	H30/26R	1951
159-160	EO 9510-11	Leyland PD2/3	Park Royal	H30/26RD	1951
50-51	EO 9765-66	Ley.PSU1/13	Leyland	B44F	1952
52	BEO 397	Ley.PSU1/13	Massey	B43F	1955
161-170	CEO 948-57	Ley. PD2/40	Park Royal	H33/28R	1958
53	EEO 468	Ley.PSUC1/1	Massey	DP39F	1959
1-10	HEO 271-80	Ley.PD2A/27	Massey	H37/27F	1961
68-73	JEO 768-73	Leyland L1	East Lancs.	B42D	1963
50-54	BEO 950-4D	Ley.PSU3/1R	Strachans	B51D	1966
55-59	EEO 255-9E	Ley.PSU3/1R	Neepsend	B51D	1967
60-64	GEO 160-4G	Ley.PSU3A/2R	East Lancs.	B51D	1968
45-49	HEO 245-9G	Ley.PSU3A/2R	East Lancs.	B51D	1969
1-5	LEO 141-5J	Daimler SRG	East Lancs.	B49D	1971
50	BJH 128F	Bedford VAM	Plaxton	C41F	1971
6-8	SEO 206-8M	Leyland National 1151/1R		B49F	1974
9-10	SEO 209-0M	Leyland National 11351/1R		DP48F	
H1-H3	HEO 341-3N	Bedford YRT	Duple	C53F	1975
11-15	NEO 829-3R	Leyland National 11351A/1R		B49F	1977
16-17	UEO 478-9T	Leyland National 11351A/1R		B49F	1978
18-19	WEO 146-7T	Dennis Domr.	East Lancs.	B46F	1979
20-23	CEO 720-3W	Leyland National 2		B49F	1980
101-3	OJD 174-6R	Ley.FE30AGR	M.C.W.	H45/32F	1982 *
104-6	LEO 734-6Y	Ley.AN68D/1R	N.C.M.E.	H43/32F	1983
107	A266 PEO	Ley.AN68D/1R	N.C.M.E.	H43/32F	1984
108	OUC 41R	Ley.FE30AGR	M.C.C.W.	H43/32F	1984 *
109	OJD 227R	Ley.FE30AGR	M.C.C.W.	H43/32F	1984 *
80	C913 XEO	Ley.TRCTL11/3R	Duple	C57F	1986
81	CEO 952	Ley.PSU5A/4R	Duple	C53F	1986 **
82	D458 BEO	Dodge S56	East Lancs.	DP22F	1986
83	D459 BEO	Dodge S56	East Lancs.	DP22F	1986
84	D460 BEO	Dodge S56	East Lancs.	B 22F	1986
85	D456 BEO	Dodge S56	East Lancs.	B 22F	1986
86	D457 BEO	Dodge S56	East Lancs.	B 22F	1986
87	E319 LHG	Talbot Pullman Talbot		B 22F	1988
88	E325 LHG	Talbot Pullman Talbot		B 22F	1988
89	E327 LHG	Talbot Pullman Talbot		B 22F	1988
90	E332 LHG	Talbot Pullman Talbot		B 22F	1988
91-100	E562-71 MAC	Talbot Pullman Talbot		B 22F	1988

* Ex London Transport, new in 1976/77.
** Ex National Travel East, MWG 499P, new in 1976.

Ambleside and five local services in the Dalton area. In addition a service from Barrow to Manchester was operated three times per week from 19th July 1927 but was withdrawn for the Winter and resumed on Tuesdays and Thursdays for the Summer of 1928 after which it was abandoned. The Lonsdale Pullman Bus Company Ltd which had been formed in July 1927 by T. Henderson, H. Such, and E. Holme of Barrow together with W. Jolly and A. Glover of Ulverston was acquired by Furness in 1928. In 1929 Furness took over the Barrow Bus Company Ltd which had been founded by F. Barrow and also another operator, J. Creighton and Sons. By 1930 the company operated 36 vehicles and attracted the attention of Ribble Motor Services Ltd which purchased it for the sum of £45,000 in May 1930. Having established itself in the Furness areas Ribble acquired the stage carriage services of Parker and Sons, Grange over Sands, in September 1930 and later entered into a co ordination agreement with the Grange Motor and Cycle Company Ltd covering services from Barrow to Ulverston, Barrow to Grange and Grange to Newby Bridge, effective from 26th September 1938 and which remained in force until Ribble purchased the stage cariage services from the Grange company on 1st July 1951 for the sum of £10,000. On 1st January 1958 Ribble purchased the excursion and tours and private hire business from Grange paying £3,000 for the goodwill and £6,500 for the property which Ribble used as its Grange depot until transfer to Cumberland in 1989. Prior to this all Ribble operations in the Furness area had been centred on its depot at The Ellers, Ulverston opened in 1932.

During wartime a joint timetable was issued for the Furness area and that dated 1st August 1944 includes the following services:–

1. Barrow Corporation Transport, Ribble 534, Grange Motor & Cycle Co Barrow-Dalton-Ulverston
2. Ribble 517, 520, Grange Motor & Cycle Co Barrow-Newby Bridge-Ambleside
3. Barrow Corporation Transport Barrow-Coast Road-Ulverston
5. Barrow Corporation Transport, Ribble 533, Grange Motor & Cycle Co Barrow-Grange
6. Ribble 536 Barrow-Gleaston-Ulverston
7. Ribble 514, 515 Ulverston-Newby Bridge
8. Ribble 535, Grange Motor & Cycle Co Grange-Newby Bridge
78. Ribble 500. Ulverston-Coniston
79. Ribble 561. Ulverston-Broughton-Millom

After the takeover of the stage carriage services of Grange in 1951, Ribble became the only operator of such services in the Furness and Grange area outside the Borough of Barrow in Furness, excluding services operated jointly with Barrow Corporation Transport.

Public transport at this time

was still in the boom period and the list of services operated in the area in 1961 as given on page 70 indicates this and also contrasts with the list on page 71 of services taken over from Ribble by Cumberland in 1989.

SOUTH LAKES.

The entry of Cumberland Motor Services into the South Lakes area occurred long before the takeover from Ribble in 1989. It was in July 1925 that Henry Meageen of Cumberland Motor Services announced to his board that he had purchased five AEC omnibuses and formed Westmorland Motor Services Ltd for operation of a service between Keswick and Kendal. He also reported that agreement had been reached with a Mr Rutter of Kendal to bring into the new company his Kendal local bus service, which, in addition to operating between Kendal and Keswick, operated services to Old Hutton, Selside and Patten Bridge plus local town services. Three Guy buses and two Thornycroft charabancs were transferred to the new company as part of this deal. Also taken into the new company was Feirn (Ambleside) Ltd and the Lake District Road Traffic Company and the service commenced on 15th July 1925. Further acquisitions in the Lancaster area of Lancaster & District Tramways Ltd, Fahy's Limited and Lambsfield Motors Ltd led to a change of name to Lancashire and Westmorland Motor Services Ltd effective from February 1926. This title was also to be short lived for in 1927 the company was acquired by Ribble Motor Services Ltd.

Another company in the Kendal area was the Kendal Motor Bus Company Ltd which had been formed in 1922 by a number of ex-service men including a Mr B. Bracken, initially to operate a service for workmen between Endmoor and the paper mills at Burneside and Bowston. As it developed there were services to Grasmere which competed with the Westmorland Motor Services operation, also to Grange over Sands, Cark, Underbarrow and Kirkby Lonsdale together with Kendal Town Services. The

This Leyland Lioness with Hall Lewis body dating from 1927 was No. 14 in the Furness Omnibus fleet and later passed to Ribble as its No. 949.

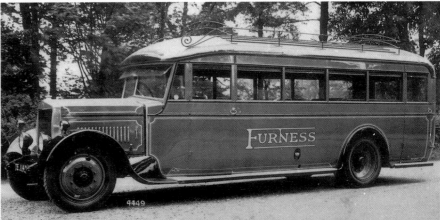

65

company was very much a thorn in the side of Ribble who introduced competing services and eventually purchased the company in 1930.

By now the only other companies of any significance in the area were Magnet Bus Service of Windermere, founded and operated by Charles Head and Dallam Motor Services of Milnthorpe, formed by the Fawcett family in 1924. Magnet operated between Windermere and Bowness and was taken over by Ribble on 1st February 1946. Dallam operated from Kendal to Arnside via Milnthorpe and from Arnside to Lancaster and survived until 1st December 1950 when it was taken over by Ribble.

From 1930 Ribble was very much the dominant operator in the central and south Lakes area and the history of this company has been well documented in *British Bus Systems No. 2 – Ribble* and in *Ribble Volume 1* and *Ribble Volume 2*. Many rural services have been withdrawn over the years and the services which survived to the Cumberland takeover are listed in the Appendices. The dominant service over the years has always been the trunk service from Keswick to Lancaster via Central Lakes and Kendal, initially numbered 68 but later numbered 555/6 and operated by

The Lake District Road Traffic Company was taken over by Westmorland Motor Services. Two of its vehicles are shown at the Shakespeare Inn, Highgate, Kendal in 1913.

Close encounter of the expensive kind – EC 7623 on the left with CARK and GRANGE labels in the back window was a Leyland Lion PLSC1 with Leyland body new to Kendal Motor Bus Company in 1927 which passed to Ribble as No.917. The vehicle facing the camera is TC 8882, a Leyland SGH7 new to Lancaster & District Tramways and Fahys in 1924 and which passed to Lancashire and Westmorland Motor Services.

Right: Kendal Motor Bus Company Ltd EC 7086, a 1926 Leyland C7, waits in Dalton Square, Lancaster with its crew, on the service from there to Kendal.

Centre: Magnet Bus Service, which operated from Windermere to Bowness, was owned by Mr Charles Head who is shown here outside the depot with JM 87, a Leyland KP2 with Burlingham body, dating from 1932.

Below: This vehicle was one of the batch of AEC 411s purchased for the commencement of Westmorland Motor Services Ltd and as the side board indicates, for operation between Keswick and Kendal.

vehicles from Ambleside and Kendal depots. Double-deck vehicles have normally been used, since the early 'fifties, giving excellent views of the Lakeland scenery from the top deck. The only other group of regular and profitable services has been the Kendal town services. These services underwent a 'mini revolution', as Ribble described it in publicity material when, prior to deregulation, minibuses were introduced on Sunday 24th August 1986. Since that time all town services in Kendal have been minibus operated apart from occasional substitution by full size vehicles.

In addition to the operation of local services Ribble had developed an extensive network of express services and the Lake District was included in this network. A service from Liverpool to Ambleside commenced on 28th May 1928, the service being cut back to Kendal for the following winter. The Ambleside service resumed on 20th April 1929 and was extended to Keswick on 22nd June 1929 when a Manchester to Keswick service was commenced. Anglo-Scottish services commenced on 13th May 1929 operating via Kendal and Carlisle. Over the years these services underwent various changes and on the formation of National Express passed to that organisation and most of the services previously terminating at Keswick were extended to operate to/from Whitehaven. Development of these services since that time is given in Chapter 7 – Coaching. Local service developments in the area since the takeover by Cumberland are given in Chapter 5.

An unidentified Leyland single-decker photographed when new for the makers and delivered to Dallam Motors, operated by John Fawcett and Sons of Milnthorpe.

This Ribble Leyland TS3 with Leyland body, CK 4465, was new in 1931 and shows 'Kendal' on the destination display at this unidentified location.

Ribble's standard single-deckers of the prewar period were familiar vehicles in the Lake District and RN 7969 was a Leyland LZ2 with body by Eastern Coachworks dating from 1936. It is waiting at Windermere with destination displays set for service 555 to Ambleside.

It was not until the postwar period that sanction was granted for the operation of double-deckers on service 555 over Dunmail Raise to Keswick. This view is thought to have been taken on the occasion of a trial run, with Ribble management as passengers, and the photograph was taken on the return journey with Dunmail Raise in the background. The vehicle is No.1773 a Leyland TD5 dating from 1938, which received a new Eastern Coach Works body in 1949.

Ribble's Leyland Olympics were regular performers on the service from Windermere to Bowness, now part of the Cumberland open top service and No. 263, dating from 1951, is shown awaiting departure from Windermere Station on 28th June 1964.

RIBBLE SERVICES IN FURNESS AND SOUTH LAKES 1961

No.	Route.
53	Kirkby Lonsdale – Sedbergh via Casterton, Barbon, Middleton.
63	Milnthorpe – Lancaster via Yealand, Beetham.
66	Kendal – Arnside via Milnthorpe.
68	Lancaster – Keswick via Kendal, Central Lakes.
69	Milnthorpe – Lancaster via Burton, Borwick.
70	Lancaster – Kendal via Burton, Milnthorpe.
71	Kendal – Milnthorpe via Hincaster.
471	Kendal – Appleby via Grayrigg, Tebay, Crosby Ravensworth.
472	Kendal – Appleby via Grayrigg, Tebay.
476	Kendal – Kirkby Stephen via Sedbergh.
477	Kendal – Dent via Sedbergh.
480	Sedbergh – Lea Yeat via Dent.
481	Sedbergh – Hawes via Garsdale.
483	Ingleton – Hawes via Ribblehead.
487	Kendal – Ingleton via Endmoor, Kirkby Lonsdale.
488	Kirkby Lonsdale – Ingleton.
493	Ambleside – Newby Bridge via Hawkshead.
500	Ulverston – Coniston via Greenodd, Blawith.
501	Foxfield – Coniston via Broughton.
510	Ulverston – Grizedale via Greenodd, Satterthwaite.
514	Ulverston – Newby Bridge via Bouth, Haverthwaite, Backbarrow.
515	Ulverston – Newby Bridge via Haverthwaite, Backbarrow.
517*	Barrow – Ambleside via Newby Bridge, Bellman Ground, Bowness.
520*	Barrow – Ambleside via Newby Bridge, Storrs Hall, Bowness.
526	Barrow – Ulverston via Little Urswick, Scales, Gleaston.
527	Barrow – Ulverston via Little Urswick, Gleaston.
528	Grange – Cartmel via Flookborough, Ravenstown, Cark.
529	Grange – Cark via Kents Bank, Flookborough, Ravenstown.
532	Newby Bridge – Grange via Cark, Flookborough.
533*	Barrow – Kendal via Newby Bridge, Seatle, Cartmel, Allithwaite.
534*	Barrow – Ulverston via Dalton.

No.	Route.
535	Newby Bridge – Grange via High Newton, Lindale.
538	Grange – Cark via Kents Bank, Allithwaite, Flookborough.
540	Grange – Cark via Allithwaite, Flookborough.
541	Kendal – Dawson Fold via Underbarrow, Brigsteer, Crosthwaite Green.
542	Kendal – Grange via Levens Bridge, Lindale.
544	Kendal – Dawson Fold via Crook, Underbarrow, Crosthwaite.
547	Grange – Cartmel via Direct Route.
549	Windermere – Bowness via Baddeley Clock.
550	Windermere – Bowness via Thornbarrow Road.
553	Kendal – Dawson Fold via Crook, Underbarrow, Bowland Bridge.
555	Kendal – Keswick via Central Lakes.
556	Ambleside – Oxenholme via Windermere, Kendal.
557	Kendal – Bowland Bridge via Crook, Bowness, Winster.
559	Kendal – Kentmere via Staveley.
560	Ulverston – Grizebeck via Broughton Beck.
561	Ulverston – Broughton via Broughton Beck, Grizebeck.
562	Ulverston – Millom via Broughton Beck, Grizebeck, Broughton.
563	Ulverston – Seathwaite via Broughton Beck, Broughton, Ulpha Bridge.
567	Dalton – Grizebeck via Ireleth, Kirkby.
639	Kendal – Selside via Direct Route.
641	Kendal – Penrith via Selside, Shap.
650	Windermere – Troutbeck via Direct Route (Summer).
667	Ambleside – Dungeon Ghyll via Langdale, Chapel Stile.
669	Ambleside – Coniston via Skelwith Bridge.
684	Kirkby Stephen – North Stainmore via Brough.
701	Kirkby Stephen – Tebay via Ravenstonedale, Newbiggin on Lune.

Dalton and Ulverston Local Services, D2,3,5,6. U1,2,3.
Kendal Local Services K1,3,7,9,10,11,13,18,19,23.

* Indicates operated jointly with Barrow Corporation Transport Department.
- Hale Grange

| 573 | Appleby – Sleagill |
| 574 | Appleby – Drybeck |

SERVICES INHERITED FROM RIBBLE IN FURNESS AND SOUTH LAKES   JUNE 1989.

Number	Route
B —	Barrow Town Services B1,2,3,4,5,7,8,9,14,15,17.
K —	Kendal Town Services K1,4,5,6,9,24.
G1-3	Grange Minilink Services
U1	Ulverston – Croftlands
W1/2	Ambleside – Bowness
502/7	Ulverston/Barrow – Dalton – Askam – Grizebeck
504/10	Grizedale – Greenodd – Ulverston – Coniston
505	Ambleside – Coniston
511	Ulverston – Broughton –Millom/Coniston
512	Ulverston – Greenodd–Coniston
514/8	Ambleside – Bowness– Newby Bridge –Ulverston – Barrow
516	Ambleside – Dungeon Ghyll
522/4/5	Barrow – Dalton – Ulverston – Croftlands
526	Ulverston – Gt. Urswick – Leece – Roose – Barrow
527/8	Ulverston – Bardsea – Roa Island – Barrow
530/3/5	Kendal – Grange –Newby Bridge –Ulverston

540	Kendal – Crook – Crosthwaite
541	Kendal – Crosthwaite – Bowness – Windermere – Lakes School
545	Lindale – Grange –Ulverston
552/3	Kendal – Milnthorpe –Arnside
555-7	Keswick – Central Lakes – Kendal – Lancaster
561	Kendal – Tebay –Appleby
563	Kendal – Kirkby Lonsdale – via Farleton
564	Kendal – Sedbergh
565	Sedbergh – Lea Yeat
566	Sedbergh – Barbon – Kirkby Lonsdale
567	Kendal – Kirkby Lonsdale Direct
568	Kendal – Old Hutton
570	Appleby – Marton
571	Appleby – Low Abbey
572	Appleby – Hale Grange
573	Appleby – Sleagill
574	Appleby – Drybeck

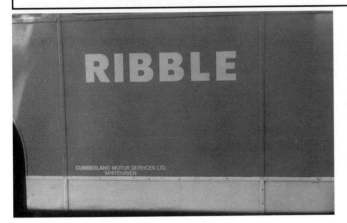

When the takeover of Ribble in the Barrow and South Lakes area took place, fleetnames were not changed immediately, as had been the case with Penrith and Carlisle. This gave the rather unusual situation of vehicles having Ribble fleetnames and Cumberland Motor Services Ltd. legal lettering. If vehicles went to Whitehaven for any reason, they tended to return with Cumberland fleetnames.

Lowbridge double-deckers are required on the service from Kendal to Arnside because of the Arnside railway bridge and Ribble 1807, a lowbridge Leyland Atlantean with MCW body, was heading south along the A6 on this service when photographed on 16th April 1974.

Chapter Seven
Coaching

In 1932 the Company took delivery of nine AEC Regal single-deckers with 32-seat rear-entrance bodies by Thomas Harrington Ltd of Hove. Six of these were finished in a reversed livery of mainly cream with red trim and were fitted with coach seating. They were the first heavyweight 'modern' coaches to be purchased and since that time coaching has played an important role in company activities. Company publicity described them as 'Luxury Sunshine All Weather Radio Coaches'. These vehicles, which were operated in Summer then delicensed for the Winter remained in service until the wartime period when they were withdrawn and sold. It is rather ironical that their fleet numbers were then allocated to wartime Bedford OWB single-deckers; a greater contrast in vehicle specification would have been difficult to imagine. There was no such thing in those days as allocating CMS fleet numbers according to vehicle type.

There was plenty of scope for private hire, excursions and tours for car ownership in west and north Cumberland was low. There had of course been excursions and tours prior to 1932, but these vehicles added a new dimension to coaching. Five Lakes tours and Eight Lakes tours were popular, as were excursions to the more distant larger resorts of Blackpool and Morecambe. It was on the return journey from Blackpool on the evening of Sunday 9th July 1939 that one of these coaches, No. 79, was invloved in an accident at Galgate and was destroyed by fire. Six people were killed and five seriously injured in the incident.

In addition to providing coaching facilities for the local population, the company provided excursions and tours for tourists staying in Keswick from which Lakes Tours were also popular together with excursions to the small resorts of St. Bees and Seascale on the west Cumberland coast.

The company decided to expand its coaching fleet and in 1935 a further AEC Regal was purchased, but this had a centre-entrance 31-seat body of new design by H. V. Burlingham Ltd of Blackpool. It was exhibited at the 1935 Commercial Motor Show but did not enter service until 1936 and was used extensively in company publicity material. Also in 1935, the businesses of Wilson Brothers, Whitehaven and N Hamilton, Workington were purchased bringing two further modern heavyweight coaches into the fleet. From Wilsons there was an AEC Regal with Burlingham body dating from 1934 and from Hamilton a Leyland TS7 with Burlingham body new in 1935. A further three coaches were purchased new in 1936 comprising Leyland TS7 chassis with centre entrance 31-seat bodies by Burlingham.

In addition to day excursions and tours, the company offered programmes of Extended Tours, a total of fifteen being included in the 'Official Handbook' issued by the

Three of the AEC Regals with coach bodies by Thomas Harrington of Hove, delivered in 1932, are shown with four Leyland TD1 double-deckers. Note the drivers in their white dust coats and with white covers to their caps. This was normal attire for crews in the Summer period.

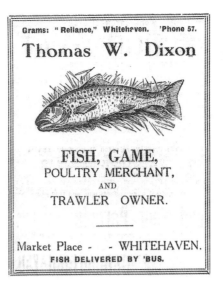

Above; A selection of advertisements which appeared in the Company's timetable booklets.

Upper left: AEC Regal No.74 with centre entrance coach body by H. V. Burlingham which was exhibited at the 1935 Commercial Motor Show and entered service in 1936. It was regularly featured in company publicity.

Centre left: The first postwar coaches to be received were Bedford OB models with Duple bodies and following prewar practice for lightweight coaches they received bus livery. Number 249 is shown in Carlisle bus station working as a service bus to Wigton. By this time it had received a Perkins diesel engine.

Left: The second batch of postwar heavyweight coaches were also Leyland PS1 models, received in 1950 but with bodies by H. V. Burlingham, of Blackpool, a more traditional supplier to the company. This view taken by the bodybuilder is of No. 283, which together with No. 284, seated only 28, the other 8 in the batch seating 31. Numbers 283-285 extended the fleet numbering system, the others being given lower numbers to fill gaps created by withdrawn vehicles. This batch, unlike the ACB bodied coaches, retained their original,bodies albeit with these rebuilt as service buses in the late 'fifties.

73

The first underfloor engined coaches were three Leyland Royal Tigers with this distinctive body design developed by Leyland for this chassis. Ribble had 120 of these coaches and used them extensively on its express services. This view of No. 345 is at Carlisle bus station, with a 'Morecambe' sticker in the window, possibly in preparation for an excursion or for a hire to Ribble to assist on an Express Service.

company in 1936. These included :-

Scottish Highlands	6 Days	£ 7 7s 0d.
London and South Coast	8 Days	£ 8 8s 0d.
Devon and Cornwall	10 Days	£11 11s 0d.
North Wales Tour	3 Days	£3 5s 0d.

In addition there were 38 day tours or excursions included.

The following year, 1937, was Coronation Year and a special brochure was issued for Extended Tours.

A number of lightweight coaches generally on Bedford or Commer chassis was purchased new or acquired with local businesses but the practice was to paint these in bus livery and only the heavyweights were painted in coach livery.

In 1939 it was decided to further expand the coach fleet by rebodying with coach bodies a number of 1929 Leyland TS2 buses and five were so treated, three by Massey Brothers, one by Burlingham and one by an unidentified builder. One of the Massey bodies, although to coach outline, was fitted with bus seating and painted in bus livery. The Burlingham body and one of the Massey bodies had seating for only 26 passengers by fitting single seats to the nearside. Cov-Rad radiators were fitted at the same time. It was ironical that soon after taking delivery of these rebodied vehicles, there came the outbreak of war with a consequent restriction on liesure travel.

During this period of considerable coaching activity,

the company had not shown any inclination to provide Express coach services from the area but was content to publicise in its timetables details of other operators' services from Keswick and Carlisle and to offer through booking facilities and connection details for these. Return fares from Whitehaven, quoted in the 1936 Summer timetable for these services included: London – 50/-, Manchester – 19/6d; Glasgow – 22/-.

Whilst the outbreak of war placed severe restrictions on coaching, it did not dampen the company's enthusiasm for the acquisition of local coaching firms. In 1943, the firms of Lewthwaite Brothers, Cleator Moor and H Crosthwaite, Frizington were acquired and with the former firm came DRM 440, a 1939 Leyland TS8 with Burlingham coach body which became the most modern coach in the fleet. It survived in the fleet until 1959, after being rebodied by Associated Coachbuilders in 1948.

Once the war had ended and attentions were turned to fleet renewal, coaches figured significantly in these. In 1947 two Bedford OBs with Duple bodies arrived and these were followed the following year by another four. All maintained the prewar tradition for lightweight coaches in being finished in bus livery. The first heavyweight coach, a Leyland PS1 with Associated Coachbuilders body, arrived in 1948 and was unusual in that it had not been ordered by Cumberland but by local coach operator H. and I.Moffat of Cleator Moor. It had been exchanged for GAO 510, one of the Leyland PS1 single-deck buses with Associated

The first Bristols to arrive in the CMS fleet, in 1954, were three LS models with luxury coach bodies by Eastern Coach Works Ltd. They were similar to No.351 shown here, photographed when new by the coach builder and which arrived in January 1955 together with No. 352. Because the Maegeens had placed orders for Leyland chassis the first Bristol did not arrive until 1954, completely by-passing the L & K models which typified Tilling companies.

Coachbuilders bodies ordered by Cumberland and which Moffats used regularly on their Miners' services.

By the middle of 1949 the company found itself short of coaches and as an interim measure, eight of the Burlingham bus bodied Leyland PS1s, which had been delivered in 1947, were fitted with coach seats, polished timber window surrounds and moquette covered lining panels but retained bus livery. It was something of a surprise to the author that these bodies were chosen for this purpose rather than the Massey bodied PS1s which were much more coach like in outline and already had polished timber window surrounds and lining panels. By contrast the Burlingham bodies when delivered had a rather spartan semi utility internal finish without lining panels. The reason may possibly have been the fact that there were only five of the Massey bodied PS1s and eight were required for conversion.

In the same year ten Leyland PS1s with Associated Coachbuilders coach bodies arrived and these were followed in 1950 by a further ten with Burlingham bodies. Including the rebodied Leyland TS8, No 194, there were now twenty eight modern coaches in the fleet. In addition to private hire, excursions and tours, interest in express coach travel had built up and whilst the company still did not operate services of its own, there were regular hirings to Ribble for duplicate vehicles on its services in the summer peak periods.

The 1950 deliveries comprised the last new front engined single-deck vehicles to enter the fleet for many years as attention turned to underfloor engined single-deckers with their greater passenger carrying capacity. Three Leyland Royal Tigers with characteristic Leyland coach bodies arrived in 1953 and thereafter, as Tilling Group policy was finally enforced on Cumberland, Bristol chassis with Eastern Coach Works bodies became the order of the day. On the coaching side this resulted initially in the delivery of Bristol LS and later Bristol MW chassis with the classic Eastern Coach Works bodies of that time. The first Bristols introduced a new coach livery of cream with black trim, a livery also used by a number of other Tilling companies at that time.

The 'fifties had been a boom time for passenger transport and to some extent this carried forward into the early part of the next decade, but by then the heyday was over and as car ownership increased so use of public transport declined. Economies were sought in many ways and this is reflected in the purchase in 1965 of a Bedford VAL coach with Duple body, the first lightweight coach since 1948. From 1965 to 1973 inclusive only lightweight coaches were purchased new, Bedfords until 1969, a Bristol LH in 1970 and Fords in 1972 and 1973 although a Bristol RELH with dual-purpose body was purchased in 1972 and two Bristol RELLs purchased at the same time were fitted with coach seating.

The decline in usage of public transport had affected the coaching operations of the company but things were about to change particularly in regard to express services.

Left: Duple Dominant bodied Leyland Leopards were the mainstay of the Cumberland provision for National Express workings for many years. Number 625 arrives at Preston bus station on 7th May 1985 operating service 952 from Whitehaven to Nottingham.

Below left: One of the first batch of Eastern CoachWorks-bodied Leyland Leopards, No.639, leaves Lancaster on 8th May 1985 operating service 735 from Barrow to Swindon. The destination display shows 735 Birmingham, as Swindon was not included on the destination blinds. Normally CMS were very quick to provide additional destinations to blinds to meet new duties for National Express.

NATIONAL EXPRESS

On formation of the National Bus Company the express service operations of the subsidiary companies were brought together under one organisation 'National Express' and coaches in an all-white livery and carrying the large red and blue NATIONAL fleetname soon became a familiar sight in many parts of the country. National Express operated services but owned no vehicles, these being hired in from other National Bus Company subsidiary companies.

In 1973 it was decided that the Express service operated by Ribble between Manchester and Keswick together with that operated by Ribble subsidiary company W. C. Standerwick, Ltd between Keswick and London, should be extended to/from Whitehaven. Initially the involvement of Cumberland Motor Services was minimal involving only the provision of a short working on the Manchester service (X40) between Whitehaven and Preston, the vehicle working out in the morning and

returning in the evening. The coach normally used for this was the solitary Bristol RELH No 600. However, this was only the start, and it was an involvement which was to grow considerably over the coming years and saw coaches of Cumberland Motor Services operating express services not only to and from west Cumbria but also in other parts of England, Scotland and Wales and covering places as far apart as Inverness and Minehead. There were at this time Summer Saturday services operating to Blackpool, Morecambe, Ayr, Filey via Scarborough, Llandudno and Cheltenham. The Ayr and Filey services remained as Cumberland services but the others were taken into or developed as part of the National Express network.

Cumberland participated in the London services by providing duplicates to Standerwick and later to National Travel West when this organisation took over from Standerwick. In Summer 1981 Cumberland commenced regular operation on the London services which at that time still included night operation. The operation was joint with National Travel West and involved Cumberland coaches operating on the London to Blackpool service. The National Travel West coaches were Blackpool-based and would operate :-

Day 1	Blackpool to London.
Day 2	London to Whitehaven.
Day 3	Whitehaven to London.
Day 4	London to Blackpool.

Three of the first Leyland Tigers to arrive in the Cumberland fleet were finished in National Express livery but the fourth, No.646 was delivered in National Holidays livery. In this view it is arriving at Preston bus station on National Express service No. 833 to Whitehaven.

This operation involved National Travel West drivers driving Cumberland coaches and Cumberland drivers driving National Travel West coaches.

The involvement in National Express work brought about a major expansion of the coach fleet and also a return to heavyweight coaches. In 1976 three second-hand Plaxton bodied Leyland Leopards were purchased from Ribble Motor Services and these were followed in 1977 by five short Leyland Leopards purchased second-hand from the Midland Red Omnibus Company Ltd. Whilst the short Leopards were purchased primarily for operation through Seascale Railway Arch and for the service to Netherwasdale, they were painted in National white livery and operated occasionally on Express Services, particularly on the 'Saturdays Only' services.

The first new heavyweight coach to be purchased since 1959 and the first Leyland vehicle to be purchased new since 1953, arrived in April 1977 and comprised a Leyland Leopard chassis with Duple Dominant 1 coach body, numbered 613. It was followed later in the year by another five similar coaches. The period between 1978 and 1980 saw the arrival of a further nine Leyland Leopards, these having Duple Dominant 2 bodies with the deeper windscreen and flat rear window. A second-hand purchase in 1979 was a Plaxton-bodied Leyland Leopard which came from National Travel (London) Ltd. A further five Leyland Leopards arrived in 1981 but these had bodies by Willowbrook of Loughborough, a make new to Cumberland. At this time Leyland Bus, through its subsidiary Eastern Coach Works of Lowestoft, developed a coach body code named B51, although it was really a

somewhat downmarket development of a previous coach body by this firm. Cumberland received ten of these in two batches in 1982, all on Leyland Leopard chassis. The first five had a modified National Express livery which incorporated red and blue stripes at skirt level whilst the second batch had a broad grey stripe at skirt level.

The long-lived Leyland Leopard was replaced with a new chassis which revived the old name 'Leyland Tiger' and in early 1983 Cumberland received four with bodies by Alexander of Falkirk, these being the first with this body to be produced and also introduced a new make of body to the company. The following year, 1984, saw the arrival of a further eight Leyland Tigers but these had the larger 245 engine and Duple 'Laser' bodies and were much more coach-like in appearance than the Alexander-bodied examples of the previous year.

By now coaches comprised a considerable proportion of the Cumberland fleet with 43 having been purchased new between 1977 and 1984.

A major development came in the winter of 1984/85 when Cumberland operated, jointly with Highland Scottish the National Express service between Leeds and Inverness. This involved Cumberland drivers operating south of Glasgow and Highland Scottish drivers operating north of Glasgow but with both operators' coaches covering the complete journeys.

National Express had at this time introduced a number of 'Rapide' services operated by coaches with toilets, servery and hostesses. This facility was extended to the Whitehaven to London service with effect from Summer 1985 and brought with it a number of changes including

a further extension of Cumberland operations. In order to cope with this situation Cumberland had to reorganise the coach fleet and the following changes took place:–

101	Upgraded to Rapide specification but National Express livery retained. Used as 'standby' Rapide vehicle.
102	Restored to National Holidays livery, having previously been repainted into National Express livery following delivery of 107.
103	Repainted from Border Clipper to National Holidays livery.
104	Repainted from Border Clipper to National Express livery and toilet fitted for Anglo Scottish services.
105	Toilet fitted for Anglo Scottish services.
106	Toilet fitted for Anglo Scottish services.
107	Upgraded from National Holidays to Rapide specification.
108	Upgraded from National Express to Rapide specification.

The Whitehaven to London Rapide service was initially provided by Cumberland which operated the early morning departure at 0700 hrs.and Ribble which operated the mid-day departure at 1200 hrs. using one of its Duple Caribbean-bodied Leyland Tigers. The early morning departure operated non-stop from Lancaster University to London with a shortening of journey time and arrival in London at 1415 hrs. The coach was then used with Cumberland driver for the 1630 hrs service from London to Minehead. The following morning it would operate the Minehead to London service and leave London for Whitehaven at 1600 hrs. This operation necessitated a complicated working schedule for drivers and a typical one is shown overleaf.

This period saw a number of other changes on express services from Whitehaven, and on other services involving Cumberland coaches. A new service was introduced from Whitehaven to Nottingham via Manchester and was operated entirely by Cumberland with a weekend short working between Manchester and Whitehaven operated by Ribble. The Inverness to Leeds service was diverted at the southern end to operate to/from Doncaster and the Cumberland coaches returned to Whitehaven once per week for servicing by operating light from Doncaster to Nottingham and returning on the Nottingham to Whitehaven working. Similarly the coach which had operated from Whitehaven to Nottingham would, once per week, operate light to Doncaster and then take over on the Doncaster to Inverness working.

Another significant event was the introduction by National Express of a service from Barrow to Swindon operated jointly by Cumberland and Black & White Motorways Ltd. This was the first time that Cumberland operated a regular service from Barrow and no one realised at that time that within four years the company would be operating all local services in Barrow and the surrounding area. Another new service was from Whitehaven to Taunton but Cumberland did not, in 1985, participate in this, the operators being Ribble and Southern National.

The services from Barrow were subject to regular change in those days and were notable for the very few passengers carried from the Furness area. In the Winter 1985/86 timetable the service operated Barrow to Catford, the operators being Cumberland and National Travel (London) Ltd. Summer 1986 saw further change with a Barrow to Swansea service operated by Ribble and South Wales Transport Co Ltd and also a Barrow to London Rapide service operated by Ribble.

In addition to carrying out work for National Express, CMS also carried out work for National Holidays and various vehicles were painted in this livery from time to time. Number 103 was in Ambleside on 4th October 1989 when so attired and employed, and working on a National Holidays duty.

TYPICAL DRIVING SCHEDULE ON WHITEHAVEN – LONDON RAPIDE 1985

Whitehaven	–	Drivers 1 & 2
		Driver 1 driving
M6 Junction 29	–	Driver 1 leaves,travelling to Preston on local service bus to take over 1200 hrs ex-Preston service 807 Inverness and driving to Glasgow.
		Driver 2 driving
London	–	Driver 3 joins
		Driver 3 driving
Yeovil	–	Driver 3 leaves
		Driver 2 driving
Minehead	–	
Minehead	–	Driver 2
		Driver 2 driving
Yeovil	–	Driver 3 joins
		Driver 3 driving
London	–	Driver 2 leaves and returns to Minehead.
		Driver 3 driving
Charnock Richard	–	Driver 4 joins
		Driver 4 driving
Whitehaven	–	Drivers 3 & 4.

In the event of driver 2 being Workington or Keswick based, driver 1 would drive from Whitehaven to Workington or Keswick. Similarly, if driver 4 was Keswick or Workington based, he would leave the coach at his depot and driver 3 would take over.

TYPICAL ROSTER FOR DRIVER ON NATIONAL EXPRESS 1985/86

Monday	Rest Day
. Tuesday	1115hrs Service 952 (Nottingham) Whitehaven to Preston.1730hrs Service 807 (from Inverness) Preston to Doncaster. Light Doncaster to Nottingham
. Wednesday	0920hrsService 952 (Whitehaven) Nottingham to Preston.1600hrs Service 850 (from Catford) Preston to Barrow. Light Barrow to Whitehaven.
Thursday	1115hrs Service 952(Nottingham) Whitehaven to Preston. 1730hrs Service 807 (from Inverness) Preston to Doncaster
Friday	0820hrs Service 807 (Inverness) Doncaster to Preston.1530hrs Service 952 (from Whitehaven) Preston to Nottingham
Saturday	0920hrs Service 952 Nottingham to Whitehaven.

This seemingly complex pattern of operation, with considerable dead mileage, was devised by Peter Townley as, otherwise, CMS would have lost some of its previous mileage and lost out on opportunities for expanding its National Express mileage.

On service 850 the coach returned to Whitehaven on Wednesday evening one week and on Thursday evening the other week. On other nights it was garaged at the Ribble depot in Ulverston.

On services 807/952 the vehicle changeovers with light running Doncaster – Nottingham and vice versa took place Tuesday evening / Wednesday morning one week and Wednesday evening/Thursday morning the other week.

From Winter 1986/87 only one service has been operated from Barrow, this being the London Rapide. Ribble lost interest in National Express work and from Winter 1988/89 the service was operated by Amberline Coaches or by Shaw Hadwin until Summer 1994 when Cumberland took over the operation.

There were various changes to services from Whitehaven to southern England. The Taunton service 735 was cut short at Swindon for the Winter 1985/86 timetable and Cumberland participated in its operation. In Summer 1986 it was extended to Bournemouth being operated by Ribble and Black & White and for Winter 1986/87 and Summer 1987 its destination was Taunton with participation by Cumberland in both these latter periods. Thereafter the service ceased.

A new destination from Whitehaven was Cambridge, this being introduced in place of Nottingham for the Winter 1987/88 period. For this first period it was operated jointly by Cumberland and Yorkshire Traction Co Ltd but after this it was operated entirely by Cumberland until its withdrawal at the end of the Summer 1989 timetable. The Winter 1989/90 timetable saw the introduction of a service to Coventry, operated by Cumberland, but for the Summer 1990 period this was cut back to terminate at Manchester Airport. The Winter timetable 1990/91 saw operation on this service omitted on Tuesdays and Wednesdays but then there came a surprise for National Express announced that the Summer timetable would commence on 10th February 1991 and on this date the Manchester Airport service was replaced by one from Whitehaven to Leeds. The Leeds service was replaced in Summer 1992 with one to Sheffield which in turn was replaced in Summer 1993 with a service to Leicester. From 11th July to 5th September 1992, the Sheffield service was extended to Lowestoft via Lincoln, King Lynn, Norwich and Great Yarmouth making it very much a 'cross country' service. A 50-minute break at Lincoln was included. The coaches for all these services were provided by Cumberland.

To return to the Rapide situation, changes were made in Summer 1986 whereby both services from Whitehaven were operated by Cumberland.

The early departure was at 0730hrs but the last pick up point was Kendal and the coach continued to operate the London to Minehead service. The later departure was advanced to 1015hrs and operated via Preston and St Helens, arriving in London at 1820hrs. The coach then operated the National Express service 097 from London to Swaffham in Norfolk arriving at 2205hrs. The following morning it operated the 0710hrs Swaffham to London service arriving in London at 1015hrs and departing to Whitehaven at 1100hrs. This caused a problem in that delays caused by traffic on the journey into London resulted in regular late departures for Whitehaven and for this reason the operation was short lived. The service was used by American Air Force personnel travelling to and from their bases at Mildenhall and Lakenheath and dollar bills were accepted for fares. Because the Swaffham service was non-Rapide, the hostess had to unload all the refreshment materials at Samuelson's garage in London and re-load the following morning.

The Summer 1988 timetable introduced further changes to the Rapide service in that only one driver was used on the service from Whitehaven and in order to comply with driver's hours regulations, a break had to be introduced and this was taken at Preston being of 60-minutes duration on the southbound working and 50 minutes on the northbound. This rather made a mockery of the description 'Rapide' and the later arrival in London meant that the Minehead service could not be operated. In place of this, Cumberland operated the London to Stranraer service jointly with Western Scottish Omnibuses Ltd with the coach operating a three day roster as follows :-

Day	1	Whitehaven to London.
Day	2	London to Stranraer.
Night	2	Stranraer to London.
Day	3	London to Whitehaven.

The drivers operated a four day roster, Whitehaven to London, London to Stranraer, Stranraer to London then London to Whitehaven. Operation of this service continued until commencement of the 1989/90 Winter timetable when it was replaced by operation of the London to Gourock service which in turn was replaced by operation of the London to St. Andrews service in Summer 1990. From the Summer 1992 timetable to the present time Cumberland has operated the London to Aberdeen service and for a short period between 15th May 1995 and 26th June 1995 operated a working on the London to Portsmouth service using the vehicle which had operated into London from Aberdeen. Vehicles operating on the Whitehaven to London and London to Aberdeen services cover about 175,000 miles per year.

The original 'Rapide' coaches, 101,107 and 108 were joined in 1987 by 109 and 110, Plaxton bodied Leyland Tigers and these vehicles between them operated the Rapide services until 1992 when the Company took delivery of its first 'Expresssliners', Plaxton-bodied Volvo B10Ms to National Express specification. These were numbered 120 to 124, and were purchased by Cumberland, not leased as was the arrangement for the majority of these coaches. A further three Expresssliners to Series 2 specification were purchased in May 1994 when the company obtained the contract from National Express for the Barrow to London Rapide service. The original

Expressliners were replaced on the Whitehaven to London and London to Aberdeen service in September 1995 by five new Expressliner 2s numbered 128 to 132.

In addition to regular workings for National Express, the company undertook extensive operation in the duplication of services operated by other companies. This was particularly so in the early and mid-1980s when the company's coaches were regularly seen in Blackpool on Saturdays duplicating services to Scotland.

A further important aspect of the work for National Bus Company was the provision of coaches for another subsidiary, National Holidays Ltd. These were generally used on tours based in the Cumbria area, and Scottish tours. On privatisation of NBC this was the first subsidiary to be sold, passing to the Pleasurama plc on 14th July 1986. This group at that time owned Shearings Holidays Ltd Coaches and the National Holidays activities were integrated with those of Shearings; for a short period use was made of the fleetname 'Shearings National'. This however was short lived and reference to 'National' disappeared. This brought about another phase in the company's coaching history as detailed below.

SHEARINGS HOLIDAYS

In 1990 the company purchased five Plaxton-bodied Volvo B10M coaches from Wallace Arnold. They were new in 1987 and were in excellent condition, and it was something of a surprise when they were painted in Shearings Holidays livery but with Cumberland Motor Services Ltd legal lettering. They were numbered 157 to 161, allocated to Kendal depot and used on hire to Shearings for its coach holidays. Two of them, numbers 159 and 160, were repainted into National Express livery and fitted with destination and service number indicators for the Sheffield service at the end of the 1991 season but the other three continued in Shearings livery and on its work until the end of the Summer 1994 season when they were all repainted in the new red 'Coachline' livery.

COACHLINE

The name 'Coachline' was originally used on five used Van-Hool bodied Volvo B10M coaches purchased from Magicbus (Scotland) Ltd, Glasgow in 1988 and numbered 151 to 155. They had originated with Cotter Tours Ltd, Glasgow which had used them on its continental tours and Cumberland repainted them in a white and red livery. Following the takeover of the Yeowart business in May 1988 the coach livery was changed to what had been the Yeowart yellow and tan scheme. Initially some coaches received the 'Yeowarts' fleetname but later all received the 'Coachline' name. This livery was continued until the end of 1994 when the three coaches still in Shearings livery were no longer required for that operator and on repaint received a new livery of all over dark red with bold 'Coachline' fleetname in gold. This then became the standard Coachline livery but some older coaches which had previously carried the yellow and tan Coachline livery were repainted in Stagecoach livery and re-classified as 'Dual-Purpose' vehicles.

Former Wallace Arnold-Plaxton bodied Volvo B10M number 160, after repainting from Shearings Holidays livery to National Express livery, leaves Windermere station on National Express service 358 from Whitehaven to Sheffield on 17th June 1992.

Chapter Eight
Buildings and Site Developments

Buildings and sites have formed a substantial part of the assets of Cumberland Motor Services Ltd since the 1920s and the company has gained fame in connection with two aspects of its buildings. In 1926 it opened, in Workington, the first purpose-built covered bus station in England and its engineering buiding in Whitehaven gained some fame from the fact of being situated on three levels. Even at the time of going to press the company has gained a reputation for its up-to-date modern maintenance facilities but more about these later.

In 1922 land was purchased at New Road, Whitehaven for the sum of £1600 and a garage costing £3500 was erected on it in 1923/24. The building is still in use as a stores unit and providing garaging facilities for management cars. The site at the corner of Tangier Street, Whitehaven, and Brackenthwaite was purchased with buildings in 1923 for £8000 and the present buildings were erected in 1933/35 at a cost of £10,800.

With the expansion of services particularly to the north of Whitehaven, the company sought premises for a branch depot and purchased land at Burnfoot, Wigton in 1924 for the sum of £320 and erected a garage costing £5000, this being opened in 1925. Further land was purchased in 1940 and a mess room was provided in 1951.

Initially no bus station was provided but land at Market Hill was rented from the local authority and used as a bus park and terminus.

The rent for the five-year period ending February 1953 was £20 per year plus £20 per year rates and the company agreed to pay a proportion of the cost of resurfacing, which averaged £110 per year over the five years.

A group of four cottages in King Street, Wigton was purchased for the sum of £1610, part of this being used to provide offices and a waiting room, the remainder being let as dwellings to provide a total weekly income from rents of £5.9.0. with the rates being paid by the company. Wigton did eventually get a bus station, this being opened in King Street in 1960. Following the closure of the depot after service on 14th August 1982, the bus station, was used for the parking of vehicles until 31st August 1991 when Wigton ceased to be an operating unit, operations being transferred to Carlisle. The bus station site was finally sold in 1992.

Land and a dwelling house in Murray Road, Workington were acquired in 1924 and this became the site for the Company's first bus station, opening in 1926. Further expansion of this site took place in 1930/33 when the garages in Vulcans Lane were erected, an additional extension being provided in 1939. The final expansion of this site took place in the postwar period when land to the west of the bus station was acquired and an annexe to the bus station was provided.

To return to the company headquarters in Whitehaven, land was acquired between the New Road garage and the

The development of the former Grand Hotel site at Whitehaven had an important side effect in that it opened up to general view the attractive elevation of the bus station, enhanced by the recently completed refurbishment. The head office building can be seen to the right of the bus station entrance whilst at the opposite end, to the left of the upper entrance, is the New Road garage which was the first building to be erected by the company. At the back at higher level is the former paint shop and body shop.

Two scenes from early days taken in the Whitehaven workshops show, in one case, four of the 1932 Harrington-bodied AEC Regal coaches delicensed for the winter and with notices hung over the radiator filler caps to denote this. The other photograph shows two Leyland TD1s with 'piano front' bodies and two contemporary single-deckers, the one nearest the camera being of the normal control type.

previously acquired premises at the corner of Brackenthwaite and this was developed into the bus station and head office building, being opened in 1931. Land also became available on the opposite side of Tangier Street and this was purchased in 1931 for £2880. The garage building which generally became known as the '1932 Workshop' was built on this land at a cost of £11,700. The company was fortunate in that its head office, bus station, garage buildings and workshops in Whitehaven were all together in one complex despite having been developed over a number of years and this must have led to considerable savings with the elimination of 'dead mileage'. Another advantage was the close proximity of this complex to Bransty Station, the town's main railway station, providing a convenient interchange for passengers.

Further premises in Whitehaven came into company ownership in 1935 with the takeover of a local operator, Wilson Brothers. These comprised two garages in Church Street and they were used occasionally for storage purposes. In the early 'fifties when business was booming and there had been a considerable growth in Whitehaven town services to serve new estates, negotiations were entered into with Whitehaven Borough Council to develop the site as a car park and second bus station to be used by town services. It was estimated that this facility would reduce mileage on some services giving a saving of around £1000 per year. However this proposal was abandoned and the site was sold in 1953 to the Borough Council which developed it as a car park.

The other major development in Whitehaven concerned the Grand Hotel site adjacent to the bus station. A major fire in January 1940 destroyed the hotel, and the site, complete with two cottages, was purchased by the company for £3400. After spending £1200 on demolition a temporary garage was erected at a cost of £2800. Further land to the west of the site was bought from Lowther Estates for £226 and the 'temporary' garage remained in use until 1991 when the area was redeveloped as detailed later. The fire had come at a time when the company fleet was expanding to meet the requirements of local industry involved in the war effort and the land which it provided was ideally situated adjacent the bus station complex. Finding similar land elsewhere in the town would have proved difficult. On the debit side it should be mentioned that Whitehaven lost an excellent building and gained a 'shed'.

There was a proposal in 1961 to further develop the Grand Hotel site as a new head office and garage complex but this did not go ahead. In the mid 'sixties, further land became available when the carriage sheds adjacent Bransty

An interior view of Whitehaven bus station showing two characteristic features which existed for many years. One is the 'slide in' destination boards which enabled stands to be changed as necessary, a feature which was used during late evenings on Saturdays when, after departure of the last Carlisle service, the St. Bees service was transferred to this stand. This meant that the bus on the St.Bees service then left the bus station via the top exit and had to do a sharp 'U' turn. The other feature visible at the bottom left hand side is the large hand painted timetable board, a feature which would have been rather expensive to maintain during the deregulation period when times were frequently changed.

railway station were no longer required following the changeover of local rail services diesel multiple-units. The land was acquired and following demolition of the carriage sheds was developed as a parking area for buses. A bus washing plant, refuelling facility and chassis cleaning unit were provided.

As the company expanded, sites were sought in other towns for bus stations and depots. In 1927/9 land was bought in Tithebarn Street, Keswick and a bus garage was erected on the site, the cost being £1500. An adjacent area of land known as Cabby Field was purchased in two sections, the first in 1932 for £815 and the second in 1933 for £1635. This land was used for the original bus station and a further garage, this complex being built in 1932/34 at a cost of £6600. Part of the bus station and garage premises was let to Ribble Motor Services Ltd at an annual rent of £250. The remainder of this land served as a coach park for many years.

In 1934 land was leased in Maryport and in 1935/37 a bus station and garage were built with further extension taking place in 1941/42. This was a very exposed site and in 1960 the bus station section was roofed over to provide a similar facility to those at Whitehaven and Workington. The arrangement of the workshop was modified at the same time to accommodate longer vehicles. However, with declining passenger numbers and services the bus station and depot were closed in 1985, the site being subsequently developed as a supermarket.

In Carlisle attempts were made to find a site for a bus station and garage and this eventually materialised as a joint venture with Ribble Motor Services Ltd which built a bus station in Lowther Street. This was an open type station and one side of it together with a garage for six buses was rented to Cumberland Motor Services Ltd for the sum of £743 per annum including rates. The garage

was closed in 1972 following the transfer of the small vehicle allocation to Wigton. Following the takeover of Ribble services in Carlisle in 1986 the station passed to Cumberland and was subsequently the subject of redevelopment as detailed later in this chapter.

The company was desirous of opening a depot in Cockermouth and following a search for sites Mr Meageen announced to the Board in 1938 that he had purchased Wordsworth's birthplace and proposed to demolish this to provide on the site a bus station and depot. This was approved by the Board. At the next Board meeting Mr Meageen announced that hardly surprisingly perhaps, difficulties had arisen regarding planning permission for this proposal and he had sold the building. No further developments took place regarding a bus station or depot in Cockermouth but a shop was rented in Main Street for a rent of £35 per year plus rates of £22 per year and used as an enquiry office and waiting room until 1970.

The other enquiry office and waiting room was in High Street, Cleator Moor where a prominent corner property formerly known as the 'Coffee House' was purchased in 1928 for £184, remaining in use until 1971.

In 1943 the Cleator Moor coach operator, Lewthwaite Brothers, was acquired and this gave the company a depot in the town which was used until 1971 when the allocation was transferred to Whitehaven.

A lease was taken on a garage in Lancashire Road, Millom at the end of 1928 and this was subsequently purchased in 1941 for £1098. There was a house next to it which was occupied rent free by the depot superintendent. One problem with this garage was that it could not accommodate double-deckers and a further small depot was purchased in King Street. In 1966 all operations were transferred to the garage in King Street, which remains in use at the present time.

Other premises taken over with the businesses of small operators included those at Little Broughton from W. & J. Kirkpatrick, High Lorton from G. Scott, Ireby from J. W. Stoddart, Seaton from W. Gilmore and Arlecdon from J. H. Clements. The company also owned a number of domestic premises which were used by staff.

MORE RECENT DEVELOPMENTS.

This section covers sites taken over from Ribble Motor Services Ltd and the subsequent development of these sites and also the many developments and improvements to the original Cumberland Motor Services Ltd sites. In 1986 with the takeover of the Carlisle and Penrith areas the

This view taken in the 'fifties shows the historic Workington bus station, the first purpose-built covered bus station in England. Inside is a Northern Coachbuilders-bodied Leyland PD1 on the town service to Harrington.

A view of the Whitehaven complex thought to date from around 1950 and showing, on the left, the 1932 workshops and on the right the engineering building and beyond this, the lower entrance to the bus station. In the centre is the former Grand Hotel site with the 'temporary' garage building with vehicle parking adjacent. Beyond to the left can be seen the original Bransty railway station building. The lamp post in the middle of the roadway was used as a turning point for vehicles which had come in from the north and would turn around it, in the opposite direction to traffic flow, to enter the bus station for the return journey. Parked outside the temporary building is a wartime Bedford single-decker with a postwar Burlingham-bodied Leyland PS1 and beyond these a Northern Coachbuilders bodied Leyland PD1 and a Leyland-bodied PD2. Outside the bus station on the town service to Hensingham is a Northern Coachbuilders wartime rebodied Leyland TD2.

Above: A view of the Maryport bus station in the days before the overall roof was added. The whole complex has since been closed and replaced with a supermarket.

Left: The 'Cumberland' side of the joint Ribble - Cumberland bus station in Lowther Street, Carlisle. Note the board advertising a 'Grand Mystery Tour' for the sum of three shillings and three pence, 16p in today's money

Below left: This view of the bus parking area at Whitehaven shows, in the centre, the area which was formerly the carriage sheds attached to Bransty Station and in the rear centre of this area, the bus wash. The parking area in the foreground occupies land to the rear of the former Grand Hotel. In the centre of the photograph is Queens Dock with coal wagons parked alongside and towards the right at the rear is the rope operated incline or 'brake' used by wagons carrying coal from Haig Colliery to the dock. Whitehaven had two such brakes.

major site acquisition was the modern depot at Willowholme Industrial Estate on the outskirts of Carlisle which had been opened in 1968 to replace the earlier premises in Corporation Road. Also in Carlisle came the bus station in Lowther Street, which Cumberland had previously shared with Ribble on a rental basis. The bus station site was sold for development and work on this commenced in February 1990, the bus station being replaced with a smaller one on an adjacent site with access from Lonsdale Street.

A major addition to the Willowholme depot took place in 1991 when a body shop and paint shop were added within the existing building, these replacing similar facilities in what had been the

Top: The building in Main Street, Wigton, one side of which served as a waiting room and the other as an enquiry office.

Centre: Some indication of the extent of the refurbishment of Whitehaven bus station carried out in 1991 is given by this photograph showing work in progress. Note that most of the roof has been removed.

Lower: This view taken on 2nd July 1991 after re-opening of Whitehaven bus station shows vehicles in three different liveries. On the left is a Bristol VR in CMS Cumberland livery, in the centre is a Willowbrook-bodied Leyland Leopard, in Border Clipper livery, whilst on the right is an Alexander-bodied Leyland Olympian in Stagecoach livery.

Central Works in Whitehaven. The main problem in Whitehaven had been the fact that the body and paint shops formed the top floor of the three storey workshop building with difficult access from the steep hill of Wellington Row, a problem which had become more severe as the length of vehicles increased.

In Penrith the company inherited the depot in Brunswick Road, which Ribble had taken over from Armstrong and Siddle Motor Services Ltd, a company which had in 1928

been purchased by Cumberland, prior to passing to Ribble. This depot was vacated for development, vehicles being stored initially at the premises of the Milk Marketing Board, later renamed Milk Marque, at Gilwilly Industrial Estate and from 1995 at the premises of Cargill Haulage Contractors on the same estate. Penrith had been an outstation of Carlisle since 18th May 1985.

The small outstation at Bowness on Solway which Ribble had taken over from White Star Motors Ltd, also passed to Cumberland and was operated until 26th October 1987 when workings were transferred to Carlisle. The building was sold in 1995. On 30th October 1987, the outstation at Kirkoswald, which Ribble had taken over from H Lace, closed. Another small depot which came into company ownership was that at Brigham which came with the business of J. Kirkpatrick's Coaches. Initially this was operated as a depot but at the time of writng was being offered for sale.

In 1989 with the takeover from Ribble of the Furness and South Lakes areas, further premises came into Cumberland ownership. The largest of these premises was the former Barrow Borough Transport Depot in Hindpool Road which was used initially to house the fleet employed on Barrow town services. The original Ribble routes in the Furness area had been operated from its depot at The Ellers, Ulverston but this did not pass to Cumberland ownership, being retained by the three Ribble managers who required Cumberland to vacate the site within a limited period of the April 1989 acquisition, by Stagecoach, of Ribble. The building was therefore leased by Cumberland until closure on 16th February 1990 following sale of the site for development. The fleet was then transferred to Barrow with a few vehicles outstationed at Ulverston and parked overnight adjacent to the railway station.

In Kendal there came the depot in Station Road which had been built in 1959 to replace both the original Station Road premises and the premises in Shap Road. This depot continues in use at the time of writing. The Ambleside depot and bus station did not pass to Cumberland as this site had been sold for development prior to the Cumberland takeover, the bus station closing on 27th May 1989. The proposed development of this site caused considerable controversy in the town resulting in various Public Enquiries and delaying the start of building work until late 1994.

In Grange over Sands, Cumberland inherited the small garage in Albert Road which Ribble had taken over from the Grange Motor and Cycle CoLtd in 1958. This was sold for development in December 1989.

To return to the original Cumberland sites, a major development took place at Whitehaven where the former Grand Hotel site had been crying out for develpoment for many years. The 'temporary' buiding erected in 1940 was in very poor condition and something of an eyesore in the town. A plan was published in 1988 which included development of the whole area to provide a large supermarket and an open type bus station to replace the existing one. Two major problems arose, one being the fact that British Rail owned a narrow strip of land within the

area and negotiations with them proved to be very tedious and long, even at one stage threatening the whole plan. The other problem was the bus station as doubts were expressed with regard to the stability of land and buildings at high level behind the bus station.

As a result of this second problem the decision was made to re-roof the existing bus station and renovate the remainder of it. In order to do this the bus station was closed from 18th February 1991 and was reopened on 14th June 1991. In this time complete renovation was carried out including a new roof, new roadway, new stands, new windows and re-pointing of the exterior and complete decoration. The problems on the Grand Hotel site were eventually sorted out and development work proceeded albeit to a different plan from that published in 1988. The supermarket was built for William Low and a petrol station was incorporated on the site, the whole complex being opened on 25th August 1992. In 1994 Tesco took over the firm of William Low and now operates this site.

It had been intended to build a new Whitehaven depot on an industrial site at Red Lonning on the outskirts of the town but the Copeland Borough Council, after granting outline planning permission, refused full planning consent following protests from residents on an adjacent council housing estate. This caused a major problem for the company at a time when work on the Grand Hotel site was progressing rapidly and an alternative site had to be found. A building on the Lillyhall industrial site opposite the Leyland National factory was purchased and converted to a depot and workshop with outside parking facilities for vehicles. In view of its location between Whitehaven and Workington, it was decided that this should form a west Cumbria depot to serve both Whitehaven and Workington. As a result of this, Copeland Borough Council lost the revenue income as the Lillyhall depot is situated in Allerdale Borough Council area.

The Lillyhall depot was officially opened by Dale Campbell-Savours MP on Friday 26th June 1992. From that time the Whitehaven depot allocation that was transferred to the site but the workshops at Whitehaven continued in use until the new workshops at Lillyhall were completed later in 1992, being Officially Opened by the North West Traffic Commissioner Mr Martin Albu on 3rd December 1992. The Workington depot was transferred to Lillyhall in February 1993.

There was a proposal to demolish the Workington bus station and sell the site for retail use and this brought protests from English Heritage in view of the historical significance of the building. An attempt was made to place a Preservation Order upon it but this failed. There had been considerable criticism directed at the building by residents and councillors in the town because of its poor condition and this culminated with presentation of the 'broken gnome' award for the most dilapidated building in the town. Following this the

company renovated the building in a similar manner to that undertaken at Whitehaven. The building was closed for this purpose on 7th March 1993 and officially reopened on 22nd June 1993 by Councillor Peter Bales.

Keswick bus station with its large adjacent coach park was another site which offered scope for development and this project also was not without its problems. There was a dispute between the company and the local council with regard to the development and this resulted in the company blocking the coach park with the Stagecoach 'reserve fleet' during the season in 1988. This created a problem for the town in that there was no coach park for touring coaches and these were directed to a lay by off the A66 road to the west of the town. Eventually the matter was resolved and the old bus station was demolished in May 1990 to make way for the new development. This comprised a supermarket with a small bus lay by adjacent and also a car and coach park. The new complex was opened in June 1991.

The premises in Hindpool Road, Barrow, taken over from Barrow Borough Transport were in very poor condition and in the winter of 1994/95 suffered extensive roof damage in gales. The company had in fact sold the premises and site in October 1994 but had been allowed six months in which to vacate the site. New accommodation was found by taking over part of the building and yard at the premises of R. Brady and Sons Ltd, Haulage Contractors in Walney Road, Barrow. The yard area was developed as a bus parking area and the building was converted to provide workshops and office accommodation. The move to the new depot took place over the weekend of 23rd/24th April 1995 with the official opening taking place on Friday, 5th May 1995. With the completion of these premises the company now had modern depot and maintenance facilities throughout its area.

The new workshop facilities are notable for their cleanliness and have certainly removed the image of bus repair workshops being dirty places.

Following completion of the work on Whitehaven bus station, similar work was carried out at Workington bus station. A view of the station after completion is shown in the colour section.

A line-up of Bristol VRs in immaculate condition in the parking area of Lillyhall depot on 21st May 1994. The maintenance building is in the background.

The most recent new depot is that at Barrow in Furness and this interior view taken on 30th January 1996 shows the standard of cleanliness which is now common in Cumberland workshop areas.

An interior view of the historic Workington bus station taken shortly after re-opening following the extensive refurbishment. Note the flower baskets hanging from the walls.

WHITEHAVEN - Indicates Operating Area.

─ ─ ─ ─ ─ Indicates Seasonal Service.

To Dumfries

Annan Gretna Longtown

Brampton To Newcastle

Bowness
Anthorn

Silloth

CARLISLE

Dalston

Wigton

Aspatria

Maryport

Penrith

WORKINGTON Cockermouth Keswick

Appleby

Harrington
Lowca Distington

Shap

WHITEHAVEN Frizington

Buttermere Patterdale

Kirkby Stephen

Cleator Moor

Seatoller

St.Bees Egremont

Grasmere

Tebay

Dungeon Ghyll

Ambleside

Gosforth

Seascale Windermere

Coniston

Hawkshead Bowness

KENDAL

Sedbergh

Newby Bridge

Milnthorpe

Millom

Kirkby Lonsdale

Ulverston Grange

Arnside

Dalton

BARROW

COMPANY STRUCTURE JANUARY 1996

STAGECOACH HOLDINGS plc
Charlotte House, Charlotte Street, Perth, PH1 5LL

STAGECOACH NORTH WEST LTD,   OTHER STAGECOACH GROUPS
Tangier Street, Whitehaven, CA28 7XF

── STAGECOACH CUMBERLAND

── STAGECOACH RIBBLE

── PSV CLAIMS BUREAU LTD

── P PHYTHIAN & SONS LTD

Stagecoach North West Ltd was first registered on 22 May 1991, Registered No. 123665, this company having previously been named
Cumberland Motor Services Ltd registered 1st June 1921 and Whitehaven Motor Services Company Ltd registered 8th August 1912.
The name CumberlandMotor Services Ltd is retained as a dormant company Registered No. 21159, previousy named Stagecoach North West Ltd,
Bee Line Buzz Company Ltd and Bulwark Transport Company Ltd.

APPENDICES

BUS OPERATORS AND SERVICES IN AND AROUND CARLISLE IN THE MID-'20s TO EARLY '30s

Mr S. P. Adair, Corporation Road, Carlisle

Joe Bell, 81 English Street, Carlisle
T/A Joe Bell's Motor Service, also as
Lonsdale Bus Company

Mr Bell, Ashgrove, Ecclefechan
T/A Bells Motor Service

Mr Fred Hart, 15 Castle Street, Carlisle
T/A Blue Bird

Mr G. Bristow, 39 Cecil Street, Carlisle
(Currock & Blackwell Services)

Mr J. G. Campbell, 68 Peel Street, Carlisle

Cumberland Motor Services Ltd, Whitehaven

Mr J. Wharton, Albert Place, Dalston
T/A Dalston District Bus Service

Downes & Todd, Kingmoor Road, Carlisle
T/A Downes & Todd's Motor Bus Services

Mr B. Everard, 36 Kingmoor Road, Carlisle

Farrer & Faulder, South Henry St, Carlisle
T/A Farraulder

Foster & Son, 33a Rickergate, Carlisle

Mr T. Graham, Burnfoot, Wigton

Mr I. Hickson, Port Carlisle
T/A Isaac Hickson's 'The Brown Buses'-
Original Service

Messrs Hodgson, Bowness on Solway,
T/A Hodgson's 'The Blue Buses'

Mr G Hudson, 1 Bedford Road, Carlisle

Messrs Huntington, Gretna
T/A Huntington's Saloon Bus Service

Mr Huntington, Warwick Road, Carlisle

Mr J. W. Campbell, Newby West
T/A Larkspur

Lochinvar Motor Service, 5 English Street, Carlisle

W. & M. S. Millican, The Croft, Hethersgill

Carlisle, Caldewgate, Raffles
Carlisle, Brampton, Hallbankgate
Carlisle, Wreay   Sundays.
Carlisle, Upperby, Belle Vue
Carlisle, Lockerbie

Carlisle, Cummersdale

Carlisle, Durdar
Carlisle, Greystones, Blackwell
Harraby, Holme Head
Carlisle, Aspatria, Whitehaven
Carlisle, Silloth, Whitehaven
Carlisle, Wigton, Cockermouth
Carlisle, Wigton, Keswick
Carlisle, Dalston, Bridge End

Carlisle, Corby
Carlisle, StAnn's Hill
Carlisle, Deer Park Rd, StAnn's Hill
Carlisle, Gretna, Annan, Dumfries
Carlisle, Rockcliffe
Carlisle, Kingstown
Carlisle, Great Orton, Wigton
Carlisle, Burgh, Port Carlisle,
Bowness on Solway

Carlisle, Burgh, Port Carlisle,
Bowness on Solway
Carlisle, Longtown, Canonbie,
Langholm
Carlisle, Penton
Carlisle, Gretna
Carlisle, Lockerbie Sundays
Carlisle, Grey St., Botcherby
Carlisle, Durranhill
Carlisle, Blackwell
Carlisle, Kirkbampton
Carlisle, Burgh
Carlisle, Gretna
Carlisle, Longtown, Blackbank
Carlisle, Houghton, Knells
Carlisle, Hethersgill
Carlisle, Roadhead
Carlisle, Dykes Terrace, Tarraby
Carlisle, Newby East, Laversdale

Mr H. I. Moore, 18 New Street, Wigton
Moore & Baty, Carlisle
T/A Moore & Baty's Bus Service

Hayton & Smith, 34 Grey St Carlisle
T/A Morris

Mr W. G. Nixon, 52 Crumnock St Carlisle

Mr T. D. Parker, 30 Port Road, Carlisle
Parker & Thomlinson, Carlisle
T/A Parker & Thomlinson's Bus Service

Richard Percival Ltd, Lowther St Carlisle
T/A Percival's Motor Services
Subsidiary of Tramway Company

Mr Thomas Graham, Gretna T/A Pioneer
Potter, Parker & Thomlinson, Carlisle

Simpson & Thompson, 1 Victoria Road, Botcherby, Carlisle

Mr W. Smith, 30 Greystone Road, Carlisle

Mr R. Vickers, 35 Westmorland St Carlisle

Mrs C. Wallis, 17 Beaconsfield St Carlisle

Mr F. Waugh, 24 Alexander Street, Carlisle

J. & S. Wood, Heads Nook

Mr T. G. Wood, Cumwhinton

N. & I. A. Wright, Parkhead, Cumwhinton
T/A Red Saloon Bus Service

J. W. Tatters, Town Foot, Alston

Henry Lace, Kirkoswald

T. J. Graham, Orchard House, Oulton

J. W. Hodgson & Co 21 Lonsdale St Carlisle

Alfred Fidler, 2 Waller St Carlisle

Mrs Kate Smith, London Rd Carlisle

E. L. Proud, Ainstable, Carlisle

Blair & Palmer, Gardenia Street, Carlisle

J. W. Pearson, Sebergham, Carlisle

Smith & Rose, Penrith

Carlisle, Wigton
Carlisle, Longtown, Springfield

Carlisle, Cummersdale

Carlisle, Croglin
Carlisle, Silloth
Carlisle, Wreay Sundays
Carlisle, Belle Vue, Upperby
Carlisle, Dumfries
Carlisle, Longtown, Gretna, Annan
Carlisle, Longtown, Langholm
Carlisle, Warwick Bridge, Brampton
Carlisle, Crosby, Irthington,
Brampton
(Connection for Hallbankgate)
Carlisle, Gretna
Carlisle, Longsowerby, Wigton
Road
Carlisle, Bitcherby
Carlisle, Talkin Tarn Sundays
Carlisle, Penrith
Carlisle, Holme Head
Carlisle, Scotby, Wetheral, via
Golf Links, Wheelbarrow Hall
Carlisle, Harraby
Carlisle, Carleton
Carlisle, Heads Nook, Talkin
Carlisle, Cumwhinton, Cotehill
Carlisle, High Hesket
Carlisle, Cumwhinton, Low Cotehill
Carlisle, Aiket Gate, Armathwaite
Alston, Carlisle
Carlisle, Renwick
Carlisle, Penrith
Carlisle, Aikton, Oulton, Wigton
Carlisle, Talkin
Carlisle, Wetheral
Carlisle, Durdar, Ivegill, Penrith
Carlisle, Upperby, Wreay
Carlisle, Croglin
Carlisle, Ainstable
Carlisle, Kirkbride, Wigton
Sebergham, Carlisle (Saturdays)
Penrith, Sebergham, Roseley,
Wigton, Carlisle

ORIGINAL RIBBLE & UNITED CARLISLE CITY SERVICES 1931

SERVICE LETTER	SERVICE NUMBER	ROUTE
A	R 185	Town Hall – Holme Head
B	R 186	Town Hall – Cummersdale
C	R 187	St.Ann's Hill – Longsowerby via Norfolk St.
D	R 188	St.Ann's Hill – Longsowerby via Nelson St.
E	R 189	Kingstown – Harraby, Garlands Road End.
F	R 190	Belle Vue – Upperby via Town Hall
G	R 191	Raffles – Blackwell – Durdar via Newtown
H	R 192	Town Hall – Raffles via Wigton Road.
	U 24	Town Hall – Warwick Road – Botcherby.
	U 30	English Street – Greystone Road – Botcherby.

R = Ribble – commenced November.
U = United – commenced December.

NB. Ribble service numbers were issued only for administrative purposes and were not displayed on vehicles.

UNITED SERVICES IN CARLISLE AT RIBBLE TAKEOVER

ORIG. No.	1968 No.	ROUTE	RIBBLE No.
22/3	322/3	Carlisle – Alston.	622/3
23	318-20	Carlisle – Brampton via Irthington.	618-20
24	328	English St. – Botcherby (Merith Ave.)	628
25	325	Houghton – Carlisle – Wetheral	625
26	326	Carlisle – Brampton via Faugh Road End.	626
26A	327	Carlisle – Brampton via Cumwhitton.	627
27	316/7	Carlisle – Noblestown.	616/7
30	329	English St.- Botcherby (Durranhill View)	629
34	334	Carlisle – Newcastle.	334
36	X36	Carlisle – Newcastle (Seasonal Limited Stop)	36.

SERVICES AT DEREGULATION DAY

* Indicates Registered Service.   TS/CS Indicates Town/City Service.

SERV.NO.	ROUTE	NOTES.
01 *TS	Whitehaven Bus Sta. – Kells.	Minibuses introduced.
02 *TS	Whitehaven Bus Sta. – Woodhouse	Minibuses introduced.
03 *TS	Whn.Bus Sta. – Hospital – Kells	Evening ser.withdrawn.
04 *TS	Whitehaven Bus Sta. – Richmond	do
05 *TS	Bransty – Bus Sta. – Mirehouse	Reduced ser.B'ty – B.Sta.
07 *TS	Whitehaven Bus Sta.- Mirehouse	Early servs. withdrawn.
09 *TS	Whitehaven Bus Sta.- Mirehouse	All now start at Bus Sta.
12 *	Whitehaven – Egremont – Seascale	Additional early journey.
15 *	Millom – Haverigg	Unchanged.
15	Millom – Festival Road	Unchanged.
16	Millom – Bootle – Ravenglass	Minor timetable change.
17 *	Whitehaven – Cross Gates	Minor timetable changes.
20 *	Whitehaven – St.Bees.	St.Bees – Egremont w'drawn.
22 *	Whitehaven – Cleator – Egremont	Local ser.in Egremont added.
26 *	Whitehaven – Ennerdale Bridge	Unchanged.
27 *	Whitehaven – Moresby Parks	Moresby – Pica withdrawn.
30 *	Whitehaven – Workington – Carlisle	Minor timetable changes.
31 *	Whitehaven – Broughton Moor	Reduced service.
34/35 *	Frizington/Whitehaven – Keswick	Minor timetable changes.
36	Workington – Greysouthen – C'mouth	Basically unaltered.
38	Maryport – Silloth	Revised Ser. S.ser.by Carrs.
38 *	Silloth – Wigton	Revised timetable.
46 *TS	Workington Bus Sta.- Brierydale	Minor timetable changes.
47 *	Workington Bus Sta.- Seaton	Minor timetable changes.
48 *TS	Workington Bus Sta.- Harrington	Minor timetable changes.
49 *TS	Workington Bus Sta.- Northside	Minor timetable changes.
50 *TS	Workington Bus Sta.- Moorclose	Minibuses introduced.
51 *TS	Workington Bus Sta.- Moorclose	Minibuses introduced.
55	Workington – B.Moor – Cockermouth	Basically unaltered.
55 TS	Cockermouth – Slatefell.	Revised timetable.
56 TS	Cockermouth – The Moor	Improved service.
57 *TS	Maryport – Ewanrigg	Reduced service.
58 *	Maryport – Cockermouth	Reduced service.
67	Wigton – Mealsgate – Aspatria	Revised timetable.
69	Workington – Ullock	Revised timetable.
74	Keswick – Penrith	Reduced service.
75 TS	Wigton Town Service	Revised timetable.
79 *	Keswick – Seatoller.	Summer ser. through Winter.
300 *	West Cumbria – Carlisle – N.East	'Border Clipper' minor changes
600 *	West Cumbria – C'lisle via C'mouth	'Border Clipper' minor changes
710 *	Keswick – Cockermouth – Carlisle	'Border Clipper'
720 *	Keswick – Castle Inn – Carlisle	'Border Clipper'
615/7 *	Carlisle – Penrith – Kendal	Reduced service.
630 *	Penrith – Renwick	Reduced service.
631 *	Penrith – Cotehill – Carlisle	Reduced service.
638	Carlisle – Calthwaite – Penrith	Revised timetable.
640	Carlisle – Caldbeck – Penrith	New service FO.
643 *	Carlisle – Cummersdale – Dalston	Some journeys op. by Palmer.
676 *	Carlisle – Faugh Rd.End-Brampton	Reduced service.
677 *	Carlisle – Cumwhitton – Brampton	Reduced service.
678	Carlisle – Irthington – Brampton	Red.ser. S. ops by WSMT.
680	Carlisle – Ruleholme – Brampton.	Red. ser.S. ops by WSMT.
682	Carlisle – Fenton-Halton Lea Gate	Reduced service.
683	Carlisle-Toppin Castle-H.Lea Gate	Reduced service.
684	Carlisle – Heads Nook -H.Lea Gate	Reduced service.
685 *	Carlisle – Hexham – Newcastle	Basically unchanged.
686	Carlisle – Noblestown	Revised timetable.
693	Carlisle – Bowness on Solway	Reduced service.
620	Penrith – Appleby	Minor timetable changes.
621	Penrith – Long Marton – Appleby	Minor timetable changes.

SERVICES AT DEREGULATION DAY – cont.

629	Penrith – Glassonby – Kirkoswald	Revised timetable.
644/5 TS	Penrith Town Schools Services	Unchanged.
646 * TS	Penrith Town Service.	Reduced service.
647 TS	Penrith – Skirsgill Park	New Service.
649 *	Penrith – Patterdale	Minor timetable changes.
634	Carlisle – Wetheral	Reduced service.
654 *CS	Carlisle T.Hall – Morton Park	Basically unchanged.
655 *CS	Carlisle T.Hall – Morton Park	Basically unchanged.
656 *CS	Botcherby – Cavray Factory	Basically unchanged.
657 *CS	Town Hall-Charlotte St.-Town Hall	Minor timetable changes.
658 *CS	Town Hall – Harraby East	Reduced service.
659 *CS	Caldewgate – City – Harraby East	Reduced service.
660 *CS	Town Hall-Botcherby-Harraby East	Basically unchanged.
661 *CS	Morton West – City – Harraby East	Basically unchanged.
662 *CS	Morton Park – City – Harraby	Basically unchanged.
663 *CS	St.Anns Hill – City – Morton Park	Basically unchanged.
664 *CS	St.Anns Hill – City – Morton Park	Basically unchanged.
668 *CS	Belle Vue – City – Upperby	Basically unchanged.
669 *CS	Brookside-City-Blackwell/Durdar	Basically unchanged.
670 *CS	Carlisle Bank St. – Houghton	Red.ser. Evenings by WSMT.
671 *CS	Sandsfield Pk.- City – Harraby E.	Basically unchanged.
672 *CS	Holme Head – City – Kingstown	Red.ser.evens.by WSMT to K.
673 *CS	Lowry Hill – City – Wetheral	Reduced service.
674 *CS	Lowry Hill – City – Wetheral	Reduced service.
675 *CS	Lowry Hill – City – Wetheral	Reduced service.

STAFF and VEHICLE LEVELS 1974

STAFF AND VEHICLES EMPLOYED IN THE COUNTY OF CUMBRIA 1974 BY CUMBERLAND MOTOR SERVICES AND RIBBLE MOTOR SERVICES.

Comy. Depot		Single Deck	Double Deck	Drivers & Cond'rs	Engin'ing Staff	Supervis'y Admin etc.
CMS	Keswick	6	1	14	3	4
CMS	Maryport	17	3	39	8	5
CMS	Millom	4	2	15	1	1
CMS	Whitehaven	53	24	162	80	71
CMS	Wigton	7	6	34	5	5
CMS	Workington	30	6	83	15	16
Company Total		117	42	347	112	102
RMS	Ambleside	9	3	23	7	5
RMS	Carlisle	26	36	121	37	18
RMS	Grange	6	-	15	1	2
RMS	Kendal	16	4	40	15	24
RMS	Penrith	16	3	38	10	8
RMS	Ulverston	26	-	37	12	8
Company Total		99	46	274	82	65

Note: The Whitehaven figures include Head Office and Central Workshops staff. The figures for Carlisle, Kendal and Penrith include Out-Stations.

01 Whitehaven Tesco – Bus Station – Newtown – Kells
02 Whitehaven Tesco – Bus Sta. – Lowther St. – Woodhouse – Greenbank
05 Whitehaven Lowther St.- Bus Station – Bransty – Parton.
06 Whitehaven Lowther St.- Bus Sta.- Hospital – Moor Row – Seascale
08 Whitehaven Bus Sta.- Lowther St.- Red Lonning – Lowther St.- Parton – Lowca
7/9 Whitehaven Lowther St.- Bus Sta.- Corkickle – Mirehouse – Newtown – Bus Sta.
9/7 Whitehaven Bus Sta.- Newtown – Mirehouse – Corkickle – Lowther St
09 Whitehaven Bus Sta. – Newtown – Mirehouse – Hospital – Richmond.
12 Whitehaven Lowther St.- Bus Sta.- Hospital – Egremont – Thornhill
17 Whitehaven Lowther St.- Bus Sta.- Cleator Moor – Frizington.
19 Whitehaven Bus Station – Hospital – Frizington – Arlecdon – Rowrah
20 Whitehaven Bus Station – Greenbank – St.Bees.
22 Whitehaven Bus Station – Hospital – Cleator – Egremont
27 Whitehaven Bus Station – Scilly Banks – Moresby Parks.
30 Whitehaven Bus Station – Workington – Maryport
   (Some workings extend south of Whitehaven via 22 service)
300 Whitehaven Bus Sta.- Workington – Maryport – Wigton – Carlisle.
34 Whitehaven Bus Sta.- Workington – Cockermouth – Braithwaite – Keswick
35 Whitehaven Bus Sta.- Workington – Cockermouth – Slatefell
36 Whitehaven Bus Sta – Workington – Greysouthen – Cockermouth – Slatefell (Occasional extension of 35/36 to Keswick via Castle Inn.)
38 Carlisle – Wigton – Silloth.   38A via Curthwaite.
39 Carlisle – Wigton – Mealsgate – Aspatria – Harriston.
46 Seaton – Workington Bus Sta. – Brierydale.
47 Brierydale – Workington Bus Sta. – Seaton.
48 Harrington – Workington Bus Sta. – Dunmail Park.
50 Workington Bus Sta.- Lorton Ave.- Moorclose – Wastwater Ave.- Bus Sta.
50A Workington Bus Sta.- Ashfield Rd. Sth.- Moorclose – Wastwater Ave.- Bus Sta.
51 Workington Bus Sta.- Wastwater Ave.- Moorclose – Lorton Ave.- Bus Sta.
51A Workington Bus Sta.- Wastwater Ave.- Moorclose – Ashfield Rd. Sth.- Bus Sta.
53 Workington – Cockermouth – Aspatria – Westnewton.
55 Workington Bus Sta.- Broughton Moor – Cockermouth.
56 Maryport – Christian Street.
57 Maryport Senhouse St. – Ewanrigg – Maryport.
58 Maryport – Broughton Moor – Dearham – Cockermouth.
59 Whitehaven Lowther St. – Bus Sta. – Workington – Cockermouth – Dovenby Hospital.
61 Harraby East – Carlisle Centre – Morton Park.
61A Harraby East – Carlisle Centre – Morton West.
62 Harraby – Carlisle Centre – St.Anns Hill.
63 Morton Park – Carlisle Centre – Lowry Hill or Kingstown Asda (63A) or Kingstown Broadway (63B)
64 Carlisle Bus Sta.- Nelson St.- Morton Park.
65 Carlisle Bus Sta.- Ridley Road – Henderson Road.
66 Carlisle Bus Sta.- Blackwell – Durdar.
67 Belle Vue – Carlisle Centre – Scalegate Road – Upperby.
68 Belle Vue – Carlisle Centre – Upperby Road – Upperby.
70 Durranhill – Carlisle Centre – Sandsfield Park.
71 Carlisle Bus Sta. – Kirkbride – Anthorn.
72 Carlisle Bus Sta. – Cumwhinton – Cotehill.
74 Holme Head – Carlisle Bus Sta.- Scotby Rd.End – Wetheral.
75 Holme Head – Carlisle Bus Sta.- Scotby School – Wetheral – Cumwhinton.
77 Keswick – Whinlatter Pass – Buttermere – Honister Pass – Grange Bridge -Keswick.
77A As 77 but opposite direction.
79 Keswick – Grange Bridge – Seatoller.
79 Carlisle Bus Sta.- Gretna – Annan.
84 Carlisle Bus Sta.- Houghton – Longtown.
90 Carlisle Lowther St. – Charlotte St. – Bus Sta.
91 Carlisle Bus Sta.- Cummersdale – Dalston – Bridge End.
92 Carlisle Bus Sta.- Heysham Park Ave.
93 Carlisle Bus Sta.- Bowness on Solway.
94 Carlisle English St.or Bus Sta.- Crosby on Eden – Brampton.
95 Carlisle Bus Sta.- Fenton – Brampton.
95A Carlisle Bus Sta.- Heads Nook – Brampton.
96 Carlisle Bus Sta.- Heads Nook – Castle Carrock – Brampton.
97 Carlisle English St.- Hethersgill – Brampton.
98 Currock – Harraby – Botcherby – Carlisle Bus Sta.- Longtown – Gretna Market.
99 Morrisons – Carlisle Bus Sta.- Botcherby – Harraby – Upperby – Bus Sta.
101 Carlisle Courts – Gretna – Longtown.
101 Cockermouth Main St.- Slatefell – Rose Lane – Main St.

102 Cockermouth Main St.- Slatefell – Highfield Rd.- Main St.
103 Cockermouth Main St. – Slatefell – Gable Ave.- Main St.
104 Cockermouth Main St. – The Moor – Main St.
105 Cockermouth Main St.- Beech Lane – Cottage Hospital – Main St.
100 Penrith Bus Sta.- Kirkby Thore – Long Marton – Appleby.
104 Penrith Bus Sta.- Carleton – Pategill – Bus Sta.- High Hesket – Carlisle.
105 Penrith Bus Sta.- Penruddock – Greystoke.
106 Gilwilly – Penrith Bus Sta.- Wetheriggs – Great Dockray – Gilwilly.
107 Penrith Bus Sta.- Hackthorpe – Shap.
108 Penrith Rly.Sta.- Bus Sta.- Yanwath – Pooley Bridge – Patterdale.
109 Gilwilly – Penrith Bus Sta.- Pennyhill Pk.- Voreda Pk.- Gt.Dockray – Gilwilly.
685 Carlisle – Hexham – Newcastle.
1 Furness Hospital – Barrow Town Hall – South Walney – Biggar Bank (1A)
2 West Shore – Barrow Town Hall – Ormsgill.
3 Barrow Ramsden Sq.- Town Hall – Ramsden St.(3A) – Newbarns.
4 Barrow Ramsden Sq.- Town Hall – Roose (4A) – Holbeck Farm.
5 Barrow Cemetery Gates – Town Hall – North Scale.
6 Barrow Town Hall – Furness Hospital (6A) – Greystone Estate (not 6B) – Ulverston – Croftlands (not 6B).
7 Barrow Channelside – Town Hall – Broughton – Millom.
8 Ulverston – Croftlands – Moorgarth.
9 Ulverston – Dalton – Askam – Kirkby.
10 Barrow Ramsden Sq. – Town Hall – Roose – Urswick – Ulverston.
11 Barrow Ramsden Sq. – Town Hall – Roa Island – Coast Road – Ulverston.
12 Barrow Ramsden Sq. – Town Hall – Roa Island – Urswick – Ulverston.
41 Kendal Town Hall – Rinkfield – Oxenholme Rd.- Oxenholme – Hospital – Town Hall.
41A Kendal Town Hall – Rinkfield – Hospital – Oxenholme – Oxenholme Rd.- Town Hall.
42 Kendal Town Hall – Castle Grove – Heron Hill – Oxenholme (Su)
42A Kendal Town Hall – Larch Grove – Heron Hill.
42B Kendal Town Hall – Parkside – Heron Hill (Evenings)
43 Kendal Town Hall – Sandylands.
43A Kendal Town Hall – Crescent Green – Sandylands.
44 Kendal Town Hall – Hallgarth Circular.
445 Kendal Town Hall – Hallgarth – Burneside (Evenings).
45 Kendal Town Hall – Burneside – Bowston.
46 Kendal Town Hall – Kirkbarrow – Colinfield.
48 Kendal Town Hall – Vicarage Park – Town Hall – Morrisons – Town Hall.
503 Whitehall – Newbiggin – Baycliffe – Low Furness School.
505 Bowness – Ambleside – Hawkshead – Coniston – Ambleside – Bowness.
506 Bowness – Ambleside – Coniston – Hawkshead – Ambleside – Bowness.
507 Millom – Broughton – Coniston.
508 Harlock – Lindal.
509 Askam – Kirkby – Grizebeck – Ulverston.
511 Millom – Broughton – Ulverston.
515 Ambleside – Hawkshead – Grizedale Visitor Centre.
516 Ambleside – Elterwater – Dungeon Ghyll.
˘517 Bowness – Windermere – Kirkstone Pass – Glenridding.
518 Ambleside – Bowness – Newby Bridge – Ulverston.
530 Kendal – Grange – Cartmel.
531 Kendal – Grange – Newby Bridge – Windermere.
535 Cartmel – Newby Bridge – Ulverston.
536 Fell Foot – High Newton – Cartmel School – Leven Valley School.
540 Kendal – Crosthwaite.
550 Kendal – Milnthorpe – Sedgwick – Kendal.
552 Kendal – Milnthorpe – Arnside.
555 Carlisle – Keswick – Central Lakes – Kendal – Lancaster.
556 Carlisle – Keswick – Central Lakes – Kendal – Borwick – Lancaster.
561 Kendal – Tebay – Appleby.
561A Kendal – Tebay – Kirkby Stephen.
564 Kendal – Sedbergh.
567 Kendal – Kirkby Lonsdale – Sedbergh.
730 Grange – Newby Bridge – Ulverston.
735 Barrow Town Hall – Ulverston – Newby Bridge – Kendal.
W1 Bowness – Windermere – Ambleside – Grasmere.
X3 Whitehaven – Workington – Cockermouth – Carlisle – Newcastle – Gateshead.
X4 Carlisle – Penrith. (Summer Sundays)
X5 Whitehaven – Workington – Cockermouth – Keswick – Penrith.
X9 Keswick (Summer) – Ambleside – Kendal – Skipton – York.
X35 Barrow Town Hall – Ulverston – Newby Bridge – Kendal.
X75 Carlisle – Annan – Dumfries.

INDEPENDENT OPERATORS TAKEN OVER BY
CUMBERLAND MOTOR SERVICES LTD

1926	Star Bus Services Ltd, Workington.	1936	W Alderson, Dearham, Maryport.
1927	Mrs J Wilson, Whitehaven.	1936	J Robley, Flimby, Maryport.
1928	Armstrong & Siddle Motor and Transport Co Ltd, Penrith.	1936	F T Smith and J T Rose, Penrith.
1930	Telford Brothers, Frizington.	1937	W Norman (Norman's Motors) Parton, Whitehaven.
1930	G W Ratcliffe, Egremont.	1939	T J Graham, Oulton, Wigton.
1932	Workington Motor Services Co Ltd	1941	J H Bennett, Millom.
1933	J B Roseby, Workington.	1941	J Hayton, Broughton Moor.
1934	J Stoddart, Ireby.	1941	W Boyes, Greysouthen, Cockermouth.
1934	H & A Mofat, Great Clifton, Workington.	1943	Lewthwaite Brothers, Cleator Moor.
1935	W Gilmore, Seaton, Workington.	1943	H Crosthwaite, Frizington.
1935	Wilson Brothers, Whitehaven.	1943	S Heron, Cleator Moor.
1935	J Ditchburn, Flimby, Maryport.	1958	Weightman's, (Keswick) Ltd Stage Carriage Operations.
1935	Kendalls (Maryport) Ltd	1965	Lake Hotel Coaches Ltd and Weightmans (Ksewick) Ltd
1935	N Hamilton, Workington.		Tours and Excursions.
1935	W & J Kirkpatrick, Little Broughton.	1967	Keswick – Borrowdale Bus Service Ltd
1936	J W Hodgson, Prospect, Aspatria.	1988	Yeowart's Coaches, Whitehaven.
1936	Jefferson Coaches, Carlisle.	1988	Kirkpatrick's Coaches, Brigham, Cockermouth.
1936	G Scott, High Lorton, Cockermouth.	1989	Stephenson's Coaches, Maryport.
1936	J J Birkett, Maryport.	1989	W A Palmer, Carlisle

PRESERVED VEHICLES

CUMBERLAND MOTOR SERVICES LTD

Having regard to the interesting vehicle types which have been operated in the Cumberland Motor Services fleet over the years it is a matter of some some regret that so few have been preserved. It is also unfortunate that one of the vehicles illustrated as preserved in British Bus Systems No.1, JAO 837, the Leyland PS1 with ECW body has since been scrapped. The Leyland Llon LT5A AAO 574 remains only as a chassis. The following are however preserved :-

BRM 596.
This Leyland TD4 was delivered to Cumberland in 1936 with lowbridge body by Massey Brothers as Fleet No. 132. The chassis cost £829 whilst the body cost £677 and at the time of delivery it carried the highest fleet number in the company. In 1950 it received a new lowbridge body by Eastern Coach Works at a cost of £1600., being renumbered 291 at this time. It was withdrawn in 1959 and sold for further service with Barton Transport Ltd, Nottingham where it was numbered 816. In 1965 it was sold to E Farnsworth, Nottingham, for preservation, passing to J Horrocks, Northampton in 1973 and to the East Pennine Transport Group in 1978. It appeared at rallies in Cumberland livery but was then off the road for some years due to an engine defect. In 1995 it passed to James Sunderland of Keighley and following rectification of the engine defect has, once again appeared at rallies.

AAO 547A – Formerly 109 DRM.
This Bristol FS with Gardner 6LW engine and Eastern Coach Works body was delivered in 1961, the chassis costing £2837 and the body £2758. Initially it was numbered C416, the 'C' prefix indicating that it had 5 speed gearbox and platform doors for country services. In the 1961 renumbering scheme it received Fleet No. 550 and numerically it was the first FS type Bristol Lodekka to enter the fleet as distinct from the earlier LD type. After withdrawal from regular service it became a Training Vehicle in June 1977 and was renumbered TV2 in December 1980.

In May 1983 it was repainted in the prewar and immediate postwar livery of Tilling Red with three cream bands and white roof, with adverts applied for British Bus Systems No. 1 – Cumberland and received it's previous fleet no. 550. In this condition it was used for private hire and promotional services including, in August 1983, a Cumbrian Coastliner Service operating on three Sunday afternoons between Workington, Whitehaven, St. Bees and Seascale. Following the withdrawal of sister vehicle 554 (TV1) it became the regular Training Vehicle. In September 1991 it was purchased by the 550 Group for preservation and was repainted into the Tilling livery in which it had been delivered, this work being carried out by Volvo at their Lillyhall Works where it was the last bus to be painted before closure of the works. It now makes regular appearances at Rallies.

AAO 34B
This Bristol MW with Gardner 6LW engine and standard ECW service bus body was delivered in November 1963 numbered 229 and registered

427 LAO but it never operated as such. It was renumbered 231 and reregistered as above in April 1964 before entering service. It spent most of its time at Keswick depot and operated regularly on service 79 from Keswick to Seatoller in Borrowdale. It was withdrawn from service in 1980 and sold to Richard Solyom of Keswick, who, at that time was only 16 years old. Difficulty in finding suitable accommodation in recent years has had its effect on the condition of the vehicle but it is hoped that restoration work will commence on it during 1996.

DAO 293K, DAO 295K.
These single-deckers formed part of the final batch of Bristol RE models delivered to CMS in 1972 with standard Eastern Coach Works service bus bodies. Following withdrawal in December 1983 they passed to Bristol Omnibus Company for further service, becoming part of the Badgerline fleet on privatisation. On withdrawal by Badgerline, both passed through various companies in South Wales and saw further service with Phil Anslow Travel, Pontypool (293) and Peak Bus, Chesterfield (295) before being purchased in December 1995 by Mr N W Frampton of Southampton for restoration in Cumberland livery and preservation.

BARROW CORPORATION / BOROUGH TRANSPORT DEPARTMENT.

EO 9177 Fleet No. 147.
This was supplied as part of a batch of 10 vehicles delivered in 1950, being Leyland PD2/3 chassis with Park Royal bodies. The complete batch was rebodied by Roe in 1959/60 and 147 received platform doors for the Ulverston service. It passed to P Cousins of Barrow in May 1981 for preservation and at the present time is awaitng restoration.

CEO 956 Fleet No. 169.
This was one of a batch of ten vehicles delivered in 1958 and comprising Leyland PD2/40 chassis with Park Royal bodies. This particular one was withdrawn in 1977 and passed to I Hodgson of Aughton on behalf of the Furness Transport Group. It later passed to Phil. Cousins of Barrow and has recently been sold to John Hambler, also of Barrow. It is preserved in the later livery.

CEO 957 Fleet No. 170.
This is a sister vehicle to 169, being supplied as part of the same batch and is owned by the Mersey and Calder Bus Preservation Group. It is preserved in the earlier livery of mainly blue with cream relief.

JEO 772 Fleet No. 72.
This Leyland Leopard L1 single-decker with East Lancashire Coachbuilders body was delivered in 1963 and is at present owned by Blue Bus, Horwich near Bolton.

EO 9051 Fleet No. 124. – Breakdown Tender.
This Leyland PD2/3 double-decker with Park Royal body was delivered 1949 as part of a batch of 30 similar vehicles. It was converted to a breakdown tender in 1963 and is at present owned by John Hambler.

FLEET SUMMARY

Compiled by Brian Pritchard

WHITEHAVEN MOTOR SERVICE COMPANY LIMITED

Vehicles Purchased New 1912 to 1920

Name	Reg	Type	Body	Seating	New	Acq.
'Lady Florence'	AO 1636	Commercial Car 30hp	-?-	Ch24	7/12	
'Lady Mary'	-?-	Leyland S3 (RAF type)	-?-	Ch32	1914	
	-?-	G.M.C.	-?-	B14	by 1917	3/17
	?-	Ford	-?-	B	by 1919	-?-
	-?-	Ford	-?-	B	by 1919	-?-
'Lady Grace'?	AK 7639	Daimler	-?-	Ch32	by 1919	1919
'Lady Florence'	CW 3166	Daimler CK	-?-	Ch22	by 1919	1919
'Lady Isobel'	-?-	Daimler CK	-?-	Ch	by 1919	1919
'Lady Molly'	-?-	Daimler CK	-?-	Ch	by 1919	1919
'Lady Nin'	AO 4620	Daimler	-?-	Ch24	1919	1919
'Lady Betty'	TB 1211	Leyland	-?-	Ch	6/19	
'Lady Mary'	TB 1051	Leyland C	-?-	Ch28	2/20	
'Lady Betty'	TB 1063	Leyland C	-?-	Ch32	1920	
'Lady Margaret'	TB 1184	Leyland C	-?-	Ch32	1920	
	TB 1197	Leyland C	-?-	Ch32	1920	
	AO 5586-7	Daimler Y 30hp	Dodson	B32R	5/20	
	AO 6009-11	Daimler Y 30hp	Birch	B32R	7/20	
	AO 6012	Daimler Y 30hp	Dodson	B32R	7/20	
	AO 6089/90	Daimler Y 40hp	Dodson	B32	10/20	

AK 7639 was reseated to Ch24 by 7/22.
AO 1636 was reseated to Ch28, date unknown. A bus body, for winter use, was ordered in 10/12.
CW 3166 was reseated to Ch28, date unknown.
TB 1051 was reseated to Ch32, by 7/22, reverting to Ch28 date unknown.
TB 1063 was reseated to Ch24, 1924, reverting to Ch32, date unknown.
TB 1051, 1063, 1184 were rebodied Tolson B32F in 7,7,9/27 respectively, and also received pneumatic tyres.

Vehicle acquired from a dealer at Knott End, near Fleetwood, 7/12

Name	Reg	Type	Body	Seating	New	Acq.
'Lady Favourite'	XS 102	Arrol Johnston	-?-	Ch24	by 1912	7/12

Vehicle acquired from Davies, Bognor Regis, 9/12

Name	Reg	Type	Body	Seating	New	Acq.
'Lady Nin'	-?-	Commercial Car	-?-	Ch	by 1912	9/12

(This may have been registered BM 1052 or BP 1285)

In addition 4 double-deckers, details unknown, were hired from British Automobile Traction from 6/20 to 2/21.

CUMBERLAND MOTOR SERVICES LIMITED

Daimler Y buses of 1921 to 1928

Fleet	Reg	Type	Body	Seating	Date
6,16,5	AO 6650-52	Daimler Y 36hp	-?-	B26R	6/21
13/14	AO 6694/95	Daimler Y 40hp	Dodson	B32R	6/21
15	AO 6899	Daimler Y	-?-	B26	7/21
24,25	AO 6900/01	Daimler Y	Birch	O32RO	8/21
27	AO 7197	Daimler Y 40hp	Tolson	O32RO	11/21
26	AO 7198	Daimler Y30hp	Dodson	O32RO	12/21
30	AO 7455	Daimler Y	-?-	B32	10/22
31	AO 7961	Daimler Y	Tolson	B32	7/22
12	AO 8911	Daimler Y	-?-	B26	5/23
11	AO 9040	Daimler Y	-?-	B26	6/23
43/44	AO 9264/65	Daimler Y	Massey	B32	9/23
48	AO 9912	Daimler Y	Tolson	B32	5/24
49-53	AO 9913-17	Daimler Y	Strachan & Brown	B32F	4-5/24
17,23,57,58	RM 304-307	Daimler Y	Massey	B32	6-7/24
59	RM 308	Daimler Y	Tolson	B32	7/24
20,21	RM 1040/41	Daimler Y	Massey	B35R	4/25
28,38,60	RM 1042-44	Daimler Y	Massey	B35	4-5/25
61	RM 1045	Daimler Y	Massey	B35F	5/25
62,63	RM 1522/23	Daimler Y	Massey	B31	7/25
64,65	RM 1970/71	Daimler Y	Massey	B32	11/25
40,71	RM 2817/18	Daimler Y	Massey	B31R	6/26

Most, but not all of the above, were surplus ex Army lorry chassis rebuilt and reregistered. The dates new shown are the dates they became buses. 17,20/1/3/8,38,40/8-53/7-65,71 are confirmed as ex Army, through British Automobile Traction, Camden Town, from various sources.
11,12 were supplied by J.M.Roberts, London and had reconditioned chassis with second hand bodies.
Both were fitted with new Massey B32 bodies in 10/23.
The double deck bodies on AO 6900/1 were acquired from London General O.C., along with 2 others.
6 was converted to Ch32 in 4/23.
5,15/6,25 were rebodied Massey B32 in 4,1,1,1/23 respectively. 15,16 became B30 by 7/23.
25 was again rebodied by Massey, along with 26, in 1/27 as B25F. It was reseated to B32 by 7/27
24 was rebodied by Tolson in 3/23 and again by Massey, as B32, in 1927.
The chassis of 30,31 were purchased 3/22. They were initially fitted with second hand bodies but new Tolson B32 bodies were fitted 12,8/22 respectively.
62,63 were reseated to B30 by 7/27.
60-63 were loaned to Westmorland Motor Services from 1-4/26.

Vehicle acquired ex Millican, Carlisle (named 'Border Queen'), 3/22

Fleet	Reg	Type	Body	Seating	Date
(40)	AO 4652	Daimler	-?-	Ch34	3/22

This was named 'Lady Maud' and only received its fleet number in 1923.

Leyland G/SG types 1923/24

Fleet	Reg	Type	Body	Seating	Date
36	AO 8967	Leyland SG6	Leyland	B40F	6/23
41	AO 9102	Leyland G7	Leyland	B32	7/23
37	AO 9103	Leyland SG6	Leyland	B40F	7/23
42	AO 9263	Leyland SG6	Leyland	B40F	9/23
45-47	AO 9378-80	Leyland SGH6	Leyland	B40F	11/23
54-56	AO 9984-86	Leyland SGH7 Special	Leyland	B32F	6/24

41 was originally a Leyland demonstrator. It was rebodied by Massey as B32 in 1927 after an accident.
54-56 were ordered as 40 seaters but delivered as 32 seaters.

Vehicles acquired from H.Meageen(t/a Happy Days), Whitehaven, 6/21

(20)	CW 3253	Vulcan 25hp	-?-	Ch14	9/20	6/21
(21)	CW 3259	Vulcan 20hp	-?-	Ch14	9/20	6/21

20,21 were reseated to Ch20 in 4/22, and both were rebodied by Massey in 11,12/22 respectively. The original body of 20 went to Massey in part exchange. The body from 21 went to G.Scott, Lorton.

New small capacity vehicles 1922-1929

32-35	AO 8088-91	Vulcan VSD	Birch	B20	8/22
38,39	EK 3194/96	Berliet	Massey	B18	5/23
5	RM 5505	Ford AA	Tolson	B14	11/2
92	RM 5529	Ford AA	Tolson	B14	2/29
97	RM 5716	Chevrolet LQ	Tolson	B14F	11/29
17	RM 5943	Ford AA	Tolson	B14F	6/29
12	RM 5944	Ford AA	Massey	B14F	6/29
90	RM 6151	Ford AA	Tolson	B14F	9/29
98-102	RM 6509-13	Chevrolet LQ	Tolson	B14F	11/29-1/30

32-35 first new vehicles with pneumatic tyres. 38,39 supplied &registered by NCME, Wigan.

Other makes 1921-1928

66	RM 1991	AEC 411	United	B31R	10/25
67	RM 2049	AEC 411	Massey	B29R	11/25
83	RM 4258	Guy FBB	Guy	B35R	7/27
74	RM 4364	Guy FCX	Massey	L52R	8/27
72,73	RM 4370/71	ADC 416	Tolson	B32R	9/27
19	RM 4442	ADC 416	Tolson	B32R	10/27
9,27,79,84	RM 5059-62	ADC 416	Brush	B32F	6/28
85, 2	RM 5068/69	ADC 416	Brush	B32F	6/28

74 was delivered as L56R but modified to L52R before entering service. It had single bucket seats upstairs back -to-back along the centre, leaving two aisles, one at either side. 66/7 were reseated to B30R by 7/27.

Leyland Lion PLSC types, 1926-28

29,32,68-70	RM 2225-29	Leyland Lion PLSC1	Leyland	B31R	4-6/26
6,3,1,4,33	RM 4106-10	Leyland Lion PLSC1	Massey	B31R	7-10/27
34,35,39,43	RM 4366-69	Leyland Lion PLSC1	Massey	B31R	10-12/27
25	RM 5058	Leyland Lion PLSC3	Tolson	B31R	5/28
8,13,24,28	RM 5165-68	Leyland Lion PLSC3	Tolson	B31R	7/28
65,86	RM 5193/94	Leyland Lion PLSC3	Massey	B31R	7/28
89	RM 5537	Leyland Lion PLSC3	Tolson	B31R	7/2
58	RM 5565	Leyland Lion PLSC3	Tolson	B31R	7/28
91	RM 5566	Leyland Lion PLSC3	Massey	B31R	7/28

29,32,68-70 were rebodied Massey B31F, 4/32.
8,13,24/5/8,58,65,86/9,91 were rebodied by Massey in 4-6/34 (8,13,24/5/8,58,89), 7/36 (65) or 1/37 (86,91).

Vehicles acquired from Star Bus Services Ltd., Workington, 11/26

	J 5050	International 25hp	-?-	B20	?-	11/26
	RM 508	International 25hp	-?-	B14	8/24	11/
75	RM 1934	Guy B	-?-	B32	9/25	11/26
77	RM 2072	Guy B	-?-	B32	10/25	11/26
76	RM 2308	Guy O	-?-	B20	2/26	11/26

J 5050, RM 508 not operated by Cumberland. J 5050 was new to J.T.Rutherford, Greenside, Co.Durham.

Vehicles acquired from Mrs J.Wilson, Whitehaven, 1/27

72	RM 558	Chevrolet	-?-	B14F	9/24	1/27
73	RM 578	Chevrolet	-?-	B14F	10/24	1/27
74	RM 2250	Guy BA	Guy	B20F	1/26	1/27

Vehicle hired from -?-, from 4/26.

-----	RM 2561	AEC 409	LGOC	H??R	4/26	4/26

This was used on a European tour c8/26.

Vehicle acquired from Leyland Motors Ltd., Leyland, 9/27

78	TD 5219	Leyland C9	Leyland	B26F	3/26	9/27

Vehicles acquired from Birmingham Corporation Transport, 59-61, 9/27

80	OK 3980	AEC 503	Fry	O28/26RO	1922	9/27
81,82	OK 8002/03	AEC 503	Brush	O28/26RO	1923	9/27

These were acquired via ADC Sales(dealer). 80 was originally a demonstrator.

Leyland Tiger TS2s, 1929-30

87	RM 5300	Leyland Tiger TS2	Leyland	B29R	7/28
88	RM 5517	Leyland Tiger TS2	Leyland	B29R	9/28
93,94,95	RM 5628-30	Leyland Tiger TS2	Leyland	B29R	3,3,6/29
7,14	RM 5635/36	Leyland Tiger TS2	Massey	B29R	5/29
15,16,30,31	RM 6015-18	Leyland Tiger TS2	Massey	B29R	5,5,5,8/29
111-114	RM 6629-32	Leyland Tiger TS2	Massey	B32R	6/30

7 was rebodied Massey B34R 4/34.
16 was rebodied Burlingham C26F, 4/39.
30,94 were rebodied Massey DP32R, 5,4/39.
15 was rebodied as C31F by an unknown builder, possibly Duple, 5/39.
31 was rebodied Massey C26F, 5/39.
14,95 were rebodied Burlingham B34F, 2/43.
111-4 were completely rebuilt by Myers and Bowman as B31R in 1938.
111-4 also received the deeper Cov-Rad Radiator conversions.

Leyland Titan TD1s, 1929-31

96,23,44,57	RM 5631-34	Leyland Titan TD1	Leyland	L27/24RO	7-8/29
10,11	RM 6019/20	Leyland Titan TD1	Leyland	L27/24RO	8/29
103-110	RM 6621-28	Leyland Titan TD1	Massey	L27/24R	2-5/30
5,17,18,21,22,42	RM 7542-47	Leyland Titan TD1	Leyland	L27/24R	1/31
48,75-77,80,81	RM 7548-53	Leyland Titan TD1	Leyland	L27/24R	1/31
36,37,45,46	RM 8120-23	Leyland Titan TD1	Leyland	L27/24R	8/31

The bodies of 103-110 were rebuilt during 1935/36. Those of 108/9 were again rebuilt after the war. 108 was in 10/48.
103/5/7/10 received new NCB L27/26R bodies and Gardner 5LW engines in 1943.
The bodies of RM 7542-51/3, 8120-3 were rebuilt by East Lancs in 1938/9. That on RM 7552 was also rebuilt but probably by Cumberland themselves.
The bodies of RM 7542-53, 8120-3 were all again rebuilt in 1947/8, by Myers & Bowman (RM 7542/9/52), Lancashire Aircraft Corporation/Samlesbury Engineering (RM 7546,8121) and by Cumberland (the rest).

Bedford WLBs 1932-1934

51	RM 9156	Bedford WLB	Massey	B20F	12/32	
100,99	RM 9564/65	Bedford WLB	Duple	C20F	6,5/33	
63,64	AAO 742/43	Bedford WLB	Duple	C20F	8/34	

51 was new with the second hand 1929 Massey body from ex Ratcliffe of Egremont 51.

Leyland Cubs 1933-1935

26	RM 9575	Leyland Cub KP2	-?-	B20F	6/33	
52	AA0 371	Leyland Cub KP3	Burlingham	B20F	5/34	
53	AAO 372	Leyland Cub SKP2	Burlingham	FC20F	5/34	
66	ARM 709	Leyland Cub SKP2	Leyland	B20F	6/35	

Vehicles acquired from Workington Motor Services Limited, Workington, 11/32

55	RM 3872	Leyland Lioness PLC1	Massey	C26	5/27	11/32
50,54	RM 4722/23	Leyland Lioness PLC1	Massey	Ch24	2/28	11/32

55 had received its second hand body from an ex Cumberland vehicle in 3/32. Originally carried a Massey Ch26 body.

Vehicle acquired from J.R.Roseby, Workington, 4/33

-	?RM 97?	Lancia	-?-	-?-	1924	4/33

This was not used by Cumberland.

Vehicles acquired from J.Stoddart, Ireby, 5/34

-	RM 3934	Dennis 30cwt	-?-	B20F	6/27	5/34
-	RM 4621	Dennis G	-?-	B20F	1/28	5/34

Both vehicles were new to Millican, Hethersgill, near Carlisle. Neither were used by Cumberland.

Vehicles acquired from H.& A.Moffat, Great Clifton, 6/34

-	RM 5716	Chevrolet LQ	Tolson	B14F	11/29	6/34
-	RM 7495	Ford AA	-?-	B20	11/30	6/34
62	RM 9797	Bedford WLB	Duple	B20F	9/33	6/34

RM 5716 was new to Cumberland, 97. RM 7495, 9797 were new to Moffat. Only 62 was used by Cumberland.

Vehicles acquired from W.Gilmore, Park View, Seaton, 4/35

-	RM 6286	Chevrolet LQ	-?-	B14F	7/29	4/35
67	AAO 394	Bedford WLB	Burlingham	B20F	5/34	4/35

Both vehicles were new to Gilmore, and RM 6286 was not used by Cumberland.

Vehicles acquired from Wilson Brothers, Whitehaven, 8/35

82	RM 8005	Reo	Burlingham	C20F	6/31	8/35
78	RM 9664	Bedford WLB	Duple	C20F	7/33	8/35
83	AAO 151	AEC Regal 662	Burlingham	C32R	3/34	8/35

These vehicles were all new to Wilson.

Vehicles acquired from Telford Brothers, Frizington, 4/30

HL 2844	Chevrolet	-?-	-?-	1926	4/30
RM 2471	Reo Sprinter	-?-	-?-	3/26	4/30
RM 3831	Bean	-?-	B14	5/27	4/30
WW 3085	Chevrolet LM	-?-	B14F	7/27	4/30
RM 4644	Chevrolet LM	-?-	B14	1/28	4/30
HH 4292	Chevrolet LO	-?-	B14F	5/28	4/30
RM 5586	G.M.C. T14	-?-	B14F	12/28	4/30
RM 6796	Chevrolet	-?-	-?-	2/30	4/30

HH 4292 was new to E.R.Shields, Carlisle.
HL 2844 may have been new to A.Telford, South Kirkby, Yorkshire.
RM 2471's origins are unknown.
RM 3831 was new to I.Hickson, Port Carlisle, Cumberland, and passed through a number of Carlisle area owners prior to arriving with Telford Brothers.
RM 4644, 5586 (and possibly RM 6796) were new to A.Telford, Frizington.
WW 3085 was new to A.Telford, South Kirkby, Yorkshire.

Vehicles acquired from G.W.Ratcliffe, Egremont, 7/30

-?-	-?-	Chevrolet	-?-	-?-	-?-	7/30
53	RM 5391	Chevrolet LO	-?-	C14	9/28	7/30
51	-?-	Chevrolet	Massey	B16	1929	7/30
20	RM 6694	Dennis G	-?-	B20	1930	7/30

53 exchanged bodies with 12(RM 5944) in 9/31, receiving the 1929 Massey B14F body from 12.

Vehicles acquired from AEC Limited, Southall (ex demonstrators), 6/31 & 9/32

12	RM 7328	AEC Regent 661	Short	H26/26R	8/30	6/31
47	RM 8032	AEC Regent 661	Massey	L24/24R	7/31	9/32

12,47 had been on hire since new.

Vehicles reacquired from Leyland Motors (as dealer), 9-11/31

97	RM 5716	Chevrolet LQ	Tolson	B14F	11/29	11/31
12	RM 5944	Ford AA	Massey	B14F	6/29	9/31
98-102	RM 6509-13	Chevrolet LQ	Tolson	B14F	11/29-1/30	11/31

These had been sold to Leyland by Cumberland in 3/31.
The body on 12 was exchanged with that on ex Ratcliffe 53(RM 5391) (q.v.).

Vehicles reacquired from Oswald Tillotson Limited, Burnley (as dealer), 5/32

(40),(41)	RM 5059/61	ADC 416	Brush	B32F	6/28	5/32
(49),(38)	RM 5068/69	ADC 416	Brush	B32F	6/28	5/32

AEC Regals from 1932

2,9,19	RM 8474-76	AEC Regal 662	Harrington	B32R	5/32
27,72,73,84,79,85	RM 8477-82	AEC Regal 662	Harrington	C32R	5/32
74	BAO 74	AEC Regal 662	Burlingham	C31C	9/35
121-125	BAO 764-68	AEC Regal II 0862	Burlingham	B32R	5/36

74 was exhibited at the 1935 Commercial Motor Show.
121-3/5 received new AEC 7.7 litre diesel engines in 1946/7.
121 had its body rebuilt in 1946. Most of 121-5 were rebuilt to some extent in the postwar period.

Vehicle acquired from J.Ditchburn, Flimby, 8/35

-	RM 5105	Reo	-?-	C20	6/28	8/35

This was not used by Cumberland.

Vehicle acquired from Kendalls (Maryport) Limited, Maryport, 8/35

-	RM 5054	Reo GB	-?-	C20F	5/28	8/35

This was new to Kendall.

Vehicle acquired from N.Hamilton, Workington, 10/35

90	ARM 553	Leyland Tiger TS7	Burlingham	C32R	4/35	10/35

This was new to Hamilton. It was rebuilt in 1947, probably by Lancashire Aircraft Corporation.

Vehicle acquired from W.& J.Kirkpatrick, Little Broughton, 11/35

98	RM 8125	Bedford WLG	-?-	C14	7/31	11/35
101	RM 9635	Commer Centaur	-?-	-?-	6/33	11/35
92	AAO 355	Commer Centaur	-?-	C20	5/34	11/35
97	ARM 56	Commer Invader B3	-?-	B20F	1/35	11/35

In addition a number of taxis and haulage lorries were purchased. The latter came with the coal haulage business which was retained by Cumberland until 1946.
The body of 92 was rebuilt by Cumberland in 1938.

Vehicle acquired from J.W.Hodgson, Prospect, 1/36

102	RM 8698	Dennis Arrow	Duple	C29F	3/32	1/36

This was new to Hodgson, and was reseated to B32F by Cumberland, date unknown.

Vehicles acquired from G.Scott, High Lorton, 6/36

131	RM 6802	Reo	-?-	B14F	2/30	6/36
130	RM 7166	Reo	-?-	B20F	6/30	6/36

130 was new to Wilson Brothers, Whitehaven. 131 was new to Scott.

Vehicles acquired from B.Graham and L.Morrison (Jefferson Coaches), Carlisle, 7/36

23	FR 9320	A.D.C. 420	Buckingham	C26	7/28	7/3
10	TY 9817	AEC Regal 662	Duple	C33F	1930	7/36

23 was new to C.Smith, Blackpool as C20.
10 was new to Easton (Tyne & Mersey Motor Company), Redcar.

Vehicles acquired from J.J.Birkett, Maryport, 7/36

44	SY 4251	Reo	-?-	B20F	7/30	7/36
57	RM 8220	Bedford WLB	-?-	B??F	10/31	7/36
96	RM 8752	Bedford WLB	Duple	C20F	6/32	7/36
128	AAO 374	Bedford WLB	Duple	C20F	5/34	7/36

44 was new to J.Dunn, Dalkeith. The rest were new to Birkett.

Vehicles acquired from W.Alderson, Dearham, 7/36

129	CK 4145	Star Flyer VB4	East Lancs	C26	5/29	7/36
-	RM 7237	Morris	-?-	-?-	7/30	7/36

RM 7237 was new to Alderson and was not used by Cumberland.
129 was new to G.E.Barnes(t/a Premier), Preston.

Vehicles acquired from J.Robley, Flimby, 7/36

126	SC 2099	Star Flyer VB4	Hoyal	B20F	9/28	7/36
-	-?-	Chevrolet	-?-	-?-	-?-	7/36

The Chevrolet was not used by Cumberland.
126 was new to Scottish Motor Traction, Edinburgh, 365.

Vehicle acquired from F.T.Smith and J.T.Rose, Penrith, 12/36

20	RM 9968	Bedford WLB	Duple	B20F	1/34	12/36

20 was new to Smith and Rose.

Vehicle acquired from W.Norman (Norman's Motors), Parton, 1/37

23	BRM 434	Commer PN4	Duple	FC26F	7/36	1/37

23 was new to Norman.

Leyland Titan TD3s, TD4s, TD5s

56,59-61	AAO 491-4	Leyland Titan TD3	Massey	L27/26R	6/34
115-120	BAO 772-77	Leyland Titan TD4	Massey	L27/26R	4,5/36
11,129,132	BRM 594-96	Leyland Titan TD4	Massey	L27/26R	10/36
133-137	DAO 48-52	Leyland Titan TD5	Massey	L27/26R	6/38
143-144	DRM 7,8	Leyland Titan TD5	Massey	L27/26R	4/39
145-146	DRM 9,10	Leyland Titan TD5	E.Lancs	L27/26R	4/39

56/9-61 were delivered with petrol engines, but were given Leyland diesel engines 1936/7.
The body of 59 was rebuilt by Massey in 1943. Its chassis was reconditioned by Leyland in 1947.
144 had its body rebuilt by Myers & Bowman, Distington in 1946/7.
The bodies of 60/1 were rebuilt in 1947.
133/7/43 had their bodies rebuilt, probably by Lancashire Aircraft Corporation/Samlesbury Engineering in 1946/7.
11, 115/7/8/29/32/4-6 were rebodied ECW L27/28R in 1950, and renumbered 286-294.
133/7/43/4 were rebodied in 1954 with the 1948 Burlingham H28/26R bodies formerly fitted to 157/8,99,152.
145/6 were rebodied in 8/54 with the rebuilt Leyland L27/24R bodies formerly fitted to 5 and 22.

Leyland Lion LT5As

38,40,41,49	AAO 574-77	Leyland Lion LT5A	Massey	B32R	7/34

Vehicle hired from AEC Limited, Southall, 8/35 to 7/36

(71?)	CMF 843	AEC Renown 0664	Weymann	B43F	7/35	8/35

This was exhibited at the 1935 Commercial Motor Show.

Vehicles acquired from Glasgow Corporation Transport, 166/4/70,68,171, 4/40

64	GE 2403	Leyland Titan TD1	Leyland	L27/24RO	9/28	4/40
63	GE 2499	Leyland Titan TD1	Leyland	L27/24R	7/29	4/40
67	GE 7200	Leyland Titan TD1	Leyland	L27/24R	10/29	4/40
62	GE 7204	Leyland Titan TD1	Cowieson	L27/24R	10/29	4/40
78	GE 7205	Leyland Titan TD1	Cowieson	L27/24R	12/29	4/40

All had been fitted with Leyland diesel engines whilst with Glasgow. 63/4/7 & 78 received new NCB L27/26R bodies in 1943/4.

Vehicle acquired from Yorkshire Traction, Barnsley, 328, 5/40

151	HE 4976	Leyland Titan TD1	Leyland	L27/24R	6/30	5/40

151 received a Gardner 5LW engine upon acquisition. Its body was rebuilt in 1946/7, probably by Lancashire Aircraft/Samlesbury Engineering.

Vehicles acquired from Preston Corporation Transport, 67, 52, 7/40

8	CK 4172	Leyland Titan TD1	Leyland	L24/24RO	7/29	7/40
20	CK 4602	Leyland Titan TD1	EEC	H29/24R	10/31	7/40

8 was fitted with a Gardner 5LW engine in 7/43. Both were rebodied NCB L27/26R in 1943/4.

Vehicles acquired from Southdown Motor Services, Brighton, 933-6/41/3-5/8, 9/40

25,28,44,65	UF 8373-76	Leyland Titan TD1	Short	H26/24R	3/32	9/40
82,86	UF 8381/83	Leyland Titan TD1	Short	H26/24R	3/32	9/40
96,99,100	UF 8844-46	Leyland Titan TD2	Short	H26/24R	6/32	9/40

99,100 received Gardner 5LW engines in 4/40. 96 followed in 9/42.
The bodies of 28,44,82 were rebuilt by Myers & Bowman in 1949.
28,44 also received Leyland diesel engines at about the same time.
96,99,100 received new Burlingham H28/26R bodies in late 1948.

Vehicle hired from Manchester Corporation Transport, 215, 11/40 to 10/41

(215)	VR 6004	Leyland Titan TD1	Crossley/MCCW	L26/26R	3/30	11/40

It had been fitted with a Leyland diesel engine by Manchester prior to coming on hire.

Leyland Titan TD7s

159-163	EAO 699-703	Leyland Titan TD7	Massey	L27/26R	1-5/41
164-168	EAO 704-08	Leyland Titan TD7	E.Lancs	L27/26R	7-10/41
169-172	EAO 724-27	Leyland Titan TD7	P.Royal	L26/26R	3-4/41
176	ERM 127	Leyland Titan TD7	Massey	L27/28R	12/41
177	ERM 128	Leyland Titan TD7	NCME	L27/28R	4/42

169-72 were a diverted order from Southdown M.S., Brighton where they were to have been numbered 292/0/89/91
162 was rebodied NCB L27/26R in 1944 after accident damage.
161/3/5/7/8 received new Burlingham L27/26R bodies in 1949/50 and renumbered 295-302.

AEC Regents

12,47	BAO 762/63	AEC Regent 0661	Massey	L27/26R	3/36

Leyland Tiger TS7s, TS8s

50,54,55	BAO 769-71	Leyland Tiger TS7	Burlingham	C31C	5-7/36
138-142	DAO 64-68	Leyland Tiger TS8	Massey	B32R	6/38

141/2 had pereimeter seating fitted during the war, but returned to B32R afterwards.
The bodies of 138-42 were rebuilt in the postwar period, that on 138 being completed 8/48, and 141 was rebuilt by Lancashire Aircraft Corporation 3/47.

Commer PN3,4s

126	BRM 169	Commer PN4	Waveney	C20F	7/36
127	BRM 170	Commer PNF4	Waveney	C25F	6/36
71	CRM 747	Commer PN4	Waveney	B20F	5/38
51,98,130	DRM 237-39	Commer PN3	Waveney	B20F	4-5/39

Vehicle acquired from T.J.Graham, Oulton, Wigton, 2/39

131	KY 9998	Leyland Cub SKP	-?-	FB26F	5/35	2/39

131 was new to Graham, being supplied by Central Garage, Bradford.

Vehicles acquired from Wilts and Dorset M.S., Salisbury, 250/15/49,10,46,9, 1/40

57	TM 3736	Leyland Titan TD1	Leyland	L24/24R	11/28	1/40
79	VW 8823	Leyland Titan TD1	Leyland	L24/24R	3/29	1/40
147	RU 9494	Leyland Titan TD1	Leyland	L27/24RO	6/29	1/40
149,150	CM 8726/29	Leyland Titan TD1	Leyland	L24/24R	1929	1/40
148	CK 4208	Leyland Titan TD2	Leyland	L24/24R	1930	1/40

57 and 79 were new to National Omnibus Co., Chelmsford, 2785/46 (later Eastern National).
147 was new to Hants and Dorset M.S., Bournemouth, E286.
148 was new to Ribble M.S., Preston, 744. 149/50 were new to Birkenhead Corporation, 99,102.
57,79,147 received new NCB L27/26R bodies in late 1943. 79, 147 received Gardner 5LW engines too.
148-50 were rebuilt by East Lancs as L27/24R in 1940, receiving Gardner 5LW engines at the same time.
These bodies were again rebuilt 11/46-2/47 by Lancashire Aircraft Corporation.

Vehicles acquired from London Passenger Transport Board, London SW1, TD11,37,29,123,12,125,28, 3/40

152	GW 550	Leyland Titan TD2	Dodson	H27/26R	12/31	3/40
156	GW 1285	Leyland Titan TD2	Birch	H30/26RO	2/32	3/40
155	EV 5860	Leyland Titan TD1	Dodson	H27/26R	4/32	3/40
157	EV 6510	Leyland Titan TD1	Dodson	H26/26R	6/32	3/40
153	GY 2042	Leyland Titan TD2	Dodson	H26/26R	7/32	3/40
158	EV 8335	Leyland Titan TD2	Dodson	H25/26R	10/32	3/40
154	HV 2822	Leyland Titan TD2	Dodson	H30/26RO	4/33	3/40

152/3 were new to A.H.Raper (Standard), London SE16. 154 was new to Renown Traction Company, London E6, 12.
155 was new to Pro Bono Publico, London E8. 156 was new to A.G.Summerskill, E.Twickenham.
157/8 were new to Reliance Omnibus Company, London E4, 14/7. All passed to L P T B in 1933/4.
152/3/5/7/8 were reengined Gardner 5LW in 1940 and rebodied Burlingham H28/26R in 11/48.
154/6 were rebodied NCB L27/26R and reengined Gardner 5LW in 9/43.

Vehicles acquired from J.H.Bennett, Millom, 1/41

13	FR 9794	Leyland Tiger TS1	Burlingham	B32R	1/29	1/41
24	GV 901	Bedford WLB	-?-	B20F	12/31	1/41
32	AAO 204	Bedford WLB	Waveney	B20F	3/34	1/41
68	FV 5690	Bedford WLB	Burlingham	B20F	3/35	1/41
91	BRM 165	Bedford WTB	-?-	C26	5/36	1/41
101	DRM 131	Dodge SBF	-?-	C26F	4/39	1/41

13 was new to J.Bracewell, Colne.
24 was new to G.Osborne, Tollesbury.
68 was new to J.Monks and Son, Leigh.
32,91 and 101 were new to Bennett.

Vehicle acquired from W.Boyes, Greysouthen, 2/41

24	DRM 542	Bedford WTB	Duple	C25F	9/39	2/41

This vehicle was exhibited at the 1939 Scottish Motor Show and was new to Boyes.

Vehicles acquired from J.Hayton, Broughton Moor, 4/41

102	WX 2100	Leyland Tiger TS2	Roe	B30F	1/30	4/41
128	BRM 284	Bedford WTB	Duple	C20F	6/36	4/41
173	BRM 328	Bedford WTB	Duple	B20	7/36	4/41
174	CAO 710	Bedford WTB	-?-	B25	6/37	4/41
175	DRM 710	Bedford WTB	Duple	C26F	6/39	4/41

102 was new to West Yorkshire Road Car, Harrogate, 514.
173 was new to W.Boyes, Greysouthen.
128/74/5 were new to Hayton.
175 was reseated to C14F in 1950 to operate over a bridge with a weight restriction.

Vehicles acquired from Morecambe Corporation Transport, 7,14,15, 4/42

178	TD 7135	Guy FCX	Short	O59RO	7/26	4/42
180,179	TE 2718/19	Guy FCX	Short	O53RO	1/28	4/42

These were for workers transport at Drigg.

Vehicles hired from the East Kent Road Car Company Ltd., Canterbury, 5/42 to 1943.

643-645	JG 1622-24	Leyland Titan TD1	Leyland	L27/24R	11/31	5/42

These were returned 3/43 (643,645) or 6/43 (644).

Vehicles hired from London Transport, ST62,204/23,332/42, 8/42 to 1943/44.

(ST62)	GF 404	AEC Regent 661	L.G.O.C.	H28/20R	4/30	8/42
(ST204)	GF 7247	AEC Regent 661	L.G.O.C.	H28/20R	6/30	8/42
(ST223)	GH 556	AEC Regent 661	L.G.O.C.	H28/20R	7/30	8/42
(ST332)	GH 8071	AEC Regent 661	L.G.O.C.	H28/20R	10/30	8/42
(ST342)	GK 3008	AEC Regent 661	L.G.O.C.	H28/20R	10/30	8/42

These were returned 11/43(ST223,ST332) or 8/44(the rest).

Vehicles acquired from Lewthwaite Brothers, Cleator Moor, 4/43

191	BRM 140	Bedford WTB	-?-	C25F	5/36	4/43
192	BRM 53	Bedford WTB	-?-	C---	5/36	4/43
193	BRM 159	Bedford WTB	Grose	C25F	5/36	4/43
194	DRM 440	Leyland Tiger TS8	Burlingham	C32F	5/39	4/43

191/3 were new to Papes Coaches, Keswick.
192/4 were new to Lewthwaites, and 194 was originally C31F. 194 was rebodied ACB C33F in 7/48.

Vehicles acquired from H.Crosthwaite, Frizington, 4/43

195	DAO 190	Bedford WTB	Burlingham	C25F	5/38	4/43
196	BAO 78	Bedford WTL	-?-	C26	8/35	4/43
197	ETE 173	Austin K3CL	Burlingham	C26F	10/39	4/43

197 was new to Darwen Corporation, 24, and was later reseated to C33F.
195/6 were new to Crosthwaite.

Vehicles acquired from S.Heron, Cleator Moor, 4/43

198	EAO 125	Commer Commando	Waveney	B26F	10/39	4/43
199	BRM 434	Commer PN4	-?-	FC26F	7/36	4/43
200	RM 8198	Reo	-?-	B20F	9/30	4/43
201	BRM 128	Commer PN3	-?-	B20F	5/36	4/43

199 was new to W.Norman, Parton, and had formerly been owned by Cumberland (23).
198,200/1 were new to Heron.

Vehicles hired from Bolton Corporation Transport, 21, 90, 120/1/4, 1941-1946

(21)	WH 6863	Leyland Titan TD4c	Roberts	L26/26R	1936	5/41
(90)	WH 5504	Leyland Titan TD3c	Bromilow & Edwards	H27/24R	4/34	5/43
(120,121,124)	WH 9218/19/22	Leyland Titan TD5c	Massey	H28/26R	7/37	5/43

These were returned 12/44 (124), 2/46 (21, 90). The return dates for 120/1 are unknown.

Vehicles hired from Morecambe and Heysham Corporation, 32-36, from 5/42

(32-34)	TF 7468-70	AEC Regent 661	Weymann	H30/26R	3/32	1943
(35,36)	TJ 2490/91	AEC Regent 661	Weymann	H30/26R	8/33	1943

These were returned 5/43.
There is also a possibility that similar 28,30/1(TF 7465-7) may have been involved, and that 33 was not.

Postwar Leyland Titan PD1s

218-222	GAO 756-60	Leyland Titan PD1	Massey	L27/26R	3/48
223-242	GAO 761-80	Leyland Titan PD1	NCB	L27/26R	1948/9
243-247	GAO 781-85	Leyland Titan PD1	Massey	L27/26R	3/48

223-42 were new 2/48 (223-6/36/8), 6/48 (227-31/3-5/9/40/2), 6/49 (232/7/41). 218-24/6-47 were rebuilt by CMS in 1955-58. 228/32/3/4/7/9/42 were altered to L31/26R in 1959 (233 - 1962). 224/38 were used as tow buses at Millom and Maryport from 1960. 221/3/4/6-40/2/3 were renumbered 329/11-28/30, 11/61.

Postwar Leyland Titan PD2s

261-282	HRM 681-702	Leyland Titan PD2/1	Leyland	L27/26R	2,3/49
-----	HRM 703-710	Leyland Titan PD2/1	Leyland	L27/26R	1949
303-322	KRM 252-71	Leyland Titan PD2/12	Leyland	L27/28R	6-11/51
328-337	LRM 102-11	Leyland Titan PD2/12	Leyland	L27/28R	7-9/52

Vehicles 303-22 were new 6/51 (303-6/8), 7/51 (307/9), 8/51 (310), 9/51 (312), 10/51 (315/20-2), 11/51 (317/9), unknown (311/3/4/6/8).
HRM 703-710 were diverted to Crosville M.S., Chester, M583-590 (later DTO 583-590), just before delivery.
They were built to Cumberland specification and registered by them too. HRM 704/5 were on hire to Cumberland from 12/60 to 4/61 (q.v.).
267/81 were rebuilt with radiused windows in 1959. 303-6 were rebuilt by Cumberland in 1959/60.
261-282, 303-337 were renumbered 340-361, 370-399, 11/61.

Vehicle Hired from West Yorkshire Road Car Co., Harrogate, 822, DX2

(822)	JWT 712	Bristol Lodekka LDX6B	ECW	H33/25R	1/51
(DX2)	MWR 618	Bristol Lodekka LD6B	ECW	H33/25R	5/53

822 was the second prototype Lodekka. It returned 2/51. DX2 was one of the 6 pre-production Lodekks. It returned 6/53.

Leyland Royal Tigers

323-327	LAO 144-48	Ld.R.Tiger PSU1/13	ECW	B45F	1/52
338-344	MAO 106-12	Ld.R.Tiger PSU1/13	Leyland	B44F	3-7/53
345-347	MAO 103-05	Ld.R.Tiger PSU1/15	Leyland	C41C	2/53

323-7 were unique in having the prototype Bristol LS type body fitted to a Leyland chassis. Few Bristol LS carried this type of body.
338-44 were rebuilt by Cumberland with no outward alteration in the 1959-61 period, and were fitted for 'Pay as you Board operation' in 1964.
323-327, 338-347 were renumbered 150-154/6/5/7/8/60/59/61/77/6/5. 11/61

Bristol LS/MW Coaches

348-50	NRM 372-74	Bristol LS6G	ECW	C39F	3/54
351,352	ORM 133/34	Bristol LS6G	ECW	C39F	1/55
370-372	RAO 734-36	Bristol LS6G	ECW	C39F	3/56
390	VAO 390	Bristol MW6G	ECW	C39F	6/58
392,393	XAO 600/01	Bristol MW6G	ECW	C39F	6/59

348-52/70-2/92/93 were renumbered 275-285, 11/61.
280-2 were refurbished by ECW in 1965/6 and were remodelled to resemble the later MW coach body. MWs 283-5 were similarly refurbished at the same time.
275 was converted to B45F 12/66-3/67 and renumbered 224. In 1970 it became a driver trainer and was reseated to B35F, and to B29F 11/71. It was again renumbered 12/71 to T1.
In 12/76 it became a mobile enquiry office, lost its fleetnumber, but became disused from late 1977.
276/8-85 were rebuilt to B41F by ECW in 11/71 and renumbered 222-4

Wartime Utility Guys and Daimlers

181-185	ERM 672-76	Guy Arab I 6LW	Brush	L27/28R	2-4/43
186-188	ERM 677-79	Daimler CWG5	Brush	L27/28R	3,4,9/43
202-206	ERM 910-14	Guy Arab II 6LW	NCME	L27/28R	2-6/43
207-215	FAO 62,51-58	Guy Arab II 6LW	NCME	L27/28R	7-9/43
216,217	FAO 59,60	Guy Arab II 6LW	Massey	L27/28R	2/44

181-188, 202-4 were originally fitted with upholstered seats. The rest had wooden slatted seats.
181-5, 202/4-15 were reseated to L27/26R in 1952 (209 to L26/26R). 205-16 received upholstered seatsafter the war – 205/6/11/2 from Leyland TD7s 169-72; 216/7from Park Royal and Massey bodies having their Massey bodies replaced; 209 from Leyland PS1s 200/54-60; 207/8/10/3-5 from Leyland Titans having their Massey bodies respectively.
Eighteen producer gas units were purchased in 1943, of which 14 came from Bristol Tramways. It is not known which vehicles they were attached to, but they were in use at Maryport and Workington until late 1944.
There is some dispute as to whether some of these vehicles carried Gardner 5LW engines or not.

Wartime Utility and immediate Postwar Bedford OWB and OBs

189,190	ERM 680/81	Bedford OWB	S.M.T.	B32F	4/43
23,68	FAO 282/83	Bedford OWB	Duple	B32F	1/44
19,32,72,128,85	FAO 505-10	Bedford OWB	Duple	B32F	6-8/44
52,72,84,174,178	FAO 686-90	Bedford OWB	Duple	B32F	11/44-1/45
248,249	GAO 465/66	Bedford OB	Duple	C29F	7/47
250-253	GAO 467-70	Bedford OB	Duple	C29F	3/48

The Bedford OWBs were originally fitted with wooden slatted seats, but were later replaced by upholstered seats amending the capacity to B30F.
248-51 were hired to West Yorkshire Road Car, Harrogate, for the summer seasons of 1949-51 (248/9), or 1949-50 only (250/1). 249/50 received Perkins P6 diesel engines in 1949.
253 was reseated to C14F in 1952, possibly as a replacement for 175(DRM 710).

Postwar Leyland Tigers 1947-1950

1,9,58,70,73	GAO 501-05	Leyland Tiger PS1	Massey	B32F	2-3/47
89,91,124,179,180	GAO 506-10	Leyland Tiger PS1	ACB	B32R	11/47-1/48
192/6,200/54-60	GAO 511-20	Leyland Tiger PS1	Burlingham	B35F	11/47-1/48
180	HRM 79	Leyland Tiger PS1	ACB	C33F	8/48
3,4,26/29,33,35,43	JAO 831-38	Leyland Tiger PS1/1	ACB	C31F	6-8/49
92,97	JAO 839-40	Leyland Tiger PS1/1	ACB	C31F	8,9/49
54,101,166,173	JRM 189-92	Leyland Tiger PS1/1	Burlingham	C31F	1-3/50
191,193,199	JRM 193-95	Leyland Tiger PS1/1	Burlingham	C31F	1/50
283,284	JRM 196/97	Leyland Tiger PS1/1	Burlingham	C28F	3/50
285	JRM 198	Leyland Tiger PS1/1	Burlingham	C31F	3/50

180(GAO 510) never entered service with Cumberland, and was delivered to H.& I.Moffat, Cleator Moor in exchange for the second 180(HRM 79). It became B31F in 1955, was rebodied by Cumberland themselves, as B34F, 2/58, and converted to pay as you board in 5/60.
Other vehicles receiving new Cumberland B34F bodies were 3,4,26/9,33/4,43,92/7 which received them in 5/58(26), 8/58(34), 11/58(3,92), 1/59(29), 2/59(33), 7/59(43), 10/59(4) or 4/60(97). All were fitted for pay as you board operation at the same time, except 26 (4/60).
35 was fitted with a new ECW FB35F body in 12/58. 4 was fitted with a Gardner 5LW engine in 9/59.
200/54/5/7 received new coach seats in 7/49, becoming DP31F. 200/55/7 reverted to B35F in 1959. 254/60 reverted to bus seating, as B34F, in 11/57, when converted to 'Pay as you Board' operation. 260 was used as a tow vehicle at Workington depot from 1960.
54, 101/66/99 were reseated to B35F by 1955(54), 4/59(101/99), or 6/59(166). In addition a full width front canopy was fitted with bus type destination blinds, and radiused windows with sliding vents were fitted. The latter were fitted to the rest of the 1950 Tigers too, but without other changes. 283/4 were reseated to C31F in 1959.
GAO 512-4/7-20, HRM 79 renumbered 100-107, 11/61. JAO 831-840, JRM 189-198 renumbered 108-127, 11/61.

Bristol Lodekka LD class

353-357	ORM 135-39	Bristol Lodekka LD6G	ECW	H33/25RD	10/54
358-362	ORM 140-44	Bristol Lodekka LD6G	ECW	H33/27RD	3-5/55
363-369	RAO 727-33	Bristol Lodekka LD6G	ECW	H33/27RD	3-6/56
375-379	UAO 375-79	Bristol Lodekka LD6G	ECW	H33/27R	10/57
380-382	UAO 380-82	Bristol Lodekka LD6G	ECW	H33/27R	1-3/58
383-386	VAO 383-86	Bristol Lodekka LD6G	ECW	H33/27RD	3-6/58
387-389	VAO 387-89	Bristol Lodekka LD6B	ECW	H33/27R	3/59
T394,395	VAO 602/03	Bristol Lodekka LD6G	ECW	H33/27R	7/59
C396-399	XAO 604-07	Bristol Lodekka LD6B	ECW	H33/27RD	9/59
T400,401	XAO 608/09	Bristol Lodekka LD6G	ECW	H33/27R	9/59

353-62 were fitted with long apron front grilles. Of these 353/60/2 were fitted with the later type short grille in 2/66(353), 1965(360) or 1968(362). By this time they were renumbered 400/7/9.
369 was fitted with Cave-Browne-Cave heating.
353-369, 383-386 had a C (for Country) prefix added to their fleetnumbers 12/59.
375-382,387-389 had a T (for Town) prefix added to their fleetnumbers 12/59.
(C/T) 353-369, 375-389, 394-401 were renumbered 400-439, 11/61.

Vehicle hired from Eastern National O.C., Chelmsford, 395, 1956

(395)	724 APU	Bristol SC4LK	ECW	B35F	1956

This was the first prototype Bristol SC.

Bristol SC4LK

373,374	UAO 373/74	Bristol SC4LK	ECW	B35F	9/57
391	VAO 391	Bristol SC4LK	ECW	B35F	1/59
402,403	XAO 610/11	Bristol SC4LK	ECW	B35F	6/59

373/4/91, 402/3 were renumbered 200-204, 11/61.

Vehicles acquired from United Counties, Northampton, 4-9/59

206-210	MPU 36-40	Leyland Titan PD1A	ECW	L27/26R	9/47	1959
211-216	MPU 41-3/5-7	Leyland Titan PD1A	ECW	L27/26R	10/47	1959
217	MPU 53	Leyland Titan PD1A	ECW	L27/26R	12/47	1959

Vehicles acquired 4/59 (206/7/11/7), 6/59 (209/15), 8/59 (208/10/3), 9/59 (212/4/6).

They were all new to Eastern National, Chelmsford, 3975-82/4-6/92. 212 had received a Gardner 5LW engine whilst with United Counties.
206-210/2-7 were renumbered 300-310, 11/61.

Vehicles hired from Crosville M.S., Chester, 12/60

DTO 584,585 HRM 704/5	Leyland Titan PD2/1	Leyland	L27/26R	1949	12/60

These were returned 4/61. These were built for Cumberland, but diverted to Crosville before delivery.

Vehicles acquired from United Counties, Northampton, 12/60

204	JEV 417	Bristol K5G	ECW	L27/28R	8/40	12/60
205	JEV 422	Bristol K5G	ECW	L27/28R	11/40	12/60

These were the only Bristol K types ever owned by Cumberland. They only lasted until 5/62.
They were new to Eastern National, Chelmsford, 3826/31.
204/5 were renumbered 600/1, 11/61.

Bristol Lodekka FSF and FLF series

C404-C408	501-05 BRM	Bristol Lodekka FSF6B	ECW	H34/26F	10-11/60
C409-C413	506-10 DRM	Bristol Lodekka FLF6LX	ECW	H38/32F	11-12/60
C421-C425	114-18 DRM	Bristol Lodekka FLF6LX	ECW	H38/32F	7-11/61
515-520	709-14 GRM	Bristol Lodekka FLF6LX	ECW	H38/32F	8-12/62
521	AAO 36B	Bristol Lodekka FLF6L	ECW	H38/32F	3/64
522-524	AAO 37-39B	Bristol Lodekka FLF6L	ECW	H38/32F	3/64
525	AAO 575B	Bristol Lodekka FLF6LX	ECW	H38/32F	11/64
526	CAO 649B	Bristol Lodekka FLF6LX	ECW	H38/32F	11/64
527	CRM 211B	Bristol Lodekka FLF6LX	ECW	H38/32F	12/64
528	CRM 472C	Bristol Lodekka FLF6LX	ECW	H38/32F	1/65
529-532	DAO 201-04C	Bristol Lodekka FLF6LX	ECW	H38/32F	2,8,8,9/65
533-535	HRM 533-35D	Bristol Lodekka FLF6LX	ECW	H38/32F	6/66

C424 had an illuminated offside advert panel.
C404-C425 were renumbered 500-514, 11/61.
522-35 were fitted with Cave-Browne-Cave heating systems.
522-524 were fitted with Leyland 0.600 engines from new.
522 was fitted with a Gardner 6LX engine in 3/76.

Bristol Lodekka FS class

C416-C420	109-13 DRM	Bristol Lodekka FS6G	ECW	H33/27RD	4/61
555-560	715-20 GRM	Bristol Lodekka FS6B	ECW	H33/27RD	10-12/62
561,562	420/21 LAO	Bristol Lodekka FS6B	ECW	H33/27RD	11/63
563,564	AAO 573/74B	Bristol Lodekka FS6B	ECW	H33/27RD	3/64
565	BRM 79B	Bristol Lodekka FS6B	ECW	H33/27RD	7/64

C416-420 were renumbered 550-554, 11/61. Of these 550 is now preserved.
561-563 were fitted with Cave-Browne-Cave heating systems.
554 was converted to a permanent driver training vehicle 4/76 and renumbered TV1, after being a temporary trainer/PSV from 11/73. It was painted in all white with a red band.

Bristol MW service buses

414,415	511/12 BRM	Bristol MW6G	ECW	DP41F	7,2/60
426,427	119/20 BRM	Bristol MW6G	ECW	DP41F	10/61
227,228	425/26 LAO	Bristol MW6G	ECW	B45F	12/63
231,232	AAO 34,35B	Bristol MW6G	ECW	B45F	4/64
233-240	DAO 205-12C	Bristol MW6G	ECW	B45F	4-11/65
241	FRM 617C	Bristol MW6G	ECW	B45F	12/65
242-246	JAO 242-46D	Bristol MW6G	ECW	B45F	9-12/66

414/5,426/7 were renumbered 225/6, 286/7 12/61. 286/7, 227/8 were renumbered 227-230 4/64.
225-228 were fitted for 'Pay as you Board' operation in 1964. All others were so fitted from new.
226/34/5/9/41 lost their front grille louvres in 1969, being replaced by blank panels.
225 was converted to a towing vehicle 8/77. 231 was sold for preservation.

Vehicles acquired from United Counties O.C., Northampton, 128-30, 2/63

205-207	ONV 428-30	Bristol SC4LK	ECW	B35F	9-10/57	2/63

These were fitted for 'Pay as you Board' operation on arrival.

Vehicle acquired from United Welsh Services, Swansea, 112, 10/63

208	OCY 952	Bristol SC4LK	ECW	B35F	12/57	10/63

These were fitted for 'Pay as you Board' operation on arrival.

Vehicles acquired from Eastern National O.C., Chelmsford, 435-437, 1/64

209-211	605-7 JPU	Bristol SC4LK	ECW	B35F	3-5/57	1/64

These were fitted for 'Pay as you Board' operation on arrival.

Bedford Coaches

300	FRM 618C	Bedford VAL14	Duple	C51F	12/65
301	GAO 38D	Bedford VAL14	Duple	C51F	1/66
302,303	LAO 580/81E	Bedford VAL14	Duple	C51F	5/67
1304	ORM 991F	Bedford VAM70	Duple	C45F	5/68
1305	TAO 263G	Bedford VAM70	Duple	C45F	4/69

300/1 were the first non Bristol vehicles delivered new since 1953.
300-303 were renumbered 1300-1303 1/68.

Vehicles acquired from United Automobile Services Ltd., Darlington, LU1-5, 4/67

162-166	RHN 763-767	Ld.R.Tiger PSU1/13	ECW	B45F	1953	4/67

These were originally ordered by Cumberland but were diverted to United A.S..
162 was used as a decimal currency training unit after withdrawal in 1970.

Bristol RELL and Bristol RELH

250,251	JAO 250/51D	Bristol RELL6G	ECW	B54F	10/66
252,253	KRM 252/53E	Bristol RELL6L	ECW	B53F	7/67
254-256	KRM 260-62E	Bristol RELL6L	ECW	B53F	8/67
257	KRM 257E	Bristol RELL6L	ECW	B53F	8/67
258-263	MRM 258-63F	Bristol RELL6L	ECW	B53F	9/67
264-276	OAO 264-76F	Bristol RELL6L	ECW	B53F	3-7/68
277-280	TAO 277-80G	Bristol RELL6L	ECW	B53F	6/69
281-288	VAO 281-88H	Bristol RELL6L	ECW	B53F	11/69-3/70
289-291	ARM 389-91J	Bristol RELL6L	ECW	B53F	6/71
292-295	DAO 292-95K	Bristol RELL6L	ECW	B53F	1/72
296-98	DAO 296-98K	Bristol RELL6L	ECW	DP50F	5/72
299	GAO 699L	Bristol RELL6L	ECW	B53F	8/72
300-302	GRM 300-2L	Bristol RELL6L	ECW	B53F	8/72
600	DRM 600K	Bristol RELH6L	ECW	DP49F	6/72

250-88 were fitted for 'Pay as you Board' operation in 1969-71. The remainder, and all future vehicles (excluding some coaches), where appropriate, were delivered as such. 293/295 were acquired for preservation late 1995.

Vehicle hired from Bristol Commercial Vehicles Ltd., 4/69

......	NHU 100P	Bristol LHX6P	ECW	B45F	1967

This was on demonstration duties 1-7/4/69.

Bristol LH saloons and Coach

100,101	WAO 100/1H	Bristol LH6P	ECW	B45F	4/70
102-105	XAO 732-35H	Bristol LH6P	ECW	B45F	8/70
106-116	XRM 106-16J	Bristol LH6P	ECW	B45F	9/70-2/71
1310	WAO 289H	Bristol LH6P	Plaxton	C45F	4/70

Vehicle acquired from Midland General O.C., Langley Mill, 251, 10/71

220	965 ARA	Bristol LS6G	ECW	B43F	1956	10/71

Vehicle hired from Eastern Counties O.C., Norwich, LHS596, during 3/72

(LHS596)	WNG 102H	Bristol LHS6P	ECW	B37F	12/69	3/72

This was on hire for evaluation.

Vehicle acquired from Ribble M.S., Preston, 1027, 4/72

1300	PCK 609	Leyland Leopard L2T	Harrington	C41F	7/61	4/72

This was originally C32F in the Ribble tours fleet. It became C41F in 4/66.

Ford Coaches

801-807	ERM 801-7K	Ford R1014	Duple	C45F	6-8/72
808	NRM 538M	Ford R1114	Duple	C53F	8/73
809	NRM 809M	Ford R1114	Duple	C53F	10/73
810-812	PAO 810-12M	Ford R1114	Duple	C53F	5-8/74

All were fitted for 'Pay as you Board' operation from new.

Leyland National 1s

350	ERM 35K	LN 1151/2R/0401	LN	B48D	3/72
351-354	GRM 351-54L	LN 1151/1R/0401	LN	B52F	1-2/73
355-358	LRM 565-68L	LN 1151/1R/0401	LN	B52F	7/73
359-362	NAO 359-62M	LN 1151/1R/0401	LN	B52F	7/73
363,364	OAO 563/64M	LN 1151/1R/0401	LN	B52F	8/73
365,366	GAO 707/8N	LN 11351/1R	LN	B52F	12/73
367-369	MAO 367-69P	LN 11351/1R	LN	B52F	11/74
					3/76

350 was the first Leyland National in public service, and was one of the pre production prototypes, and entered service 16/3/72 on Whitehaven town service 05(West Cumberland Hospital to Bransty) after an initial run on service 41 (Workington - Lowca - Whitehaven).
367-9 were diverted from a Western Welsh, Cardiff, order, where they were to have been N32-N34.75.

Bristol VRT double deckers

400-405	HHH 271-76N	Bristol VRT/SL2/6LX	ECW	H43/34F	3-4/75
406	NHH 406P	Bristol VRT/SL3/6LXB	ECW	H43/31F	6/76
407-9	PHH 407-9R	Bristol VRT/SL3/501	ECW	H43/31F	12/76
410-413	SAO 410-413R	Bristol VRT/SL3/501	ECW	H43/31F	5-6/77
414-416	WHH 414-16S	Bristol VRT/SL3/501	ECW	H43/31F	5/78
417-429	FAO 417-29V	Bristol VRT/SL3/6LXB	ECW	H43/31F	1-2/80
430-437	KRM 430-37W	Bristol VRT/SL3/6LXB	ECW	H43/31F	10/80

All these vehicles were of the lowheight 13'5" variety. Alternative heights were standard at 13'8" and highbridge at 14'6". Cumberland never bought any of the latter 2 types new, but acquired examples of both from Ribble.

Vehicles acquired from Ribble M.S., Preston, 780/3/91, 6/76

610	ARN 780C	Ld.Leopard PSU3/3RT	Plaxton	C49F	2/65	6/76
611,612	ARN 783/91C	Ld.Leopard PSU3/3RT	Plaxton	C49F	1/65	6/76

Vehicles acquired from Midland Red O.C., Smethwick, 6154/41/3/6/7, 1-2/77

601	SHA 654G	Ld.Leopard PSU4A/4R	Plaxton	C36F	5/69	1/77
602-605	SHA 641/3/6/7G	Ld.Leopard PSU4A/4R	Plaxton	C36F	5/69	2/77

These were all reseated to C40F and modified for 'Pay as you Board' operation in 1977. They were mainly for use on the sparsely used services from Millom area, including the Millom to Seascale leg of the Millom to Whitehaven service, which passed through the tight Seascale railway arch.

Leyland Leopard Coaches 1977-1982

613	PHH 613R	Ld.Leopard PSU3D/4RT	Duple D1	C49F	4/77
614-618	THH 614-18S	Ld.Leopard PSU3E/4RT	Duple D1	C49F	9-11/77
619-622	VRM 619-22S	Ld.Leopard PSU3E/4RT	Duple D2	C49F	5-6/78
623,625,626	GRM 623/5/6V	Ld.Leopard PSU3E/4RT	Duple D2	C49F	7/80
624,627	LAO 624/27W	Ld.Leopard PSU3E/4RT	Duple D2	C49F	8/80
628-632	PRM 628-32X	Ld.Leopard PSU3F/4RT	Willowbrook	C49F	12/81
633-637	RRM 633-37X	Ld.Leopard PSU3G/4RT	ECW	C49F	4/82
638-642	VAO 638-642Y	Ld.Leopard PSU3G/4RT	ECW	C49F	10/82

623-627 were named 'Lady Florence', 'Lady Nin', 'Lady Betty', 'Lady Margaret', & 'Lady Mary'.
623/5 did actually carry the above names until early 1982. The names on 623/6 were exchanged in mid 1982.
These names were the same as those carried by the Whitehaven M.S. charabancs in 1912-21.
628-632 were named 'River Ehen', 'River Waver', 'River Esk', 'River Cocker', & 'River Derwent'. These names only lasted until 10/84 when they were allocated the following, in order - 'River Calder', 'River Cocker', 'River Ehen', 'River Waver', 'River Derwent', 632 being the only coach retaining its former name. 633-637 were named 'Great Gable', 'Scafell Pike', 'Helvellyn', 'Skiddaw', & 'Pillar Rock' with a painting of the location above the name.

Vehicles acquired from Ribble M.S., Preston, same fleetnumbers, 2-8/78

629	CRN 629D	Ld.Leopard PSU4/2R	Marshall	B44F	4/66	3/78
630	CRN 630D	Ld.Leopard PSU4/2R	Marshall	B44F	4/66	2/78
632	CRN 632D	Ld.Leopard PSU4/2R	Marshall	B44F	4/66	8/78
633	CRN 633D	Ld.Leopard PSU4/2R	Marshall	B44F	4/66	3/78
634,635	CRN 634/35D	Ld.Leopard PSU4/2R	Marshall	B44F	5,4/66	2/78
636,637	CRN 636/37D	Ld.Leopard PSU4/2R	Marshall	B44F	5,4/66	7/78
638,639	CRN 638/39D	Ld.Leopard PSU4/2R	Marshall	B44F	4/66	2/78
640,644	CRN 640/44D	Ld.Leopard PSU4/2R	Marshall	B44F	5,4/66	2/78
641,642,646	CRN 641/2/6D	Ld.Leopard PSU4/2R	Marshall	B44F	5/66	3/78

Leyland National B type 'Country Cousins'

201-205	AHH 201-5T	LN 10351B/1R	LN	B44F	10/78
206-209	AHH 206-9T	LN 10351B/1R	LN	B44F	3/79
210-215	CHH 210-5T	LN 10351B/1R	LN	B44F	4-5/79

Vehicle acquired from National Travel (London) Ltd., London SE6, 4/79

610	VYM 505M	Ld.Leopard PSU3B/4RT	Plaxton	C49F	4/74	4/79

This vehicle was new to National Travel(South East) Ltd., London SE6. It was converted for 'Pay as you Board' operation 4/80.

Vehicles acquired from Trent Motor Traction, Derby, 41-4, 7/80

606-609	ACH 141-44H	Ld.Leopard PSU4A/4R	Plaxton	C40F	4/70	7/80

These were replacements for earlier 601-5.

Leyland National 2s

370-373	HHH 370-73V	LN 2 NL116L11/1R	LN	B52F	5-6/80
374-378	KHH 374-78W	LN 2 NL116L11/1R	LN	B52F	8-10/80
379-382	NHH 379-82W	LN 2 NL116AL11/1R	LN	B52F	6/81
383-386	RRM 383-86X	LN 2 NL116AL11/1R	LN	B52F	11-12/81
387-394	SHH 387-94X	LN 2 NL116AL11/1R	LN	B52F	1-5/82
395-399	WAO 395-9Y	LN 2 NL116HLXB/1R	LN	B52F	11-12/82

395-399 were the first Leyland Nationals to be fitted with Gardner engines.

Leyland Olympians 1982

801,802	URM 801/02Y	Ld.Olympian ONLXB/1R	ECW	H45/32F	12/82

They were renumbered 1001/2 in 9/85 and 4/86 respectively, and were reseated to CH45/30F in 4-5/86. 1002 was reseated to H45/30F (bus seats) in 1994.

Leyland Tigers from 1983

643-646	WAO 643-46Y	Ld.Tiger TRCTL11/2R	Alexander	C47F	3/83
101,102	A101/2 DAO	Ld.Tiger TRCTL11/3R	Duple L1	C50F	2/84
103-108	B103-8 HAO	Ld.Tiger TRCTL11/3RH	Duple L2	C53F	10-11/84
109,110	C109/10 OHH	Ld.Tiger TRCTL11/3RH	Plaxton	C46FT	4,3/86

101 was reregistered 109 DRM, 4/90, the mark formerly carried by Bristol Lodekka 550.
107 was reregistered TCK 841, 8/92, a mark formerly carried by a Ribble Leyland Titan PD3/5.
108 was reregistered WLT 713, 3/92, a mark formerly carried by Cumberland Routemaster 900.
Several seating changes took place among the above vehicles as follows:-

101 to C44FT c2/86; to C51F 2/88.
103 to C49FT c4/85; to C50F 3/86.
104 to C49FT 5/85; to C50F 4/86.
105 to C49FT 3/85; to C53F 4/87.
106 to C49FT 3/85 and remained so.
107 to C44FT 4/85; to C51F 4/89; to C44FT 11/89; to C46FT 3/92.
108 to C44FT 4/85.
109, and possibly 110, to C48FT 3/92.

Vehicles acquired from Ribble M.S., Preston, same numbers, 23/2/86

with the transfer of Carlisle and Penrith depots to Cumberland.

748	UHG 748R	LN 11351A/1R	LN	B49F	9/76	2/86
752	UHG 752R	LN 11351A/1R	LN	B49F	10/76	2/86
756	UHG 756R	LN 11351A/1R	LN	B49F	1/77	2/86
801	GCW 461S	LN 10351B/1R	LN	B44F	1977	2/86
802	TRN 802V	LN 10351B/1R	LN	B44F	7/79	2/86
809-812	TRN 809-12V	LN 10351B/1R	LN	B44F	8-9/79	2/86
882,883	RHG 882/83X	LN 2 NL116AL11/1R	LN	B52F	5/82	2/86
885,887	RHG 885/87X	LN 2 NL116AL11/1R	LN	B52F	6/82	2/86
895-898	ARN 895-98Y	LN 2 NL116HLXB/1R	LN	B52F	3/83	2/86
1000	TRN 801V	Ford Transit	Dormobile	B16F	10/79	2/86
1082	PCW 682P	Ld.Leopard PSU3C/4R	Duple D1	C49F	7/76	2/86
1086	VRN 86R	Ld.Leopard PSU3D/4R	Duple D1	C47F	12/76	2/86
1108,1109	KRN 108/9T	Ld.Leopard PSU3E/4R	Duple D2	C47F	12/78	2/86
1110	KRN 110T	Ld.Leopard PSU3E/4R	Duple D2	C47F	1/79	2/86
1115,1116	KRN 115/16T	Ld.Leopard PSU3E/4R	Duple D2	C47F	4,3/79	2/86
1118,1119	KRN 118/19T	Ld.Leopard PSU3E/4R	Duple D2	C47F	5,4/79	2/86
1126,1127	WCK 126/27V	Ld.Leopard PSU3E/4R	Duple D2	C51F	11/79	2/86
1128,1129	WCK 128/29V	Ld.Leopard PSU3E/4R	Duple D2	C49F	11/79	2/86
1133	WCK 133V	Ld.Leopard PSU3E/4R	Duple D2	C49F	12/79	2/86
1136,1140	WCK 136/40V	Ld.Leopard PSU3E/4R	Duple D2	C49F	1/80	2/86
1449-1459	LHG 449-59T	Bristol VRT/SL3/501+	ECW	H43/31F	3-6/79	2/86
1460-1465	TRN 460-65V	Bristol VRT/SL3/501+	ECW	H43/31F	11/79	2/86
1467-1485	TRN 467-85V	Ld.Atlantean AN68A/1R	ECW	H43/31F	7/79-1/80	2/86
2002,2017	CBV 2,17S	Bristol VRT/SL3/501+	ECW	H43/31F	7-10/77	2/86
2024,2032	DBV 24,32W	Bristol VRT/SL3/6LXB	ECW	H43/31F	8-10/80	2/86
BD3	FWB 563S	Leyland Buffalo		Recovery Vehicle	1977	

+ - Vehicles were fitted with Gardner engines by Ribble around 1982/83.

Vehicle acquired from Ribble M.S., Preston, 309, 4/86

For spares	LRN 309J	Bristol RESL6L	Marshall	B47F	3/71	4/86

This was acquired in burnt out condition. The mechanical parts were used for spares and the rest sold for scrap.

Vehicles acquired from Bristol O.C., Bristol, 1307/21-4/6/8-30, 4/86

900	HHW 920L	Bristol RELL6L	ECW	B44D	11/72	4/86
901-904	MHW 281-84L	Bristol RELL6L	ECW	B44D	6-7/73	4/86
905-908	OHU 34/6-8M	Bristol RELL6L	ECW	B44D	7-8/73	4/86

These vehicles retained National Bus Company leaf green when repainted, and were for use on Sellafield internal site services.

Fellrunner Ford Transit

3000	C209 PAO	Ford Transit	Mellor	C16F		4/86

This was purchased partly by Cumbria County Council and partly by Cumberland M.S. and was operated by Langwathby and District Community Transport. Like its predecessor, 1000(TRN 801V), it was named the 'Fellrunner'. Maintenance was carried out by Cumberland.

Minibuses 1986/87

21-32	D21-32 SAO	Renault Dodge S56	Reebur	B23F	9-10/86
33,34,36,38,40	D33 UAO etc.	Mercedes-Benz L608D	Reebur	B20F	12/86
35,37,39	D35 UAO etc.	Mercedes-Benz L608D	Reebur	B20F	1/87
41-46	D41-46 UAO	Mercedes-Benz L608D	Reebur	B20F	2/87

Vehicle acquired from S.Rae, Whitehaven, 6/87

MTV1	RSM 520S	Bedford CF	Reebur	C17F	6/78	6/87

This was new to Gallacher, Eastriggs, near Annan, passing to Rae in 1986. It was used on the Sellafield internal site services as well as for minibus driver training.

Vehicles hired from Carlyle, Birmingham (bodybuilder), from 7-8/87

S1,S2	D736/5 OOG	Freight Rover Sherpa	Carlyle	B18F	c3/87	7/87
S3	E105 SOG	Freight Rover Sherpa	Carlyle	B18F	7/87	8/87
S4	D275 OOJ	Freight Rover Sherpa	Carlyle II	B20F	7/87	8/87

These were on hire to work the Sellafield internal site services after the former Bristol Omnibus Bristol REs were sold. They were all returned 10/87.

Vehicles acquired from London Transport, RM713, RM2024, 8/87

(via Stagecoach, Perth)

900	WLT 713	AEC/PRV Routemaster	P.Royal	H36/28R	1961	8/87
901	ALM 24B	AEC/PRV Routemaster	P.Royal	H36/28R	1964	8/87

These vehicles were used in Carlisle on city service 61(Morton Park-Harraby East). See below for further details. 900 was reregistered TSK 270, 3/92.

Vehicles acquired from Kelvin Scottish, Bishopbriggs,
RM1941/83/33,706,875,824, 8/87

902	ALD 941B	AEC/PRV Routemaster	P.Royal	H36/28R	1964	8/87
903	ALD 983B	AEC/PRV Routemaster	P.Royal	H36/28R	1964	8/87
904	ALD 933B	AEC/PRV Routemaster	P.Royal	H36/28R	1964	8/87
905	WLT 706	AEC/PRV Routemaster	P.Royal	H36/28R	1961	8/87
906	WLT 875	AEC/PRV Routemaster	P.Royal	H36/28R	1961/2	8/87
907	WLT 824	AEC/PRV Routemaster	P.Royal	H36/28R	1960/1	8/87

These vehicles were used in Carlisle on service 61 (Morton Park-Harraby East), along with 900/1 above, and were painted Ayres red with a large oatmeal diagonal stripe. The fleetname CMS Carlislebus was carried. These were some of the last vehicles to receive Cumberland livery rather than the impending Stagecoach colours. They were new to London Transport RM1941,1983,1933,706,875,824. 905,907 were reregistered TSK 269/71, 3/92. 906 was reregistered OVS 940, 12/92.

Vehicles acquired from Kirkpatrick's, Brigham, 12/5/88

560	XNE 884L	Ld.Leopard PSU3B/4R	Plaxton	C49F	6/73	5/88
561	LHU 661L	Ld.Leopard PSU3B/4R	Plaxton	C47F	4/73	5/88
562	JAD 880N	Bedford YRQ	Duple D1	C45F	4/75	5/88
563	JRM 381N	Bedford YRT	Duple D1	C53F	7/75	5/88
564	MRA 347P	Bedford YRT	Duple D1	C53F	1/76	5/88
565	LAO 316P	Bedford YRT	Duple D1	C53F	10/75	5/88
566	SDD 144R	Ld.Leopard PSU3D/4R	Plaxton	C53F	3/77	5/88
567	FWP 566S	Bedford VAS5	Duple D1	C29F	5/78	5/88
568	EHE 226V	Bedford YMT	Duple D2	C53F	1/80	5/88
569	LUA 275V	Ld.Leopard PSU3F/4R	Plaxton	C51F	5/80	5/88
570	SND 710X	Ld.Tiger TRCTL11/3R	Plaxton	C53F	3/82	5/88
571	D52 URM	Ford Transit	Mellor	B16F	2/87	5/88

These vehicles were acquired with Kirkpatrick's business, 5/88, and were new to the following:-
560 to SELNEC PTE, Manchester, 72.; 561 to Bristol O.C., Bristol, 2300.;
562 to Warner, Tewkesbury; 564 to Butler, Kirkby-in-Ashfield.; 565 to Rae, Whitehaven.;
566 to National Travel South West, Cheltenham, 144.; 567 to Coaches, Catshill.;
568 to National Travel East, Sheffield.; 569 to Wallace Arnold, Leeds.;
570 to Yelloway M.S., Rochdale.; 563/71 were new to Kirkpatricks.

Vehicles acquired from United Counties, Northampton, 237/40, 150-4, 5/88

1148,1149	KVV 237/40V	Ld.Leopard PSU3F/4R	Willowbrook	C49F	2/80	5/88
1150	UVV 150W	Ld.Leopard PSU3F/4R	Willowbrook	C49F	5/81	5/88
1151,1154	UVV 151/54W	Ld.Leopard PSU3F/4R	Willowbrook	C49F	6/81	5/88
1152,1153	UVV 152/53W	Ld.Leopard PSU3F/4R	Willowbrook	C47F	6/81	5/88

In the main these were purchased to replace the former Kirkpatricks Bedfords.

Standard Stagecoach Vehicles —

47-50	E47-50 CHH	Mercedes Benz 709D	Alexander	B25F	4/88*

(*Note - 49 was new 5/88)

Standard Stagecoach Vehicles —   Leyland Olympians 1988-1992

1003-1011	F803-11 FAO	Ld.On ON6LXB/2RZ	Alexander	H51/36F	9/88
1201,1202	F201/2 FAO	Ld.On ON6LXCT/5RZ	Alexander	CH55/41F	2/89
1012-1019	H112-19 SAO	Ld.On ON2R56G13Z4	Alexander	H51/34F	8/90
1020-1024	J120-24 XHH	Ld.On ON2R56G13Z4	Alexander	CH47/27F	9/81
1025-1027	J125-27 XHH	Ld.On ON2R56G13Z4	Alexander	CH47/27F	10/81
1020-1022	J120-22 AAO	Ld.On ON2R56G13Z4	Alexander	CH47/27F	11/81
1028-1035	K128-35 DAO	Ld.On ON2R50G13Z4	Alexander	CH43/27F	10/92

1020-2/4 (J120-2/4 XHH) were hired to Northern Scottish, Aberdeen, from new for use inInverness. 1024 finally arrived with Cumberland 11/91. 1020-2 never arrived with Cumberland and were sold to Northern Scottish 11/91 and replaced at Cumberland with the new 1020-2(J120-2 AAO).
1028-35 were shorter vehicles.
1003-35 were retrofitted with front electronic blinds 11-12/93(1003-19), 3-5/93(1020-35). Side/rear electronic number blinds were fittedto 1020-35 when new. 1016 was fitted with an experimental 3 line electronic blind in 1995.

Vehicles hired from Hampshire Bus, Eastleigh, 1928-30/5, from 9/87

1928,1929	LWB 379/80P	Volvo Ailsa B55-10	VHMA	H44/31D	6/76	9/87
1930	LWB 383P	Volvo Ailsa B55-10	VHMA	H44/31D	6/76	9/87
1935	NAK 415R	Volvo Ailsa B55-10	VHMA	H44/31D	c10/76	9/87

Disused from 10/87 and left 12/87, direct to Magic Bus, Glasgow.

Vehicles acquired from Hampshire Bus, Eastleigh, 1917-26, 3618, 180, 10/87-1/88

1917,1918	OUC 39,40R	Ld.Fleetline FE30AGR	MCW	H44/32F	10/76	10/87
1919,1920	OJD 170/94R	Ld.Fleetline FE30AGR	MCW	H44/32F	11/76	10/87
1921	OJD 203R	Ld.Fleetline FE30AGR	MCW	H44/32F	1/77	10/87
1922	OUC 55R	Ld.Fleetline FE30AGR	MCW	H44/32F	10/76	10/87
1923,1924	OJD 169/97R	Ld.Fleetline FE30AGR	MCW	H44/32F	12/76	10/87
1925	OJD 224R	Ld.Fleetline FE30AGR	MCW	H44/32F	4/77	10/87
1926	OJD 245R	Ld.Fleetline FE30AGR	MCW	H44/32F	6/77	10/87
358	NEL 861M	LN1151/1R/2402	LN	B49F	11/73	11/87
111	B180 RLJ	Ld.Tiger TRCTL11/3RH	Plaxton	C48FT	1/85	1/88

1917-26 and the Routemasters 900-907 came in part exchange for highbridge VRs 1449-65 at Carlisle.

Vehicles acquired from Kelvin Scottish, Bishopbriggs 1275/61/2/5/8, 2006/9, 1201-3, 11/87-1/88

300	YFS 305W	LN2 NL116AL11/1R	LN	B52F	2/81	11/87
301,302	SNS 831/22W	LN2 NL116AL11/1R	LN	B52F	12/80	11/87
303,304	SNS 825/28W	LN2 NL116AL11/1R	LN	B52F	12/90	11/87
612	GLS 267S	Ld.Leopard PSU3D/4R	Alexander T	DP49F	1/78	12/87
613	GLS 275S	Ld.Leopard PSU3E/4R	Alexander T	DP49F	1/78	12/87
216	OLS 806T	LN 10351B/1R	LN	B44F	9/78	1/88
217,218	OLS 807/9T	LN 10351B/1R	LN	B44F	9/78	12/87

All were refurbished by Cumberland on acquisition. 612/3 were placed on the 685 service from Carlisle to Newcastle.

Vehicle acquired from Stagecoach, Perth, 2/88

600	PVO 22X	Volvo B58-61	Duple D3	C57F	by7/82	2/88

This vehicle had been on hire since 10/87.

Vehicles acquired from Yeowart, Whitehaven, 12/5/88

500	YHA 333J	Ford R192	Plaxton Dt	B45F	12/70	5/88
501	VOD 102K	Bristol RELL6G	ECW	B53F	1971	5/88
502	NFM 843M	LN1151/1R/0405	LN	DP48F	11/73	5/88
503	HWU 74N	Ld.Leopard PSU3C/4R	Duple D1	C53F	1975	5/88
504	SKO 273R	Ford R1014	Plaxton D1	B45F	3/77	5/88
505	LUA 273V	Ld.Leopard PSU3F/4R	Plaxton Sup	C53F	6/80	5/88
506	A459 FHH	Ld.Tiger TRCTL11/2R	Duple D4	C53F	6/84	5/88
507	C293 PAO	Mercedes Benz L608D	Reebur	B20F	3/86	5/88
508	D895 VAO	Mercedes Benz 609D	Reebur	B20F	3/87	5/88
509	E986 AHH	DAF SB2305DHTD585	Plaxton P3	C53F	1/88	5/88
------	C801 KBT	Leyland Cub	Optare	DP33F	5/86	5/88

These vehicles were acquired with Yeowart's business, 5/88.
C801 KBT was not used by Cumberland and was on the premises of Hughes(dealer), Cleckheaton at the time of sale as Yeowarts had placed it up for sale. 506-509 were new to Yeowart

Vehicles acquired from Ribble M.S., Preston, 18/6/89, on the transfer of Ribble's South Cumbria operations to Cumberland

Fleet	Reg	Chassis	Body	Seating	New	Acq
70,71	D78/79 RVM	Peugeot Talbot Pullman	Talbot	B20F	6/87	6/89
72-74	D80-82 RVM	Peugeot Talbot Pullman	Talbot	B20F	7/87	6/89
75	E509 UNE	Peugeot Talbot Pullman	Talbot	B20F	8/87	6/89
76,77	E717/27 UNA	Peugeot Talbot Pullman	Talbot	B20F	8/87	6/89
78	E737 UNA	Peugeot Talbot Pullman	Talbot	B20F	8/87	6/89
79	D86 RVM	Peugeot Talbot Pullman	Talbot	B20F	7/87	6/89
156	B156 WRN	Ld.Tiger TRCTL11/2R	Duple L2	C53F	1/85	6/89
271,272	FBV 271/72W	Bristol LHS6L	ECW	B35F	10/80	6/89
426,434(Loan)	NTC 606/14M	LN 1151/1R/0402	LN	B49F	c9/73	6/89
440	NTC 620M	LN 1151/1R/0402	LN	B49F	10/73	6/89
446	NTC 626M	LN 1151/1R/0402	LN	B49F	12/73	6/89
517	D517 RCK	Mercedes Benz L608D	Reebur	DP19F	9/86	6/89
518-520	D518-20 RCK	Mercedes Benz L608D	Reebur	DP19F	10/86	6/89
522-534	D522-34 RCK	Mercedes Benz L608D	Reebur	B20F	8/86	6/89
557,558	D557/58 RCK	Mercedes Benz L608D	Reebur	B20F	9/86	6/89
559-562	D559-62 RCK	Mercedes Benz L608D	Reebur	B20F	10/86	6/89
716	UHG 716R	LN 11351A/1R	LN	B49F	1977	6/89
744(Loan)	UHG 744R	LN 11351A/1R	LN	B49F	1977	6/89
755	NEO 829R	LN 11351A/1R	LN	B49F	3/77	7/89
757,758	NEO 830/1R	LN 11351A/1R	LN	B49F	3/77	7/89
760	NEO 833R	LN 11351A/1R	LN	B49F	3/77	6/89
761,762	UEO 478/79T	LN 11351A/1R	LN	B49F	8/78	6/89
803,804,806	TRN 803/4/6V	LN 10351B/1R	LN	B44F	7/79	6/89
807,808	TRN 807/8V	LN 10351B/1R	LN	B44F	8/79	6/89
813,814	YRN 813/14V	LN2 NL106L11/1R	LN	B44F	5/80	6/89
842	DBV 842W	LN2 NL106L11/1R	LN	B44F	11/80	6/89
847	JCK 847W	LN2 NL106AL11/1R	LN	B44F	6/81	6/89
856,857,860	LFR 856/7/60X	LN2 NL106AL11/1R	LN	B44F	9/81	6/89
861-864	LFR 861-64X	LN2 NL106AL11/1R	LN	B44F	10/81	6/89
872,873	LFR 872/73X	LN2 NL116AL11/1R	LN	B44F	12/81	6/89
881	RHG 881X	LN2 NL116HLXB11/1R	LN	B52F	5/82	6/89
892	ARN 892Y	LN2 NL116L11/1R	LN	B52F	2/83	6/89
895	CEO 720W	LN2 NL116L11/1R	LN	DP45F	9/80	6/89
896-898	CEO 721-23W	LN2 NL116L11/1R	LN	B49F	9/80	6/89
1044,1045	UTF 724/25M	Ld.Leopard PSU3B/4R	Duple D1	C49F	5/74	6/89
1052,1055,105	UTF 732/5/6M	Ld.Leopard PSU3B/4R	Duple D1	C49F	8/74	6/89
1088,1091	YFR 488/91R	Ld.Leopard PSU3E/4R	Duple D1	C47F	5/77	6/89
1094	YFR 494R	Ld.Leopard PSU3E/4R	Duple D1	C47F	6/77	6/89
1103	KRN 103T	Ld.Leopard PSU3E/4R	Duple D2	C47F	9/78	6/89
1104,1105	KRN 104/5T	Ld.Leopard PSU3E/4R	Duple D2	C47F	10/78	6/89
1113	KRN 113T	Ld.Leopard PSU3E/4R	Duple D2	C47F	2/79	6/89
1117	KRN 117T	Ld.Leopard PSU3E/4R	Duple D2	C47F	5/79	6/89
1169,1175	MRJ 269/75W	Ld.Leopard PSU5C/4R	Plaxton	C50F	2/81	6/89
1199	FDV 799V	Ld.Leopard PSU5C/4R	Plaxton	C49F	11/79	6/89
1237	BNB 237T	Ld.Leopard PSU5C/4R	Duple D2	C50F	2/79	6/89
1247	BNB 247T	Ld.Leopard PSU5C/4R	Plaxton	C50F	8/79	6/89
1253	HNE 253V	Ld.Leopard PSU5C/4R	Plaxton	C53F	1/80	6/89
1405-1411	RFR 405-11P	Ld.Atlantean AN68/1R	ECW	H43/31F	4/76+	6/89
1413/15/17-24	RFR 413P etc.	Ld.Atlant eanAN68/1R	ECW	H43/31F	5/76+	6/89
1425/26	SFV 425/26P	Ld.Atlantean AN68/1R	ECW	H43/31F	6/76	6/89

(+ 1406 was new 3/76 and 1417 was new 4/76)

2134	DBV 134Y	Ld.Olympian ONLXB/1R	ECW	H45/32F	5/83	6/89
2175-2177	C175-77 ECK	Ld.Olympian ONLXB/1R	ECW	CH42/30F	11/85	6/89
3781	PTF 724L	LN 1151/2R/0401	LN	B49F	10/72	6/89
5031,5041	D503/4 RCK	Mercedes Benz L608D	Reebur	DP19F	8/86	6/89
HGV1	D994 SCW	Leyland Roadtrain 8-12	Drop sided lorry		1986	6/89

Vehicles acquired from Cook & Marshall, Egremont, 9/88

Fleet	Reg	Chassis	Body	Seating	New	Acq
80	D217 NUR	Iveco 49.10	Robin Hood	C21F	11/86	9/88
70	D639 VAO	Ford Transit	Mellor	B16F	3/87	9/88
90	E317 BRM	MCW Metrorider MF150	MCW	C25F	3/88	9/88
91	E855 BRM	MCW Metrorider MF150	MCW	B25F	3/88	9/88
---	E 66 BVS	Iveco 49.10	Robin Hood	B25F	1/88	9/88
---	RRR 515R	Bedford YRT	Plaxton	C53F	1976	9/88
---	OAG 175P	Ld.Leopard PSU3C/4R	Plaxton	C49F	7/76	9/88

The above vehicles were acquired when Cook and Marshall ceased their stage carriage services in the West Cumbria area. E66 BVS, RRR 515R and OAG 175P were not used by Cumberland.

Vehicles acquired from Magic Bus(Scotland), Glasgow, 10/88

151	VLF 578	Volvo B10M	Van Hool	C40FT	4/81	10/88
152	RUT 842	Volvo B10M	Van Hool	C40FT	3/82	10/88
153	LJC 800	Volvo B10M	Van Hool	C40FT	4/82	10/88
154	VRR 447	Volvo B10M	Van Hool	C40FT	4/82	10/88
155	ORY 640	Volvo B10M	Van Hool	C40FT	4/82	10/88

These vehicles were refurbished by Stuart Johnson, Worksop (dealer) before entry into service. They lost their toilets and were reseated to C48F. 151 was originally registered TGD 766W. They were the first vehicles in the fleet with non age related registrations.

Vehicles acquired from Southdown M.S., Brighton, 3200, 10/88

(3200)	PRX 186B	Leyland Titan PD3/4	N.Counties	FH39/30F	1964	10/88

This was acquired for driver training but was never used. It was dismantled 6/90 and the remains sold. Originally registered 400 DCD.

Vehicles acquired from Hampshire Bus, Eastleigh, 50-2, 2-3/89

51	E510 PVV	Mercedes Benz 709D	Alexander	B25F	6/88	3/89
52,53	E511/12 PVV	Mercedes Benz 709D	Alexander	B25F	6/88	2/89

These were new to United Counties, Northampton, 10-12.

Vehicles acquired from Stephenson, Maryport, 2/5/89

---	PWR 646K	Ld.Leopard PSU5/4R	Plaxton	C57F	c4/72	5/89
---	JNB 653N	Bedford YRQ	Plaxton	C45F	4/75	5/89
---	SCK 405P	Bedford YRT	Duple D1	C53F	4/76	5/89
---	OAO 530R	Bedford YRT	Plaxton	C53F	8/76	5/89
580	OFR 929T	Volvo B58-61	Duple D2	C57F	4/79	5/89
581	KGF 306T	Ld.Leopard PSU5C/4R	Plaxton	C55F	6/79	5/89
582	PGH 341V	Ld.Leopard PSU5C/4R	Plaxton	C50F	4/80	5/89
583	OTU 510V	Bedford YMT	Plaxton	C53F	8/80	5/89
584	KHH 724W	Bedford YMT	Plaxton	C53F	8/80	5/89
585	JMA 312Y	Bedford YMT	Plaxton	C53F	8/82	5/89

These vehicles were acquired with the business of Stephenson, Maryport, 2/5/89. PWR 646K, JNB 653N, SCK 405P and OAO 530R were not used by Cumberland.
They were new to the following operators:-
JNB 653N to Stott, Oldham.; SCK 405P to Premier, Preston.; 580 to Battersby, Morecambe; 581/2 to Epsom Coaches, Epsom.; 583/5 to Lloyd, Bagillt; OAO 530R and 584 were new to Stephensons.

Left panel

*426/34 were returned 7/89 on the arrival of 757/8. *744 was returned 27/6/89 on the arrival of 716.

895 was originally B49F, being converted to DP45F by Barrow Corporation in 5/87. It was converted, by Cumberland, to B45F in 10/91.

156(B156 WRN) was reregistered PCK 335 4/92. This registration was formerly carried by sister vehicle 1155, originally registered B155 WRN, which had come on hire to Cumberland from 11/91.

520/58/60 received the Southdown style apple green and cream livery 3-4/91 and were named 'William Wordsworth', 'John Ruskin', and 'Beatrix Potter' respectively.

560/1 were originally numbered and registered 561/0(D561/0 RCK) (i.e. the reverse way round). They had been corrected prior to acquisition by Cumberland.

Of the above the following were not new to Ribble:-

70-79 were new to United Transport Buses, Manchester, 070-079, passing to Ribble 3/88.

755/7/8/60-2, 895-8 were new to Barrow-in-Furness Corporation, 11-13,15-17,20-23.

1199 was new to Western National O.C., Exeter, 3543.

Leyland Lynx

251,252	F251/52 JRM	Ld.Lynx LX112L10ZR1	Leyland	B51F		6/89
253	F253 KAO	Ld.Lynx LX112L10ZR1	Leyland	B51F		6/89

Vehicle acquired from Leyland Bus (demonstrator), 7/89

254	E709 MFV	Ld.Lynx LX112L10ZR1	Leyland	B51F	3/88	7/89

Vehicles acquired from Magic Bus (Scotland) Ltd, Glasgow/Perth, 201/2/13, 12/89

350	ORP 475M	LN 1151/1R/0401	LN	B49F	1/74	12/89
351	GRM 351L	LN 1151/1R/0401	LN	B52F	12/72	12/89
353	GRM 353L	LN 1151/1R/0401	LN	B52F	2/73	12/89

350 was new to United Counties, Northampton, 475.

351/3 were new to Cumberland M.S., being sold to Stagecoach, Perth in 6/89.

Vehicles acquired from Southdown M.S., Brighton, 610/2/8/20, 4/90

2035,2036	UWV 610/12S	Bristol VRT/SL3/6LXB	ECW	CO43/31F	12/77	4/90
2037,2038	UWV 618/20S	Bristol VRT/SL3/6LXB	ECW	CO43/31F	2/78	4/90

These vehicles were acquired for the open top service introduced 5/90 from Bowness to Ambleside, and retained the Southdown apple green and cream livery which was introduced for special 'Lakeland Experience' services.

The tops for these vehicles remained in store at Worthing.

Vehicle hired from Ribble M.S., Preston, 1927, from 5/90

1927	ABV 669A	Ld.Atlantean PDR1/1	MCCW	(C)O44/31F	1961	5/90

This was also painted into the green and cream 'Lakeland Experience' livery. It was originally registered 927 GTA, being reregistered by Ribble. It passed to Fife Scottish, Kirkcaldy, 2/92, being sold to them by Ribble Although technically a convertible open topper, the top had been absent for some time.

This was new to Devon General, Exeter, 927.

Vehicle acquired from Ribble M.S., Preston, 723, 5/90

723	UHG 723R	LN 11351A/1R	LN	B21FL	1977	5/90

This vehicle was purchased for use as disabled persons transport.

Right panel

Vehicles acquired from Hampshire Bus, Eastleigh, 40-42, 6/90

24,25	E934/35 NBK	Renault Dodge S56	Alexander	B25F	6/88	6/90
26	E615 NBP	Renault Dodge S56	Alexander	B25F	6/88	6/90

These vehicles have automatic gearboxes.

Vehicles acquired from Magic Bus, Perth (Inverness Traction), L16/7/9, 5-7/90

3001	CMS 376L	Ld.Leopard PSU3/3R	Alexander	C49F	c9/72	5/90
3003	OGM 608M	Ld.Leopard PSU3/3R	Alexander	B53F	1974	5/90
3002	SCS 359M	Ld.Leopard PSU3/3R	Alexander	C49F	9/74	7/90
......	EDS 341A	AEC/PRV Routemaster	Park Royal	H36/28R	1961	6/90

3001-3 were acquired for driver training, replacing front engined double deckers. They did not enter service until 8-10/91, being converted to circa 11 seaters with tables.

EDS 341A was used for spares until 6/92, when sold.

3001 was new to W.Alexander & Sons (Midland). Falkirk, MPE146.

3002 was new to Western SMT, Kilmarnock, L2490.

3003 was new to Central SMT, Motherwell, T208.

EDS 341A was new to London Transport, RM831.

Vehicles acquired from Magic Bus, Perth, 263-9/93-301, 8/90-2/91

61,62	G263-64 TSL	Mercedes Benz 709D	Alexander	B25F	2/90	11/90
63,64	G265/66 TSL	Mercedes Benz 709D	Alexander	B25F	2/90	10/90
57-59	G267-69 TSL	Mercedes Benz 709D	Alexander	B25F	2/90	9/90
70,68	G293/94 TSL	Mercedes Benz 709D	Alexander	B23F	3/90	2/91
67	G295 TSL	Mercedes Benz 709D	Alexander	B23F	3/90	1/91
60	G296 TSL	Mercedes Benz 709D	Alexander	B23F	3/90	9/90
65,66	G297/98 TSL	Mercedes Benz 709D	Alexander	B23F	3/90	10/90
55,56	G299,300 TSL	Mercedes Benz 709D	Alexander	B23F	3/90	9/90
54	G178 PAO	Mercedes Benz 709D	Alexander	B23F	3/90	8/90

Vehicles acquired from Plaxton(dealer), Anston, 8/90

157,158	D202/3 LWX	Volvo B10M-61	Plaxton 3500	C50F	1987	8/90
159,160	D205/6 LWX	Volvo B10M-61	Plaxton 3500	C50F	1987	8/90
161	D207 LWX	Volvo B10M-61	Plaxton 3500	C53F	1987	8/90

These were new to Wallace Arnold, Leeds. In 12/90 they received non year letter plates acquired from Southdown - WVT 618, DSV 943, LJY 145, YDG 616 and JPU 817. They were first painted into Shearings Holidays tan livery for use on contracted services. 159/60 were converted to C48FT in 3/92 for National Express services, receiving that livery. The pair were sold to Ribble M.S., Preston, 5/93, but were reacquired mid 1995 (q.v.).

Vehicle acquired from Ribble M.S., Preston, 901, 1/91

255	C544 RAO	Ld.Lynx LX112bLXCTFR1	Leyland	B51F	1985	1/91

This was new as a demonstrator for Leyland Bus.

Vehicle acquired from Southdown M.S., Brighton, 11, 1/91

1928	ERV 251D	Ld.AtlanteanPDR1/1MkII	MCCW	O43/33F	6/66	1/91

This was new to Portsmouth Corporation Transport, 251, as H43/33F. It was converted to open top by Portsmouth in 1979.

Vehicles acquired from Rainworth Travel, Shirebrook, 88,90/2, 5/93

| 149,150 | IIL 3503/05 | Volvo B10M-61 | Van Hool | C49FT | 1987 | 5/93 |
| 163 | IIL 3507 | Volvo B10M-60 | Plaxton 3500 | C50F | 1988 | 5/93 |

149,150 were new to Smiths Shearings Ltd., Wigan, 625,623(E625/3 UNE), passing to Park, Hamilton who reregistered them TXI 2426, XIA 257 and again to E936/42 XSB 10/92, just prior to sale. They were again reregistered as above c11/92.

163 was new to Wallace Arnold, Leeds, and was originally registered F410 DUG. It passed to Rainworth Travel 10/92 and was reregistered IIL 3507 c11/92. It was converted to C46FT for Nationa Express work by Plaxton in 6/93. It was sold to Ribble M.S., Preston, 1163, but was reacquired in 1995 (q.v.).

Standard Stagecoach Mercedes Benz minibuses 1993-95

| 71-78 | K871-78 GHH | Mercedes Benz 709D | Alexander(NI) | B25F | 5-6/93 |
| 1-15 | N201-15 UHH | Mercedes Benz 709D | Alexander(NI) | B23F | 10-11/95 |

1-15 have electronic destiantion equipment.

Vehicles acquired from Ribble M.S., Preston,

511, 626/3/2, 594, 601/6/3, 593, 1162, 514/39/47, in 1994

511	D511 RCK	Mercedes Benz L608D	Reebur	DP19F	8/86	1/94
79-81	K626/3/2 UFR	Mercedes Benz 709D	Alexander(NI)	B25F	1/93	4/94
82,83	K114/21 XHG	Mercedes Benz 709D	Alexander(NI)	B25F	7/93	5/94
84,85	L126/23 DRN	Mercedes Benz 709D	Alexander(NI)	B25F	7/93	5/94
86	K113 XHG	Mercedes Benz 709D	Alexander(NI)	B25F	7/93	5/94
1162	WLT 980	Volvo B10M-61	Plaxton 3500	C53F	5/86	5/94
31	D514 RCK	Mercedes Benz L608D	Reebur	DP19F	8/86	9/94
32,33	D539/47 RCK	Mercedes Benz L608D	Reebur	B20F	9/86	9/94

1162 was new to Wallace Arnold, Leeds, registered C103 DWR.

New Expressliner IIs

| 125-127 | L125-27 NAO | Volvo B10M-62 | Plaxton Prem. | C46FT | 7/94 |
| 128-132 | N128-32 VAO | Volvo B10M-62 | Plaxton Prem. | C46FT | 8/95 |

Vehicles acquired from Stagecoach Grimsby Cleethorpes, 185/78/84, 6/95

| 112,113 | PSU 775/88 | Ld.Tiger TRCTL11/3RZ | Duple Car. | C48FT | 5/85 | 6/95 |
| 114 | PSU 787 | Ld.Tiger TRCTL11/3R | Duple Car. | C49FT | 5/86 | 6/95 |

112,113 were new to Ribble M.S., Preston, 148/6(B148/6 ACK), being reregistered by Grimsby 4,3/91.
114 was new to Peter Sheffield, Cleethorpes, whose fleet was acquired by Grimsby 2/90. It was originally registered C495 LJV, being reregistered 3/91. It originally seated 51 without a toilet, and became C45FT by 9/87 and C49FT by 12/93.
113/14 were hired to Ribble by Cumberland from 6/95 to 9/95, when 112/13 were sold to Ribble and 114 arrived with Cumberland. 113 never saw service with Cumberland before being sold.

Vehicles acquired from Ribble M.S., Preston, 2075, 1159/60, during 1995

2075	XRR 175S	Bristol VRT/SL3/6LXB	ECW	O43/27F	6/78	5/95
159	LJY 145	Volvo B10M-61	Plaxton	C48FT	3/87	6/95
160	YDG 616	Volvo B10M-61	Plaxton	C48FT	3/87	6/95

159/60 were previously owned by Cumberland from 8/90 to 5/93.
2075 was new to East Midland M.S., Chesterfield. It is painted in a variation of Stagecoach livery with coffee cream instead of white.

Vehicle acquired from Midland Travel(East Midland), Chesterfield, 11/90

| 95 | D639 VAO | Ford Transit | Mellor | B16F | 3/87 | 11/90 |

This was new to Cook & Marshall, Egremont, passing to Cumberland, 70(later 95), 9/88. It was sold to Midland Travel 8/89. This was not used by Cumberland and was sold 4/91.

Vehicles acquired from Northern Scottish, Aberdeen, LO73-5/80/1, 7/91-1/92

1090,1091	GSO 3,4V	Ld.Olympian ONLXB/1RV	Alexander	H47/30F	6/86	7/91
1092	GSO 5V	Ld.Olympian ONLXB/1RV	Alexander	H47/30F	4/87	7/91
1093,1094	D380/81 XRS	Ld.Olympian ONLXB/1RV	Alexander	H47/30F	4/87	1/92

1090-92 were originally registered C473/74 SSO, D375 XRS. All five were new as H47/26D for Aberdeen City Services.
1090-92 were reregistered C382/83 XAO, D384 XAO in 2/93.

Vehicles acquired from Ribble M.S., Preston, 1151/3/4, 155/62, 11/91

1151/53/54	B151/3/4 WRN	Ld.Tiger TRCTL11/2RH	Duple L2	C49F	1/85	11/91
1155	PCK 335	Ld.Tiger TRCTL11/3RH	Duple L2	C53F	1/85	11/91
162	B162 WRN	Ld.Tiger TRCTL11/3RH	Duple L2	C53F	2/85	11/91

These vehicle were initially on long term hire but at some point the vehicles were acquired by Cumberland. 1155 was originally registered B155 WRN, being reregistered by Ribble. It was further reregistered by Cumberland to B43 MAO 4/92. 'PCK 335' was transferred to 156(B156 WRN) acquired from Ribble 6/89.

Volvo/Plaxton Expressliners 1991/92

| 120-122 | J120-22 AHH | Volvo B10M-61 | Plaxton | C46FT | 12/91 |
| 123,124 | J123/24 AHH | Volvo B10M-61 | Plaxton | C46FT | 3/92 |

Dennis Darts, 1991

| 701-703 | J701-3 YRM | Dennis Dart 9.8SDL3017 | Alexander | B41F | 12/91 |

These vehicles passed to the Stagecoach South (Hampshire Bus) fleet in 10/92.

Volvo B6 single deckers, 1992-1993

704	J704 BRM	Volvo B6R	Alexander	B40F	6/92
270-272	K270-72 ERM	Volvo B6-50	Alexander	B40F	10/92
273	K273 ERM	Volvo B6-50	Alexander	B40F	11/92
275-9/81-283	L275 JAO etc.	Volvo B6-50	Alexander	B40F	8/93
270-274	L270-274 LHH	Volvo B6-50	Alexander	B40F	12/93

Note that there was no vehicle numbered 280 due to difficulties in obtaining a matching registration. 704 was renumbered 274 before entering service. The 'new' 270-274, delivered 12/93, replaced the original vehicles, which were built in Austria. The latter were sold back to Volvo. The L registered vehicles have electronic destination equipment.

Volvo B10M Buses 1992-1995

699,704	K699,704 ERM	Volvo B10M-55	Alexander	B49F	12/92
700-3/5-46	K700 DAO etc.	Volvo B10M-55	Alexander	B49F	12/92-2/93
748-771	K748-71 DAO	Volvo B10M-55	Alexander	B49F	2-3/93
772-791	K772-91 DAO	Volvo B10M-55	Alexander	DP48F	4-5/93
789,790	N789/90 VRM	Volvo B10M-55	Alexander	DP48F	8/95

Note that there was no vehicle numbered 747 due to difficulties in obtaining a matching registration.
The original 789-791 were sold to Stagecoach East Kent in 1994. All have electronic destination equipment.

Leyland-bodied PD2/12 No. 395, formerly numbered 333, displays the three cream bands livery which was a feature of Cumberland double-deckers for many years. It is pictured in the bus station annexe at Workington awaiting departure on a miners' service to Harrington No. 10 colliery at Lowca.

Pre NBC years

The first Leyland Royal Tigers to enter the Cumberland fleet had Eastern Coach Works bodies to this design which was based on the prototype body for the Bristol LS. Number 150, formerly numbered 323, is parked in Aspatria after being rebuilt with fixed windscreen mounted in cream rubber. Behind No. 150 can be seen the rear of one of the Bristol SC4LKs known in the CMS fleet as the 'Sputniks.'

Pre NBC years

The second and final batch of Leyland Royal Tiger service buses had Leyland bodies to this rather box like design. Number 155, formerly No. 339, is shown at the coach park adjacent Keswick Bus Station ready to take up its next duty on service 79 to Seatoller. This photograph was taken after a rebuild when the cream band below the windows was omitted and the window surrounds were painted cream.

The Bristol FLF was a popular vehicle in the Cumberland fleet, a total of 31 being delivered. Number 533, pictured here in Wigton Bus Station on service 71 to Keswick, was one of the last three delivered in 1966. These three were the only FLF examples for CMS which did not have the top cream band below the upper-deck windows.

Bristol RE No. 266 with flat front, shallow windscreen and 'T' type destination display waits in Carlisle bus station on service 38 to Silloth in the Tilling red and cream livery with black lining out in which these vehicles were delivered.

The Leyland PD3s with attractive full fronted bodies by H. V. Burlingham were regular operators on Carlisle City Services before the introduction of one-person-operation. Here, No. 1580 heads into English Street southbound on service 660 to Harraby East.

Pre NBC years

The Burlingham-bodied PD3s were followed by a batch with similar bodies by Metro Cammell Weymann which, although lacking the attractive lines and proportions of the Burlingham examples, were an improvement on the standard MCW 'Orion' body of the time. Number 1789 picks up passengers at the Town Hall on service 660 to Harraby East.

With the transfer of United operations in Carlisle to Ribble in 1969, Ribble inherited some vehicles not normally associated with an ex-BET company. Among these was this Bristol MW, 5042 HN, which became Ribble 274. Here it is leaving the United bus station in Scotch Street en route to Hethersgill on service 617, still in Tilling red and cream but with Ribble fleetname.

One-person-operation was introduced in Carlisle with a fleet of Bristol VR double-deckers with Eastern Coach Works bodies, supplemented by a number of Leyland Atlanteans with lowbridge MCW bodies. Bristol No. 2000 is shown in the city centre heading for Harraby on service 662 followed by one of the Atlanteans.

The NBC era

Now-preserved Bristol MW No. 231 spent most of its life at Keswick depot working service 79 to Seatoller. It is depicted at Middle Howe, Borrowdale on 5th January 1979 working the 1.05pm journey from Keswick

Number 601 one of the ex-Midland Red short Leyland Leopards purchased by Cumberland for operation through the Seascale railway arch and for the service to Netherwasdale, is pictured at Ravenglass, having arrived there on a schools service on 30th May 1980. Much criticism has been directed at the use of 'Service' on destination blinds and this was particularly unhelpful when there was no facility for the service number.

The NBC era

On 1st June 1981, Leyland National B type No. 210 departs from Keswick Bus Station for Seatoller in Borrowdale.

Cockermouth Main Street provides the setting for this view of Keswick based Bristol VR No. 426 as it picks up passengers on its return from Whitehaven on service 34.

The ex-Midland Red short Leyland Leopards were replaced by similar vehicles purchased from Trent Motor Traction of Derby. Number 606 from this second batch had just turned at Netherwasdale for the return journey to Gosforth when this view was taken in July 1983. This service had formerly operated through from Whitehaven but was then shortened to operate from Gosforth to Netherwasdale, connection being made at Gosforth with service 12 to and from Whitehaven. With this change operation was transferred to Millom Depot.

Willowbrook-bodied Leyland Leopard No. 628 had been painted in the dual-purpose NBC livery when this view was taken. It is seen in the village of St. Bees as it arrived there on a works service from Sellafield in July 1983.

Cars parked without due consideration for other road users can cause problems, especially for bus drivers as illustrated by this view of Leyland National B type No. 215 as it enters the village of Papcastle en route from Cockermouth to Wigton in August 1983.

The Summer Saturday express service from Whitehaven to Blackpool was popular in the 'seventies and 'eighties and Duple Dominant 2-bodied Leyland Leopard No. 620 in NBC dual-purpose livery leaves Blackpool Coliseum coach station for Whitehaven on 29th June 1985.

Overall Advertising Buses

Above: In overall advert livery for Jennings brewery, Bristol VR No. 420 operated the Border Clipper service on 13th June 1990 and heads along the A595 south of Distington towards Whitehaven.

Left: In the mid-'eighties a number of Leyland Nationals were repainted in 'Cumberland Advertiser' liveries and one of these was No. 387 in this green scheme shown leaving Whitehaven for Keswick on service 34 in June 1984. In addition to providing revenue, they provided a welcome change to the drab NBC unrelieved poppy red.

Another Leyland National to receive 'Advertiser' livery was No. 391 shown in August 1983 en route from Keswick to Whitehaven and about to turn off the A66 at the west end of Bassenthwaite.

Vehicles in the overall advertising livery for Heyes Garden Centre, Ambleside have featured in first Ribble, then Cumberland fleets for some years. Olympian 1020, with its distinctive Alexander-profiled bodywork and so attired, is shown entering the Windermere Railway Station area in June 1992 en route from Kendal to Carlisle and incorporating the intermediate points roller blind before being retrofitted with electronically operated destination display.

Looking well in the summer sunshine of 1995 is Volvo B10M No. 737, in overall advert livery for 'Finesse', as it turns into Lowther Street, Carlisle operating city service 62 to Harraby on 26th July.

Border Clipper

Displaying the Border Clipper livery, Willowbrook-bodied Leyland Leopard No. 631 leaves Carlisle on 29th April 1987 operating the 1520 journey from Carlisle to Egremont.

Photographed on New Road, Whitehaven, shortly after repainting in Border Clipper livery, but before the fitting of coach seating, is Olympian 1002, formerly 802.

The CMS Cumberland double-deck livery was particularly attractive and is illustrated by Bristol VR No. 433 in Duke Street, Whitehaven in August 1987. Its pristine condition confirms the vehicle was photographed shortly after repainting.

CMS Cumberland

A Bristol VR with highbridge Eastern Coach Works body leaves Carlisle city centre on city service 661 to Morton West in the CMS Carlislebus version of the CMS Cumberland livery on 27th May 1987. This batch of vehicles was later, under Stagecoach ownership, transferred to Hampshire Bus.

CMS Cumberland

This view taken in Lowther Street, Whitehaven, on 14th August 1987 illustrates the level of competition faced by CMS at that time in that town. At the front is Yeowart's Mercedes Minibus C293 PAO on its service to Lowca, followed by CMS Minibus No. 21, CMS Duple-bodied Leyland Leopard No. 1119 in the 'Bargain Bus' livery and at the rear Brownriggs's Leyland Leopard PWK 7W.

Mercedes 608 minibus No. 40 heads out of Carlisle city on service M3 to Kingstown (Asda) as sister vehicle No. 46 heads in the opposite direction on 27th May 1987.

Coach-seated Bristol VR No. 436 displays one version of the double-deck dual-purpose CMS Cumberland livery as it passes the Howgate Hotel heading for Whitehaven from Broughton Moor on service 31 on 22nd July 1987. Sister vehicle No. 437 had a similar livery but the red finished at the top of the lower saloon windows.

One of the first vehicles to receive the CMS Cumberland livery without the brown skirt was Leyland National 1 No. 360 shown at Flatt Walks, Whitehaven on service 17 to Wath Brow on 11th May 1988.

Leyland National 2 No. 380 displays the original single-deck version of the CMS Cumberland livery, complete with brown skirt, in Duke Street, Whitehaven on 11th May 1987 as it operates Town Service O4.

On the last day of Yeowarts independent operation, 11th May 1988, its Plaxton bodied Ford, SKO 273R, passes Whitehaven Castle on Flatt Walks operating town service Y2.

Turning from George Street into Church Street, Whitehaven, is Eastern Coach Works-bodied Leyland Leopard No. 641 in the dual-purpose version of the CMS Cumberland livery on 5th August 1987, operating on service 310 from Workington to Egremont. The service was commenced in response to Brownriggs' operation on this route.

Two Alexander-bodied Leyland Leopards with coach seating were acquired from Kelvin Scottish and both were based at Carlisle. Here No. 613 leaves Penrith Bus Station for Carlisle on 4th May 1990.

Routemaster No. 906 is shown on the outskirts of Carlisle on 26th May 1990 operating service 61 from Morton Park to Harraby East.

CMS Cumberland

The Duple Dominant bodied Leyland Leopards carried the dual-purpose CMS Cumberland livery very well as displayed by No. 1140 seen leaving Carlisle bus station for Newcastle on Service 685, jointly operated with Northumbria Motor Services, on 7th September 1990. The fleetname in this case is CMS Carlislebus.

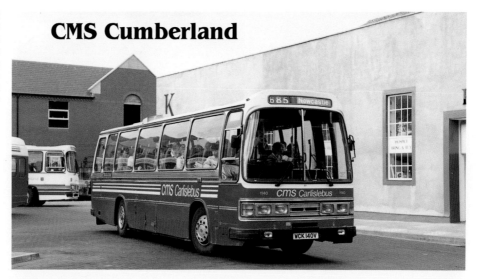

Leyland National 2 No. 382 displays the dual-purpose version of the CMS Cumberland livery as it leaves Keswick for Whitehaven in June 1992.

A Reeve Burgess-bodied Dodge minibus, No. 32, one of the first batch of minibuses to enter the fleet, travels along Scotch Street, Whitehaven on town service 01 to Kells on 11th May 1988. The CMS Club shown on the left of the photograph has nothing to do with Cumberland Motor Services – it belonged to the Catholic Mens Society.

The Stagecoach era

In the towns

Number 1201, one of the two six-wheeled 'Meggadeckers' in the fleet, has just emerged from Whitehaven bus station into New Road to commence its journey on Border Clipper service 600 to Carlisle on 8th August 1991.

On the takeover of Yeowarts, a number of Cumberland Vehicles received 'Yeowart' fleetnames and one of these was Leyland National B type No. 218 shown in Duke Street, Whitehaven on town service 07 on 5th May 1989.

The Volvo B10M service buses are to be found operating town services in all the major towns with the exception of Kendal. Against a background of some of Whitehaven's many restored buildings, No. 745 turns from Duke Street into Scotch Street operating Haven Link Service 3/9 to the West Cumberland Hospital via Ullswater Avenue. The 3/9 service number indicates that it would operate outward via service 3 and return via service 9.

'Kells Bus' has been a feature of the Whitehaven scene since the 'twenties, so much so that when fleet numbering was commenced in 1950, it was given the number '01'. Minibus No. 75 climbs New Road to Seacliffe and Kells on 20th October 1995 with the northern part of the town and the Solway Firth visible in the background.

The Border Clipper service from Whitehaven to Gateshead, now numbered X3, continues to be popular and in late 1995 Plaxton-bodied Volvo B10M No. 159 was painted into Stagecoach livery and lettered for the service. A day return fare of £5.00 must be good value for a journey of over 100 miles each way. It is shown on 23rd January 1996 in Carlisle bus station on the outward journey to Gateshead.

An experimental 3-line destination display was fitted to Olympian No. 1016 with a notable improvement in the clarity of the display. In this view in Duke Street, Whitehaven, on 15th September 1995, it is showing Whitehaven and Egremont via Workington – 30.

The first delivery of Volvo B10M single-deckers were used to carry out a major replacement of vehicles operating Carlisle city services and No. 710 is illustrated in the city centre on 26th July 1995 on city service 67 to Upperby.

Leaving Carlisle bus station on 26th July 1995 on the Summer Tourist Route to Hadrian's Wall is Volvo B6 No. 270, one of the replacement vehicles received in place of the original batch.

Leyland National 2 Number 397 operates Workington town service 46 to Brierydale on 25th April 1992 and is shown on Vulcans Lane, having just left the bus station.

Crossing Goat Bridge into Cockermouth on service 58 from Maryport on 15th September 1995 is Olympian 1015.

The X5 'Lakes Link' service from Whitehaven to Penrith, introduced in May 1993, has proved popular and is generally operated by the Volvo B10M single-deck service buses with dual-purpose seating. Number 773 is shown approaching Keswick on 2nd May 1995 heading for Penrith.

Mercedes 608 minibuses operated Kendal town services from 1986 until the arrival of the larger Mercedes 709s at the end of 1995. Number 5041 is pictured in Kendal in August 1991. It was formerly Ribble 504 but at the time of takeover by Cumberland there was already a 504 in the CMS fleet so this vehicle was renumbered 5041.

Replacement of the Mercedes 608 minibuses in Kendal commenced in late 1995 when 10 of the batch of 15 Mercedes 709s with Alexander bodies were allocated to the town. Number 7 is shown at the Town Hall terminus on service 44 to Hallgarth on 24th January 1996.

Turning into Abbey Road, from Ramsden Square, Barrow on 31st May 1995 is Bristol VR No.433 operating on town service 3A to Newbarns. The excellent condition of the vehicle is typical of the VRs which continue to be turned out in immaculate condition despite being, in this case, 15 years old.

131

The Stagecoach era

In the lakes

For the 1995 season, Volvo B6 midibuses were introduced on the Conistion Rambler service in place of Mercedes minibuses and No. 282 is shown at Clappersgate heading towards Coniston on 2nd May. For the 1996 season the two vehicles concerned were painted in Lakeland Experience livery.

On 2nd May 1995 Duple Dominant 2 bodied Leyland Leopard No. 1119 approaches Clappersgate near Ambleside on the return journey from Dungoen Ghyll in Langdale on service 516.

On 28th June 1995 Leyland Lynx No. 253 was deputising for the normal bus, Leyland National No. 810, on the Borrowdale Service from Keswick to Seatoller. Here, on the outward journey, it enters the village of Rosthwaite with not very much room to spare.

The Seatoller terminus is at the foot of Honister Pass and, having turned there, No. 253 makes its way back to Keswick.

In the Summer of 1995, following a relaxation of the Traffic Regulation Order for Honister Pass, Cumberland commenced a regular bus service over the pass by modifying the Keswick to Buttermere service No. 77. Here, on 28th June 1995, Mercedes 709 minibus No. 77 climbs the last part of Honister Pass from the Seatoller end en route to Buttermere. It was on service 77A and would return from Buttermere via Whinlatter Pass. Workings on service 77 operated the opposite way round.

More of the spectacular Lakeland scenery is apparent in this view as Leyland Leopard No. 1105 reaches the top of Kirkstone Pass, en route to Glenridding, at 0930 hrs. on 26th July 1995 on another of the Lake District tourist routes.

Double-deckers are sometimes used on the service from Penrith to Patterdale and Bristol VR No. 2024 is senn leaving Glenridding for Patterdale on 29th July 1995.

Service 555

On the takeover of the Barrow and South Lakes areas from Ribble, two low height Bristol VRs were transferred from Whitehaven to meet the requirement for such vehicles for operation under the Arnside railway bridge. One of these, No. 422 was in the attractive CMS Cumberland livery and is shown at Milnthorpe on a northbound journey from Lancaster to Keswick on 7th August 1989.

A former Ribble coach-seated Leyland Olympian, No 2175, rejoins the main road from Grasmere in August 1991 operating the 555 service to Keswick.

Leyland Olympian 1023 leaves Ambleside for Lancaster in September 1993 on service 555. The bold branding on the upper-deck panels adds a little variety and neatly fills an otherwise large area of white.

Service 555

An unusual vehicle on the 555 service on 13th July 1995 was this Duple Laser bodied Leyland Tiger coach No. 105 shown heading south along the A6 road from Kendal towards Milnthorpe.

Leyland National No. 372 crosses the picturesque Ouse Bridge at the Western end of Bassenthwaite Lake on its journey from Keswick to Whitehaven and Frizington on service 35 on 19th June 1990.

Some vehicles in the Barrow and South Lakes area, following takeover by Cumberland, received 'Cumberland' fleetnames on their Ribble livery. One of these was Atlantean 1425 photographed at Greenodd on 2nd September 1991.

Entering the village of Haverigg on 26th June 1995 operating the local service M1 from Millom is Mercedes 608 minibus No. 44, one of those from the original Cumberland fleet, purchased for the commencement of minibus operation in Carlisle.

Heading along the causeway from the 'mainland' to Roa Island is Volvo B10M No. 755 operating on the coast road service from Ulverston to Barrow on 10th July 1995. After calling at Roa Island the bus would return along the same road to Rampside and Barrow. Careful scrutiny will reveal water on either side of the causeway.

Mercedes Minibus No. 520 in Lakeland Experience livery waits in Bowness on Windermere for departure on the Coniston Rambler service in September 1993.

Lakeland livery

The only Leyland Atlantean remaining in the fleet at the time of writing was open-topper No. 1928 which commenced life with Portsmouth City Transport in 1966. It came to Cumberland following the withdrawal of the previous open-top Atlantean, No. 1927 which had commenced life with Devon General, later passing to Ribble. Number 1928 is shown leaving Grasmere for Bowness on 7th July 1994.

Lakeland livery

Leyland National No. 810, which came to Cumberland from Ribble with the takeover of the Carlisle and Penrith areas, is now the only Leyland National in the fleet. It is retained in 'Lakeland Experience' livery for the Borrowdale service and is illustrated at Keswick bus station awaiting departure to Seatoller on 24th July 1992.

Bristol VR 2002 was converted to open top in the body shop at Lillyhall following an accident with a low canopy and at a time when an additional vehicle was required to cater for the extension of the service to Grasmere. In mid-afternoon on 28th June 1995 it arrives at Grasmere carrying a good number of passengers.

Newly repainted into the green and cream Lakeland livery for the 1996 season are the two Volvo B6s Nos. 276 and 282 which in 1995 had operated the Coniston Rambler service in Stagecoach livery. Number 276 is shown at the car park in Ambleside used for layovers, having just worked into Ambleside on service 505 on 24th January 1996.

When originally purchased the ex-Wallace Arnold Plaxton bodied Volvos operated on hire to Shearings Holidays in their livery and No. 161 is pictured at the Prince of Wales Hotel, Grasmere in May 1991 on a Shearings Tour.

Coaching

The 'Coachline' name was first launched on the ex-Cotters Van Hool-bodied Volvo B10Ms, and to mark the occasion the company took a party of senior citizens on a day tour to the Lakes. The two coaches used for this purpose are shown in Cockermouth Main Street on the outward journey.

Coaching

Showing the former Yeowarts livery, adopted as the CMS 'Coachline' livery are Plaxton bodied DAF No.509 taken over with the Yeowart business and Plaxton bodied Leyland Tiger No. 111 behind. They are parked at Bowness on Windermere in June 1992.

Number 162, in the 'Yeowart' style Coachline livery, is depicted in Skipton operating the X9 service from York to Ambleside on 5th August 1994.

In the glorious sunshine enjoyed in the summer of 1995, Plaxton-bodied Volvo B10M number 161 arrives in Grasmere on 28th June operating an afternoon excursion in the latest Coachline livery of red with gold lettering.

National Express

Number 102, one of the first two Duple Laser-bodied Leyland Tigers to enter the CMS fleet, was delivered in National Holidays livery and is shown in this scheme approaching Preston bus station on the return journey from London to Whitehaven whilst operating service 831 on 4th May 1984.

Plaxton-bodied Leyland Tiger No. 109 is about to enter Preston bus station on 10th August 1987, operating National Express service 921 from London to Stranraer. It would return from Stranraer to London overnight and operate the London to Whitehaven service the following day. This vehicle and fellow No. 110 were the first examples in the fleet to have electronic destination displays but these lacked clarity.

In the early morning of 9th July 1987, Duple Laser-bodied Leyland Tiger No. 108 passes Thirlspot, just south of Keswick, in typical Lakeland scenery. It is heading for London on the 7.20am Whitehaven to London National Express Rapide service 575 which was later renumbered 570.

National Express

In the Summer of 1995 the Forton service area on the M6 was used as a changeover point for CMS drivers working on National Express turns. Here, on 27th September 1995, No. 132 arrives at Forton from Whitehaven for this purpose.

National Expressliner No. 124 operating the 0950 Whitehaven to London National Express Rapide service on 13th July 1995 travels along the A591 road north of Kendal.

Ex-Shearings Van Hool-bodied Volvo B10M No. 149 enters Ambleside on the Whitehaven to Leicester service 398 in September 1993.